Pursuit of National Interests Through Neutralism :

India's Foreign Policy in the Nehru Era

SAURIPADA BHATTACHARYA

FIRMA KLM (PRIVATE) LIMITED
CALCUTTA   * * *   1978

Published by
Firma KLM Private Limited,
257B, B. B. Ganguly Street,
Calcutta-700012.

1st Edition, Calcutta, 1978

Distributed by:
South Asia Books
Box 502
Columbia, MO 65201

Printed by
N. Anwar
A. S. Printing Concern
249, B. B. Ganguly Street
Calcutta-700012.

PREFACE

There have been quite a number of studies on non-alignment-cum-neutralism as a new movement in international affairs of the second half of the twentieth century and on India's role in it. Of the general studies of it as a world diplomatic movement, the following deserve honourable mention :

Crabb, Cecil V., Jr., *The Elephants and the Grass : A Study of Nonalignment* (New York : Praeger, 1965)

Jansen, G. H., *Nonalignment and the Afro-Asian States* (New York : Praeger, 1966)

Karunakaran, K. P., ed., *Outside the Contest : A Study of Nonalignment and the Foreign Policies of some Nonaligned Countries* (New Delhi : People's Publishing House, 1963)

London, Kurt, *New Nations in a Divided World : The International Relations of the Afro-Asian States* (New York : Praeger, 1964)

Martin, Lawrence W., ed., *Neutralism and Nonalignment : The New States in World Affairs* (New York : Praeger, 1962)

Power, Paul F., ed., *Neutralism and Disengagement* (New York : Scribner, 1964)

Of the studies documenting India's diplomacy dominated by the posture of non-alignment-cum-neutralism, the following would be considered representative, although by no means complete or exhaustive :

Kundra, J. C., *Indian Foreign Policy, 1947-1954* (Groningen, Netherlands : J. B. Wolters, 1955)

Mallik, D. N., *The Development of Nonalignment in India's Foreign Policy* (Allahabad, India : Chaitanya Publishing House, 1967)

Power, Paul F., *India's Nonalignment Policy :
Strengths and Weaknesses* (Boston : D. C. Heath,
1967)

Brecher, Michael, *Nehru : A Political Biography*
(London : Oxford University Press, 1959)

Berkes, Ross N. and Bedi, Mohinder Singh, *The
Diplomacy of India : Indian Foreign Policy in the
United Nations* (Stanford : Stanford University
Press, 1958)

Both the kinds of studies, general studies of nonalignment and more specialised studies of India's Foreign
Policy of nonalignment-cum-neutralism, particularly the
latter, while being very probing in regard to its motivations which have been shown to contain elements of national
interests, have yet remained basically indifferent to the
all-important question of relationship between national
interests and nonalignment-cum-neutralism as a means of
securing them, notwithstanding Karunakar Gupta's early
study, *Indian Foreign Policy : A Study in National Interest*
(Calcutta : World Press, 1964). So far as the present author
is concerned, there has not been any detailed study yet
either of nonalignment-cum-neutralism in general or India's
neutralism in so far as it is considered as a means of securing national interests. The present work is intended to
remove this lacuna at least in so far as India's nonalignment-cum-neutralism in the Nehru Era is concerned : indeed, the title of the present work is : "Pursuit of National
Interests through Neutralism : India's Foreign Policy in
the Nehru Era" and is a study of the *leitmotif* of India's
foreign policy of neutralism. The purpose of this study is to
establish this correlation between India's national interests
and nonalignment/neutralism as defined by her decision-
makers during the period 1947-1964 and to aver that in
most important respects India's national interests were
indeed served by her chosen diplomatic instrument of nonalignment-cum-neutralism.

The study is made up of several chapters. In Chapter I

an attempt has been made to discuss the concept of neutralism as regards what it is not and what it is. The most important point that has been made in this chapter appears to be this : Neutralism is only an aspect of India's foreign policy, that it does not seem to be inherent in every aspect of it, that it was part of India's stances in regard to global problems affecting the Super Powers ; also that it is a means or a technique of securing national interests, and that it is not primarily a goal of foreign policy and is not to be confused as a goal of foreign policy. There is a discussion of the philosophic bases of neutralism to emphasize that there is nothing casual about it. Yet the philosophic bases have been shown to be overwhelmed by the concrete situations of contemporary world which had an important role in settling the minds of Indian decisionmakers in favor of national interests. It has been shown also that nonalignment/neutralism is an evolutionary concept—from certain initial general negative propositions like anti-colonialism, anti-racialism (that did not necessarily include anti-alliance postures), it came to have more positive characteristics, including willingness to solve international disputes and to extend the idea of peace area, through, among others, Panch Sheel of Peaceful Coexistence, and finally, in the aftermath of Chinese invasion of India, it became almost synonymous with bialignment, or equidistance. Neutralism is also discussed in terms of its relations with powerpolitics and the point is made that while it appears to reject the assumptions of powerpolitics of the Super Powers, it is not entirely against the idea of Balance of Power : and that in fact it is a variant or substitute of balance of power although not quite balance of power itself.

In Chapter II an attempt is made to define the national interests of India as articulated by such spokesmen as Nehru. There is first of all a discussion of the general world view of Nehru with a view to finding out whether or not he could be labelled as a hard-core nationalist or a starryeyed internationalist. The conclusion that has been reached is that his was a sort of rational nationalism which would not go against the interests of humanity. But the most important aspect of this chapter seems, at least in the eyes of this author, to consist in the study of the speeches of Nehru (supplemented wherever possible by a study of speeches of other spokesmen of India) chosen not at random but casually. This study is claimed as an exploration of a hitherto untrodden field in the manner of content analysis, only conceived in a limited way, because it does not attempt to project the findings to a much larger universe. The findings from the study seem to emphasize India's greater preoccupation with national interests as opposed to interests that are more or less altruistic and internationalist in character.

Chapter III deals with India's nonaligned/neutralistic postures in some of the most representative cold war conflicts of the period of our study, such as those relating to China's recognition, Korea, Suez, Hungary and the Congo. Some pains have been taken to show that India's stances differed from one case to another, with one characteristic remaining constant all through—independence of judgment that always led her to the 'merits' of the case as her policymakers saw them and refusal to be directly aligned with any power bloc. An attempt has also been made to show what calculations of national interest these particular stances of India, subsumed under the rubric of nonalignment/neutralism, were based upon. Analysis in this chapter of India's nonaligned/neutralistic postures tries to make it obvious that that nonalignment/neutralism did not mean equidistance from the blocs—rather that India did indeed come closer to one bloc or the other on some occasions, while on rare occasions only maintained a posture of equidistance. These specific postures were determined by particular circumstances of the cases and by her own reading of her interests and obligations. The thrust of the argument in this chapter is to show that India's nonalignment-cum-neutralism, while not entirely remote from ideological considerations, was essentially pragmatic and interest-oriented—its essential purpose being to subserve her own national interests which required constant honing of means and methods subsumed under the general label of nonalignment/neutralism.

Chapter IV is an analysis of the contents of India's national interests as defined by her policymakers. This is in a sense a follow-up of the study of national interests as was undertaken in Chapter II. That is to say, the present chapter outlines the contents of the national interests the broad areas of which have already been identified on the basis of content analysis of the speeches of decision-makers. It is pointed out that there are certain interests that were involved in such cases as Korea, Hungary, Suez and the Congo where India experimented with the technique of nonalignment ; these were the interests that were *directly* involved. On the other hand there were other interests that although invisible seemed to be of abiding value and were matters of real concern to India, that were sought to be pursued even though she was trying to negotiate these global conflicts affecting the super powers. Such interests included strengthening internal affairs, making Indian economy strong ; laying the foundations of a strong defense against foreign aggression, strengthening the democratic framework under which independent sovereign India will make her mark in the comity of nations. The present chapter goes to prove that mere idealism was *not* the whole of India's credo in so far as her foreign policies were concerned. India had strategic as well as tactical interests and the latter included non-alignment-cum-neutralism. Strategic interests are divided into three categories : A. Territorial/geographic and B. General. Among the first are included such questions as Kashmir, Goa, Northern areas contiguous to China (it must be noted also that all these territorial questions involved India's neighbors). Among the general strategic questions are included such interests as security (as inherent in Kashmir and northern boundary questions), anti-colonialism and the elimination of racial discrimination, etc. These abstract general interests, when divorced from such territorial questions as have been pointed out, were only tactical in nature.

The third category of strategic interests are internal in nature and import (which did not involve foreign powers *per se*). These include maintenance of political stability and organization of the economy geared to removing mass poverty without doing away with parliamentary democracy. Internal wellbeing, a most important national interest, is construed by India's policymakers in terms largely of economic wellbeing. A discussion of the Five Year Plans and their major objectives is undertaken with a view to bringing out Indian leaders' conception of economic wellbeing. The most important point to emerge in this discussion is that such plan objectives could not be realized without a liberal dose of external assistance, which could not be unrelated to questions involving relations with powers that were in a position to give aid.

Next discussed in the same chapter are a number of tactical interests, including maintenance of peace, and avoidance of war. Neutralism which includes nonalignment is also included here since it suggested India's interest in a balance between India's alignment with the two Super Powers. Through nonalignment/neutralism, India, her leaders felt, "must seek the optimum path of taking advantage of US-Soviet hostility and to induce the two powers to prevent the growth of a preponderant power in Asia". Finally, in bringing out the nature of tactical interests a reference is made to those interests that were involved in the global disputes in which India cared to intervene.

In the following two chapters, Chapters V and VI, an attempt is made to deal with consequences of India's policies. Consequences are seen first in terms of change in disposition of the Super Powers resulting from or occurring simultaneously with India's interventions in world politics. This is discussed in Chapter V. This chapter brings out first a vague leftward orientation in India's nonalignment/neutralism at least in so far as Asian issues were concerned. This inferred that this might have had some impact on the disposition of the Super Powers toward India. The study reveals that the United States, mood towards India was one of cool tolerance not untouched by misunderstandings. India played a relatively minor part in the scheme of things as seen by the US policymakers. But there was no marked *hostility* between these two democracies. The *overall* Soviet mood as apparent from the study was, on the other hand, one of friendliness and understanding. The Soviets seemed to encourage India to continue her policy of nonalignment/neutralism and to support the Indian Government's domestic social and economic policies which, to the local Communists, appeared perverse. But Communist China's mood, crystallizing slowly but surely, appeared to be distinctly *unfriendly,* as evinced from events after 1954. Interestingly, with the development of conflictual relations between India and China, the mood of the Super Powers vis-a-vis India underwent some change—the US and USSR both seemed to become more concerned toward India. Indeed India emerged as 'the area of agreement' in the policies of the two Super Powers. The discussion of the change in the disposition of the Super Powers is followed by a discussion of the state of international milieu to which India's policies in regard to Korea, Suez, Hungary, and the Congo contributed to some extent. The discussion of the above hopefully brings out the framework under which the specific Indian national interests could be preserved and satisfied.

In Chapter VI other consequences are discussed : in terms first of strategic interests and then tactical interests. In regard to strategic interests, such as Kashmir, although the US stand was not definitely pro-India, India continued to hold on to the disputed territory because of Soviet help. The point has been made that India's continued hold on Kashmir was largely because of Soviet help which in turn was helped largely by India's global stances and partly by the Western stances that such Indian stances induced or provoked. In regard to Goa again India's interests prevailed, thanks again to Soviet help and in spite of US opposition. The Soviet help came in the shape of veto when the Security Council of the UN was seized with the Goa situation in 1961. This veto killed the Western resolution that sought an immediate cessation of hostilities which would have hampered India's interests in Goa. This meant in effect that India could secure her national interests—

territorial and security—as symbolized by Goa's full integration with the rest of India.

In regard however to the Sino-Indian dispute, India's overall success if any has been questionable and failure more conspicuous. On the diplomatic front, India got US and USSR assistance only after a period of some hesitancy on the latter's part. After the outbreak of the war in 1962 India did get immediate support from the Western powers led by the US. This support, if measured in material terms, was not great but its psychological and symbolic value went a long way toward convincing the Chinese that the ceasefire was the best way to halt a further worsening of the situation that was fraught with unacceptable consequences from their point of view. The Soviet position in regard to the dispute was no less helpful ; the initial neutrality of the Soviets (as suggested by such statements as "Indian friends and Chinese brothers") that was favourable to India later gave place to outright support for India as indicated in such stands as continued arms delivery to India, even tacit endorsement of Western arms support to India, encouragement of Colombo Powers' mediation in the dispute. Despite her overall defeat in the war and loss of sizable segments of territory in the North, India made substantial gains on the diplomatic front as testified to by her emergence as the 'area of agreement' in the policies of the Super Powers.

It has also been shown in this Chapter that India's strategic interests as determined by her domestic requirements such as foreign economic assistance, foreign defense assistance, industrialization, consolidation of domestic consensus in regard to democratic governmental experiment in India have also been helped by India's foreign policy stances. Indeed India's foreign policy seems to have succeeded in keeping both the Super Powers inclined to offer economic assistance to India. Although this assistance has not been sufficient enough to help India bridge the financial resources gap, the point however is that without it India would have been in direr straits. In military assistance also, India succeeded in drawing at least token American and Western assistance, whereas the Soviet Union emerged as the major supplier of defense equipments. Thus India having been able to get supplies from both power blocs was freed from the necessity to rely upon one particular source at any moment of time. Her socialism which depended upon successful launching of statemanaged projects also prospered a little, thanks to such aid as she received from the Soviet Un.on and others in such key industries as Steel and Oil refining. American aid was also helpful in supplementing India's own efforts in agriculture, etc. The point is also made that because of the Soviet Union's greater understanding of India's objectives and policies in foreign affairs, the local Indian communists gradually moved to support the Ind.an democratic experiment, but of course as an independent national force—the opposition that it retained was that of a party of Opposition. In spite of such aid, which was sometimes accompanied by strings, India retained in substantial measure her independence in making decisions, domest:c and external, because of her size and other factors inherent in her situation. All these consequences further helped her consolidate a position of prestige in the international community. The chapter recounts the failures also, but the point is made that most of the failures followed the Chinese invasion of India in 1962.

In the final Chapter, some concluding observations are offered, including the ones relating to the linkage between consequences and nonalignment/neutralism. It is pointed out that consequences in terms of disposition of the big powers are not *necessarily* to be seen as following from India's nonalignment/neutralism pertaining as they did to global issues. The point is also made that such stances might have been somewhat irrelevant in regard to big powers' overall attitude to India, for they had their own global strategy already developed even before they could react to neutralism. It is further pointed out in this chapter that some of the failures of neutralism might have followed not from its conceptual framework but from its faulty implementation and by some outright wrong perceptions about the world situation, especially vis-a-vis

China ; which it is suggested could be remedied by restructuring the decisionmaking apparatus of the government to the extent of making it free from personal elements. Finally an evaluation is made that relative success of the policy is due to a careful, conservative and modest definition of India's national interests, taking into account the domestic milieu and the international situation dominated by cold war. A hint is made, rather obliquely, that since international situation shows flexibility India's nonalignment/neutralism might have undergone a subtle change—the change is noticeable in its nonalignment component through bialignment to the decisionmakers' final readiness to enter into 'friendship agreements' with major powers.

It is difficult to acknowledge in a few lines the many debts that I have incurred during the course of this undertaking. Notwithstanding the difficulty, any such attempt will have to include the names of the following individuals and institutions : Dr. Soon Sung Cho, who having first obliged me by agreeing to become my dissertation supervisor, has been helpful in many ways since—the early correction that he made in the outline of the dissertation set the writer on the right trail, which, although since proved lengthy and tortuous, has yet led to the final objective, completion of the dissertation ; Dr. Louis G. Kahle, who was my chairman during the days of coursework in Columbia, has also given me the right advice on many an occasion ; Southeastern State University for the sabbatical leave and research assistance that enabled me to return to Columbia to do the research on the dissertation ; and the many libraries (including the Library of Congress in Washington, D. C.) that opened their doors to me ; and, finally, Mrs. Anima Bhattacharya, my wife, who, during these difficult years, risked my displeasure to remind me of the unfinished work. I am grateful to all these people and institutions for their help and cooperation. Whatever merit this work has is due to their help.

TABLE OF CONTENTS

LIST OF TABLES

Chapter II

Chapter IV

Chapter VI

CHAPTER I

NEUTRALISM—A CONCEPTUAL ANALYSIS

Of the numerous principles current in international relations of the twentieth century, none is more abused or misunderstood than that which goes by the name of neutralism. It is a principle that came into use in its contemporary form in the immediate post-World War II period when the two Super Powers, the United States of America and the Union of Soviet Socialist Republics, found themselves locked in tight, painful embrace, as it were, too immobilized, because of their very antagonism, ideological, political, military, social and economic, to carry on even the semblance of a dialogue between themselves. As if this situation were not bad enough, they found it necessary to have allies and cohorts from all the five continents, and offensively armed themselves to the teeth, threatening thus to engulf the whole world in their war —a war for securing their interests—which could be truly called total and totalitarian. At such a critical juncture in the history of the world, Mr. Jawaharlal Nehru, later to become the Prime Minister of India, rather unobtrusively made this not so unimportant statement in the course of a radio broadcast as the newly installed Vice-President of the interim Government of India[1] :

We propose as far as possible to keep away from the power-politics of groups, aligned against one another, which have led in the past to world wars and which may again lead to disasters, on an even vaster scale....

And, significantly, he sent the following messages to the two Super Powers :

We send our greetings to the people of the United States of America to whom destiny has given a major

---

[1] The broadcast was made from New Delhi on September 7, 1946, almost a year before India was to be bifurcated to give birth to the independent dominions of India and Pakistan. August 15, 1947, was the day of independence for India.

role in international affairs. We trust that this tremendous responsibility will be utilized for the furtherance of peace and human freedom everywhere. To that other great nation of the modern world, the Soviet Union, which also carries a vast responsibility for shaping world events, we send greeting. They are our neighbours in Asia and inevitably we shall have to undertake many common tasks and have much to do with each other.[2]

In the paragraphs just quoted we find expressed for the first time the idea of "keeping away" from power alignments while simultaneously carrying on friendly relations of cooperation with, and deliberately avoiding any hostility to, the two Super Powers, the USA and the USSR, the main participants in the contest and the main mobilizers of power alignments.

This very seed of an idea has now sprouted into a huge tree of a movement, under whose capacious shade have taken shelter many a new nation of the socalled Third World—*le tiers monde*—which includes Asia, Latin America, Africa, and even parts of Europe.[3] But this

---

2 For the full text of the broadcast talk, see Jawaharlal Nehru, *Independence and after* : *A Collection of Speeches, 1946-1949* (New York : The John Day Co., 1950). The First American edition lithographed from the original edition published by the Publications Division, Ministry of Information and Broadcasting, Government of India, Delhi, pp. 339-343. Hereafter referred to as *Speeches, 1946-1949.*

Four months later, Nehru expressed the same ideas in a note circulated to all the Indian ambassadors. For excerpts from the note, see K. P. S. Menon, *Many Worlds* (London, New York, Bombay : Oxford University Press, 1965), pp. 229-30.

3 By the time the Belgrade Conference was held in September, 1961, neutralism as a policy was adopted by the following nations as evidenced by their presence in this conference of nonaligned (*sic*)powers : Afghanistan, Burma, Cambodia, Ceylon, India, Indonesia, Nepal, Iraq, Lebanon, Saudi Arabia, Yemen (Asia) ; Congo, Ethiopia, Ghana, Guinea Mali, Morocco, Somalia, Sudan, Tunisia, the UAR (Africa) . Cuba (Latin America) ; and Cyprus and Yugoslavia (Europe). The Provisional Government of Algeria was also admitted to the Conference. Bolivia and Ecuador and Brazil sent observers.

By 1963, the number of neutralist countries proliferated further. The number of neutralist countries of all categories, Belgrade non-aligned, neutrals and those informally nonaligned was 54 in the General Assembly of the United Nations, which contained 113 members. See J. W. Burton, *International Relations* : *A General Theory* (Cambridge, England, Cambridge University Press, 1965), p. 157.

very popularity of neutralism has, while making it highly important, made it at the same time, a source of extreme confusion to laymen and scholars alike. It behoves us therefore to understand the concept in a way we would be freed of any confusion. It would be our endeavour to do this by referring mostly to aspects of Indian foreign policy, whose themesong it became, especially under late Mr. Nehru, the first Prime Minister of India and the acknowledged father of neutralism and nonalignment.[4]

Section I : Neutralism : What it is Not.

It appears that quite a number of terms are in circulation as synonyms of neutralism, the subject of our discussion and Georg Schwarzenberger, for one, mentions isolationism, non-commitment, neutrality, neutralization, unilateralism, nonalignment, and non-involvement as terms related to neutralism.[5] To this may be added neo-neutrality, coined first by George Cohn, long before the advent of neutralism, but resurrected only comparatively recently by J. W. Burton to explain neutralism of today.[6] Although in some way or another these terms do indeed bear some resemblance to or comparison with our term, it would be difficult to sustain the proposition that they are synonymous with neutralism.

If isolationism is the policy of aloofness, as was followed by the United States of America in the nineteenth and the second and third decades of the present century and by the Soviets for a brief period of time in the thirties

---

[4] But, as Robert A. Scalapino has so acutely observed : "Nehru may be the father of neutralism, yet Nehru for all of his unique qualities, is, in a certain sense, a type. In this sense, there are many Nehrus in Asia—Nehrus without India, Nehrus without Gandhi, Nehrus of right and left, with and without power. They are a response to the broad forces...." See "Neutralism in Asia," *American Political Science Review*, XLVIII (March, 1954), 51.

[5] "The scope for Neutralism, *The Yearbook of World Affairs*, 1961 (New York : Praeger, 1961), pp. 234-236.

[6] J. W. Burton, ed., "Introduction to Non-alignment," in *Non-Alignment* (London : Andre Deutsch, 1966), pp. 23-24. Also see George Cohn, *Neo-Neutrality* (New York : Columbia University Press, 1933), pp. 253, 281, 282, 340.

of the present when the Stalinist "Socialism in One State" was the prevailing dogma,[7] then it is difficult to see how neutralism is the exact replica of isolationism.

Non-commitment is not neutralism either, for it lacks the latter's characteristic of being very much committed to happenings around the world.

Neutralization (also known as permanent neutrality) and neutralism are cognate terms, no doubt, and we might say that a neutralist nation would be more inclined toward making a country permanently neutralized[8] if that helps free it from being a constant and easy bone of contention between the rival powers or power-blocs,[9] but this is not to say that they are identical.

If unilateralism means a policy of "going it alone"[10] "a policy of calculated risk, like the destruction of stockpiles of nuclear weapons irrespective of similar action by other powers"[11] then we hardly see any resemblance between the two, for the neutralist, however alliance-free he might be, may not gamble upon such a risk without consulting other states, especially those who are members of an informal grouping of nations, like the (ex-British) Commonwealth of Nations, or of any other informal or non-rotating organization, like the Bandung Conference.

Nonalignment, a political status, is traditionally understood as a "policy of keeping out of entangling alliances,"[12] and the United States foreign policy before the first World

---

[7] It was Isaac Deutscher who remarked that "Socialism in one state" was nothing but a doctrine of isolationism expressed in Bolshevik idiom. See Peter Lyon, *Neutralism* (Leicester : Leicester University Press, 1963), p. 25.

[8] Cecil V. Crabb says that 'solution by neutralization' is a typically neutralist method. *The Elephants and the Grass* (New York : Praeger, 1965), p. 93.

[9] A neutralized state (ex. Laos or Austria) is sought to be removed from the arena of conflict. "In time of war, those states accept the obligations and demand the rights of all other *neutral* states. In times of peace, they accept the fundamental obligation *never* to join an alliance which could conceivably involve them in war" (my italics). See Michael Brecher, "Neutralism : An Analysis, "*International Journal*, XVII (1961-62), 224-36.

[10] Schwarzenberger, "The Scope for Neutralism," p. 235.

[11] *Ibid.*

[12] *Ibid.*, p. 236.

War could be termed the policy of non-alignment.[13] Should we say then that the United States of America was a neutralist power then in the same sense as India is now ?

As regards non-involvement, in which, as Schwarzenberger puts it, "the emphasis is as much on the struggle between contending ideologies, as on that between rival power-groupings,"[14] it signifies "an attitude of tolerant detachment from the squabbles between the world powers and a resolve not to be deflected more than is absolutely unavoidable from the task of developing one's own country."[15] Neutralism certainly includes a bit of this signification, but it is only one among so many others. There remain two other terms to dispose of—neutrality and neo-neutrality.

Neutrality is indeed a very old concept or principle in international affairs ; indeed, as someone has said, "the problem of neutrality is as old as the problem of politics."[16] Even the warring Greek city-states and Rome and Carthage found it necessary and desirable at times to resort to neutrality. Kautilya, the Indian author of *Arthashastra* and Machiavelli, the Italian author of *The Prince*—the two kindred souls, adept in statecraft and diplomacy but divided only by intervening millenium and a half, allude to it. But neutrality as a viable doctrine came into play only after the emergence of the sovereign nation-state system in Europe during the period ushered in by the Peace of Westphalia (1648) and increasingly out of vogue after the Treaty of Versailles (1919). During this period, punctuated by the warring activities of the belligerent nations, the behavior of some was characterized by non-partiality (rather than impartiality), and non-commitment as well as a lack of concern and responsibility in regard to world affairs.[17] Because of this very behavior, of course, these nations, which came

---

13 *Ibid.*
14 *Ibid.*
15 *Ibid.*
16 R. T. Jangam, "The Problem of Neutrality in World Politics," *United Asia,* VIII (1961), 147.
17 For a brief history of neutrality, see *Ibid.,* pp. 147-48.

to be identified as "neutral" (following a policy of neutrality), "came to enjoy certain rights from the belligerents and obligations towards those belligerents"[18] during the same time under international law so much so that their neutrality became as much a legal concept as a political-diplomatic stance, capable of objective verification or scrutiny. Thus traditional neutrality coming into existence *after* a war has begun,[19] is therefore linked to *overt* war,[20] but at the same time, linked to war of a special kind—non-ideological as well as non-totalitarian.[21] In other words, diplomatic or political neutrality connotes a state of fact, two parties in conflict of a special kind and a third adopting a policy of being on neither side.[22] Also, neutrality tends to be isolationist ; a neutral would stay out of war by being non-partial to all the belligerents[23] and by equally evaluating them,[24] which seems to lend credence to the observation that it is of an amoral type.[25]

Neo-neutrality, on the other hand, is a :

...part of the system of war prevention...is based on an equal devaluation of the war in all cases ...does not seek its own *raison d'etre* in reflections as to whether it has in one situation or another a moral or legal claim to assert its non-participation as a right ; it takes an exception in principle to participation in war in any form ; it replaces it instead with a system of combined sanctions...it recognizes no obligations of impartiality...it disqualifies and rules out war...and it requires that really effective measures must be applied against both belligerents.[26]

18 Michael Brecher, "Neutralism."
19 *Ibid.*
20 Peter Lyon, "Neutralism and the Emergence of the Concept of Neutralism," *The Review of Politics,* XXII (April, 1960), 257. Cf. his statement : "Recognition of legal neutrality depends on differentiating clearly between peace and war as two distinct situations defined by international law." *Ibid.*
21 Peter Lyon, *Neutralism,* p. 18.
22 Peter Lyon, "Neutralism and the Emergence etc.", p. 257.
23 Michael Brecher, "Neutralism," p. 224.
24 J. W. Burton, "Introduction to Non-alignment," p. 23.
25 Peter Lyon, *Neutralism,* p. 71.
26 George Cohn, *Neo-Neutrality,* as cited by J. W. Burton, *Non-Alignment,* p. 23.

Now, neutralism is a doctrine that covers and contains most of the concepts we have discussed above one way or the other, excepting one—neutrality. Thus, neutralism is more than either isolationism, or non-commitment, or neutralization or unilateralism, or non-alignment, or non-involvement. Now, the element of negation in non-commitment, non-alignment or non-involvement is so pertinent that it makes it difficult for us to consider it synonymous with neutralism. But since non-alignment as an "attitude" values negation as something positive,[27] we can accept Michael Brecher's consideration of it as "the passive first stage of neutralism."[28] Neutralism, a product of recent times with unique characteristics, however, is very decidedly not neutrality, although substantially "it might have begun as a continuation of the old concept of neutrality."[29] The only term that comes closest to, and seems almost co-terminous or co-extensive with, neutralism is neo-neutrality—its temper and attitude being the same, it is a positive enough doctrine allowing its advocate to take a position on the merits of the case independent of the contending parties. Even so, neo-neutrality could not be the same as neutralism, because the former could not anticipate the problem, or rather the problems, of a world organized into two rival camps propagating two opposing ideologies and threatening a conflict to the finish that may be global in scope. Also, neo-neutrality badly needed a practitioner to give it more content than it had, but unfortunately he never made his appearance.

Section II : What is Neutralism ?

The first and the most important point to remember

---

27 U. R. Ehrenfels, "The Culturological Approach to Non-Alignment," *The Indian Yearbook of International Affairs*, XIV (Madras : University of Madras, 1955), 126.

28 Michael Brecher, "Neutralism," p. 225.

29 *Ibid.*, p. 227. Pradip Sarbadhikari says the same thing in his *India and the Great Powers : A Study of the Politics of Non-Alignment and of India's Relations with the USA and the USSR* (1947-1961) (London : By the Author. Printed in the Netherlands by J. C. Baan, The Hague, 1962), p. 17.

is that it is a highly subjective phenomenon admitting of various interpretations, the complexity of which is further accentuated by the fact of its being an evolutionary concept which can hardly be explained at any point of time with any degree of finality. In the world of today, just as there are all kinds of communists, who can at best be put on one political spectrum, similarly there are all kinds of neutralists deserving to fare no better. There are at least two,[30] although it is not inconceivable to think of more,[31] categories of them—(1) Neutralist-idealists and (2) Neutralist-realists, and the same nation may very well in one period of world history be neutralist-idealist and in other neutralist-realist, and suffice it to say at this point that the neutralists of the first category would tend to give less consideration to their country's interests narrowly conceived, to be more doctrinaire, think of their policy as something absolute and permanent;

---

[30] Peter Lyon, *Neutralism,* p. 13. Pradip Sarbadhikari also expresses the same idea a little differently : "The evolution of neutralism brings to light two concepts. First, there is the idealistic concept of which neutralism is regarded as a safeguard of wider interests common to many nations. It particularly provides an insurance for the peaceful economic development of states and the inauguration of a phase in world history in which relations between states will only be peaceful. The second conception is that of realists. To them, neutralism is like legal neutrality, an expression of political weakness, that neutralism owes its existence to the cold war as well as to a state of continued preparation of war between states. Based essentially on national interests, it is the natural expression of the policy of many an emerging state." *India and the Great Powers,* p. 18.

[31] Hans J. Morgenthau, for example, conceives of four types of it— (i) escapism, (ii) political non-commitment in the cold war, (iii) moral indifference toward pressing world problems, (iv) surreptitious alignment with the Soviet bloc. *The New York Times Magazine,* August 27, 1961, pp. 25, 76-77.

The Economist, on the other hand, divides neutralist countries according to the nature of their alignments with the two power blocs. Still others classify neutralists according to the political institutions and philosophies represented in the movement. Holla Fick, "From Neutralism to Non-alignment," *The Spectator,* No. 6960, September 8, 1961, p. 310. Another classification talks in terms of "right neutralists," "left neutralists." *The Times of India,* May 20, 1961. Still another classification speaks of positive, negative, messianic, ideological, pragmatic neutralism. Nazli Choucri, "The Non-alignment of Afro-Asian States : Policy, Perception, and Behavior," *Canadian Journal of Political Science,* II, (March, 1969) 1. Another interesting classification finally, includes "status quoist neutralist" and "revisionist neutralist." Samir Anabtawi, "Neutralists and Neutralism," *Journal of Politics* XXVII (May, 1965), p. 357.

while neutralists of the second category, consumed as they seem to be by their passion of serving national interests, would tend to be more pragmatic and think of their policy as something instrumental and transitory.[32] It is moreover a political doctrine, and not a legal status, although attempts have been made to give it a legal facade.[33] It may refer to a policy as well as an attitude,[34] although the distinction if any seems to lose its validity when the neutralist in question is a Nehru or a Bandaranaike.[35] Last, it is not simply a doctrine applicable in the international arena, but also a doctrine geared to domestic considerations as well ; what is more, one doctrine in one arena suggests the other doctrine in the other arena, and vice versa.[36] In other words, it is a Janus-faced doctrine.

There are certain characteristics of the international system in which it may be operative. It must be plagued by the phenomenon known as the cold war, a *status mixtus* of war and peace,[37] which is at best fuzzy ; it is given an ideological coloring and carried out by methods that smacked of totalitarianism.[38] Also, it is a system which includes more than just two states ; in fact, it may be coextensive with the whole world, but nonetheless tending to be dominated by the two Super Powers. In spite of the attempt by the latter to make the struggle one for the establishment of a millenium of morality, the neutralists try to practice a sort of moral neutralism, because they think that there are indeed no

---

32 Ernest Iefever, "Nehru, Nasser and Nkrumah on Neutralism," in *Neutralism and Non-alignment,* ed. by Lawrence W. Martin (New York : Praeger, 1962), p. 132.

33 See J. W. Burton, "Rights and Obligations of Nonalignment, *"The Australian Outlook,* XVI (December, 1962), 292-303.

34 Robert Scalapino, "Neutralism in Asia," p. 50. Also, Peter Lyon, "Neutralism and the Emergence etc.", 266.

35 *Ibid.*

36 In our next section, it will be argued that both domestic and non-domestic compulsions dictate this neutralism, and that both these compulsions are related to each other. This, it is expected, will justify our statement above.

37 Peter Lyon, "Neutralism and the Emergence," 251.

38 Peter Lyon, Neutralism, p. 18.

moral issues involved in this struggle. So neutralism involves a feeling of equidistance from both the West and the East.[39]

Unlike neutrality, which was a policy for individual countries to follow, it is one that is followed simultaneously by many nations—after all, the formation of a "peace area" including many nations is one of the goals of neutralism.[40] Neutralism is not withdrawal, but a kind of selective participation, and hence not a passive thing, but quite activistic, and this is relevant only at the global level in the context of the cold war and the bipolar phase of world politics, and no attempt is made to reduce it to regional proportions.[41]   Or, better still, it is a sort of opting out of direct involvement in the central power struggle to play the role of a referee in that game.   Hence, neutralism is participating in the play, yet not quite in it, "like the Greek Chorus."[42] Thus, cold war conciliation, moral suasion and compromise are very definitely elements in neutralism.[43]   It is an attempted "existence alongside both power groups" of those non-powers who espouse it, and therefore "logically a demonstration that co-existence rests upon the continued existence of this third agency."[44] The neutralist does not seem to have any "official enemy" in the global context,[45] and hence can be on friendly terms with all, and someone, therefore, has called neutralism "the doctrine of defence by friendship."[46]   This friendship does not call for any commitment—yet, "it is only being uncommitted up to the time when it commits itself, as it does on each occasion when it arises.   Neutralism is the expression of a right to make up its own mind in every case,

---

[39] *Ibid.*
[40] K. P. Karunakaran, "Nonalignment," *Seminar,* XIX (March, 1961), 13-16.
[41] Nazli Choucri, "The Nonalignment of Afro-Asian States," 6.
[42] Coral Bell, "Nonalignment and the Balance of Power," *The Australian Outlook,* XVII (August, 1963), 118.
[43] Pradip Sarbadhikari, *India and the Great Powers,* p. 107.
[44] J. W. Burton, "Rights and Obligations of Nonalignment," 303.
[45] Nazli Choucri, "The Nonalignment of Afro-Asian States," 6.
[46] Michael Edwardes, "Illusions of the Nehru Bequest," in *India's Nonalignment Policy : Strengths and Weaknesses,* ed. by Paul F. Power (Boston : D. C. Heath, 1967), p. 41.

but in accordance with the merits of the case and its own national interest," as defined by itself.[47]   Representing the third type of anti-alliance policy, which opposes all formal alliance, including those among other powers,[48] it is not opposed to membership of an informal organization, like the Commonwealth of Nations,[49] which might obviate the danger of isolation.[50]   In a world split among rival blocs, it is a kind of making separate peace,[51] but perhaps, as Georg Schwarzenberger points out, "it underlines a negative type of peace...it is characterized by the absence of war rather than a common struggle for the realization of positive values of world civilization, and, in the cold war atmosphere of the post-1945 world, this has been the unhappy lot of a world divided against itself.[52] Yet finally it is an anti-status quo, revisionary, if not revolutionary, doctrine in the sense that it "not only rejects the existing world reality, reflecting the dominance of the developed Powers, which happen to be Western also, but tries to change for the better their own present inferior position in it,[53] and that means, it is a way of attaining importance and leadership in the world.   While rejecting the proposition that the principal crisis of our time is the struggle between capitalism and communism, it stands foursquare on its belief that the failure to resolve the problems of colonial slavery, poverty, and under-development in general of three-fourths of the world's humanity is the real crisis.[54]   Mr. Nehru himself said in a speech to the joint session of the Boards of Governors of IMF, IBRD and IFC at New Delhi, October 6, 1958 :

...And yet the major division of the world today,

---

[47]Vincent Sheean, *Nehru : The Years of Power* (New York : Random House, 1960), p. 123.
[48] George Liska, "The Third Party : The Rationale of Non-Alignment," in *Neutralism and Nonalignment*, p. 83.
[49] India in fact continued her membership in the Commonwealth of Nations even after becoming a republic in 1950.
[50] George Liska, "The Third Party," p. 83.
[51] *Ibid.*, p. 81, although Krishna Menon once describe it as "collective Peace."
[52] Georg Schwarzenberger, "Scope for Neutralism," 237.
[53] Peter Lyon, *Neutralism*, p. 120.
[54] *Ibid.*, pp. 75,82.

I think the real division, is the division of the indus-
trialized communities or the developed communities
and the underdeveloped communities. That is the real
division of the world today.[55]

Lastly, neutralism means independent policy rejecting
the claim of either of the Super Powers to have exclusive
responsibility for decisions as to whether peace or war
should not be preserved or prevented.[56] Thus by itself it
appears to be a sufficiently positive concept ; yet other
aspects of a neutralist nation's foreign policy, especially
India's, like crusades against colonialism and racialism,
etc., go to make it more positive, even dynamically so. It
was this awareness of the dynamic character of India's
policy that led Mr. Krishna Menon to react to the appellation "neutral" (as a description of India's policy) in this
way :

We want it understood that we do not welcome
this appellation of being called a neutral....We are
not a neutral country...We are not neutral in regard
to peace. We are not neutral in regard to domination
by imperialist or other countries. We are not
neutral in regard to ethical values. We are not neutral with regard to the greatest economic and social
problems that may arise...We would take part, we
would participate, we would express our views. Even
that expression, "positive neutrality" is a contradiction in terms. There can no more be positive neutrality than there can be a vegetarian tiger.[57]

Section III : Roots of Neutralism

Although neutralism is a twentieth century phenomenon, it could be traced to sources dating back to much
earlier times. A look at India's neutralism makes this
quite clear. As someone has pointed out, neutralism has

55 *Foreign Affairs Review,* IV (October, 1958), 191.
56 J. W. Burton, "Introduction to Nonalignment," 17-18.
57 Quoted in N. D. Palmer, "India's Foreign Policy, "*The Political
Quarterly,* XXXIII (October-December, 1962), 402-403.

its roots in the "mind and heart" of India. There are certain historical experiences and attitudes, philosophical bases and personality factors which are abstract and non-material ; these have joined forces with some more concrete and material things like geographical configurations, internal political and economic situations in the context of a particular global confrontation between two Super Powers to produce the phenomenon known as neutralism.

According to some, it is the first category of factors, essentially nonmaterial or abstract in character, that are among the most important sources of influence on neutralism in India,[58] and these are matters of attitudes and beliefs, profoundly affecting the Indian character, that could be traced to earlier times. Dr. K. S. Murty for one suggests that by history and temperament Indians have a horror of concerning themselves with affairs of other people. Ancient Hindus were insular and wanted to be left alone and to leave others alone. Hindu ethics is essentially individualistic, and not social. The *Gita*, the sacred scripture of the Hindus, taught *anasakti*, nonattachment. Samkhya and Advaita Vedanta (systems of ancient Hindu philosophy) held that the world is an illusion (*Maya*), and we should be mere detached spectators of the world show.[59] Hinduism, as revealed in the *Gita* is, if anything, catholic in temperament and is essentially tolerant of all views and faiths. And, both Buddhism and Jainism, two other religions developed in India, extolled non-violence, role of Reason, and moral appeal, and denigrated very clearly paths of violence and war. The central message of India's philosophical tradition, dating from the Buddha, says Michael Brecher, has revolved round the rejection of absolutes and extreme positions ; on the contrary, it has stressed philosophical relativity, intellectual catholicism, and coexistence of good and evil ; in short the golden middle path of compromises and tolerance of oppo-

---

58 Krishnalal Shridharani, "The Philosophic Bases of India's Foreign Policy," *India Quarterly*, XIV (April-June, 1958), 197.
59 Satchidananda Murty, *Indian Foreign Policy* (Calcutta : Scientific Agency, 1964), p. 35.

sites.[60] This philosophical tradition has yielded "the idea of the independence of the two powerblocs in making up her own mind as to the rights and wrongs of a given problem, the use of methods that relax inflexibility and counter-inflexibility."[61] Gandhi, the father of the Indian Nation, bequeathed to his followers the technique of non-cooperation. The philosophical tradition and attitudes and Gandhian technique, when transferred to the international sphere, says Dr. Murty, "result in confirming neutralist tendencies and in trying to keep one's country as a political monad, whereas other concepts such as 'the whole world is one family' (*Vasudhaiva kutumbakam*), the good of all beings' (*sarvabhutahita*), and 'the welfare of the people' *(lokasamgraha)*, tend to make Indian policy a dynamic one concerned with freedom and welfare of people all over the world . . ."[62]

This apart, India has certain historical experiences of British colonialism, which in spite of its having certain good features, was yet harsh and humiliating for the people of India since it was not free from exploitative and racist overtones. That India did not decide on any formal alignment with the Western bloc is because there is still, "a residual antipathy" to the West, as one Western diplomat in New Delhi observed, "clouding their assessment of the contemporary world power struggle in which the Western bloc is one of the principal antagonists."[63]

If Gandhian legacy were allowed to have its full impact, then of course the residual antipathy to the West could have been overcome, for had not Gandhi written, "India's greatest glory will consist not in regarding Englishmen as her implacable enemies fit only to be turned out of India at the first available opportunity, but turning them into friends and partners in a new Commonwealth of Nations."[64] But

60 For a fuller treatment of the point, see *Ibid,,* pp. 197-200. Also, Michael Brecher, "Neutralism : An Analysis," 227-229.

61 Krishnalal Shridharani, "The Philosophic Bases," 200.

62 Satchidananda Murty, *Indian Foreign Policy,* p. 35.

63 William Henderson, "The Roots of Neutralism in Southern Asia," *International Journal,* XIII (Winter, 1957-58), 30.

64 Quoted in A. P. Rana, "The Intellectual Dimensions of India's Nonalignment," *Journal of Asian Studies,* XXVIII (February, 1969), 301.

Nehru, a keen student of contemporary history, of imperialism-colonialism, and emotionally, if not dogmatically,
attracted to socialism as he was, could not accept it in toto,
thereby "whittling away the Gandhian essence."[65]   As A. P.
Rana puts it :

> Nehru considered Gandhi's ideas basically sound,
> but the firm association in his mind of capitalism with
> imperialism, his great attraction to the socalled demo-
> cratic experiment to raise the lot of the poor, and his
> desire not to tie a future foreign policy of India to a
> great European power like England's, and so merely to
> perpetuate the old system of power-politics instead of
> scuttling it, these impulses in the young Nehru were
> too heady to be checked by Gandhi's cooler vision.[66]

Some culturologists, who see an element of 'non' in
India's neutralism and who would rather prefer to call it
nonalignment, see a profound connection between India's
ageold, hoary, indigenous culture and the main theme of
India's foreign policy, which is of much more recent vintage.
Neutralism seen only in a negative light resembles, as U. R.
Ehrenfels says, the idea of nonresistance, nonviolence and
nirvana (non-illusion)." Also, as the same writer suggests,
the formulation of a concept in a negative way may remind
us of the fact that one of the most far-reaching contributions
to world civilizations by India was the "invention" of zero
as a mathematical entity and its mathematical use in its
positional value.[67]   Seen from a wider angle, the expression
as well as the contents of neutralism (as a developed variant
of nonalignment) may be found suggestive of a deeper connection with Indian cultural traditions.[68]

If these are some of the less obvious abstract factors,
then there were other concrete and more objective factors
that unmistakably influenced the emergence of neutralism.
In the first place, the state of the world into which India
emerged as an independent entity wore certain character-

---

65 *Ibid.,* 301.
66 *Ibid.,* 301-302.
67 U. R. Ehrenfels, "The Culturological Approach to Nonalignment,"
126-127.
68 For elaboration, see *Ibid.,* 127-136.

istics. The immense technological innovations, with all the rapid means of transportation and communications, have tended to reduce the world into a rather small and compact unit. Presence of terrible nuclear weapons threatens a complete doom for *all* nations—obliterating the difference between neutral and belligerent, peace-loving and warlike ; a war fought with such weapons would only leave ashes, no victor, nor any vanquished.[69] In such a world, there happned to be two Super Powers, armed with opposite ideologies and awesome armies, engaged in a cold war (to which reference has been made already), which may turn into a hot war. This situation does not leave any scope for complacency even for those who are not directly involved, because they are destined to be involved if a war breaks out. The radically transformed character of the international milieu however does allow scope for a kind of "manipulative diplomacy," known as neutralism, which is subject, however, to a minimum of defense capability.[70]

The appropriateness of the technique of nonalignment-cum-neutralism is further underscored by the failure of a policy of alignment and armament tried by both the principal power blocs. The international situation has not changed for the better from either point of view ; neither has got any victory—communism has not been defeated, nor even fully contained ; nor has communism's threat of burying capitalism been successfully carried out. On the other hand, both sides seemed to be delicately balanced in a system known as the "balance of terror," losing all flexibility for initiative. As a result problems have risen, continue to rise, accumulate and get insoluble. Requirement of the situation seems to be a new approach, neutralism, an approach to international relations geared to reduction of tensions, building bridges, even providing solutions, at least temporary.[71]

---

[69] For a description of the changes in the world, see H. T. Jangam, "The Problem of Neutrality in World Politics," 147-150.

[70] Jayantanuja Bandyopadhyaya, *The Making of India's Foreign Policy* (Bombay, Calcutta : Allied Publishers, 1970), p. 22.

[71] H. T. Jangam, "The Problem of Neutrality in World Politics," 149-150.

The Super Powers might have lost all initiative in tackling their problems directly, but in their quest for securing more allies they felt the necessity for wooing the undeveloped or developing countries, especially the more important ones among them.   India felt their needs keenly ; to be able to meet their needs is to have an opportunity to be "areas of agreement."[72]   The problem is : How to use this opportunity ?

Against this international background, one has to remember the geopolitical factors of India.   India has a strategic geopolitical location, large physical area, tremendous human and material resources.   Such a situation rules out any possibility of compromising one's prestige by playing second fiddle.   As regards the strategic location of India, J. Nehru had this to say as early as in 1949 :

When we talk of Asia, remember that India, not because of ambition of hers, but because of geography, because of history, and because of so many other things, inevitably has to play a very important part in Asia.   And not only that ; India becomes a kind of meeting ground for various trends and forces and a meeting ground between what might roughly be called the East and the West.

And he said further :

Whichever problem in Asia you may take up, somehow or other India comes into the picture.   Whether you think in terms of China or the Middle East or South-East Asia, India immediately comes into the picture.   It is so situated that because of past history, traditions, etc., in regard to any major problem of a country or a group of countries of Asia, India has to be considered.   Whether it is a problem of defense or trade or industry or economic policy, India cannot be ignored.   She cannot be ignored, because as I said, her geographical position is a compelling reason....[73]

---

[72] Peter Lyon, *Neutralism.*

[73] See Dorothy Norman, ed., *Nehru : The First Sixty Years* (New York : The John Day Co., 1965), p. 462.

K. M. Panikkar, one of Nehru's closest advisers in earlier years, also drew attention of his countrymen to the pivotal position India occupied in the Indian Ocean and strongly advocated India's pursuit of interests in the oceanic problems which the British policy-makers in pre-Independence days had so grossly neglected or even ignored.[74]

Anyway proper utilization of this geographical situation must be done. But how? At the same time sealed as she undoubtedly appeared to be in the north by the Himalayas, India was still a neighbor of the People's Republic of China and the Soviet Union. What does the logic of the situation suggest? India must be on friendly terms with both, but not at the same time at the expense of the USA, which was and perhaps still is mightier of the two Super Powers. What is the technique of being on friendly terms with both?

The internal political situation of India at the time of her independence, on the other hand, was one of latent instability,[75] the presence of Jawaharlal Nehru and his Congress Party notwithstanding. Apart from the factor of nationalism[76] which remained quite strong suggesting a foreign policy of independence, there were certain other factors which suggested that this foreign policy should not be carried on in the traditional way of the big powers. Also, forces of division, reaction, and disruption within the Congress Party itself, not to speak of the country at large,

---

74 K. M. Panikkar, *India and the Indian Ocean* (London : 1951), pp. 17-18. As regards Britain's failure to give adequate consideration to the geopolitical problems of India, he suggested that the obsession of geopolitical thinkers, whom the British followed so blindly, with the question of world strategy in pursuit of the view that the control of land, air, and sea must ultimately pass to the power which controlled the pivotal land area in Europe, was the basic reason. Even MacKinder, the founder of geopolitical school, thought equally in terms of the continent and consequently the Indian Ocean was considered only as a link area of the "World Island" of which the only effective political boundaries were the Atlantic and the Pacific. *Ibid.*, p. 18.

75 For an account of the relationship between nonalignment/neutralism and stability, see J. W. Burton, "Nonalignment and Stability," 62-98.

76 For the influence of nationalism on India's foreign policy, see N. Parameswaran Nayar, "Nationalism as a Factor in India's Foreign Policy," *Indian Yearbook of International Affairs,* XI (Madras : University of Madras, 1962), 433-458.

were too formidable to be played fire with, with thought-less policies and attitudes. That is to say, the delicate balance of political forces within the country was seen to brook no interference from factors outside the country. Nehru understood this better than anybody else and he felt the need for not "going too far in one direction" in international affairs. There was the need for preventing the polarization of the effective public opinion within the Congress Party and interparty affairs, involving the Congress and other all-India parties.[77] Those needs have to be fulfilled, but how ?

There was also the question of stability in another context. The socio-cultural problems—of linguism, provincialism, communalism—after partition were gigantic. These were sources of disunity in the bodypolitic of India. These problems could not be removed immediately, but an attempt could be made not to add more to the list. This could be done by a technique of quarantining the country against the "cold war epidemic" in order to ensure normal political evolution. What is the best technique of serving the functions of an "isolation hospital" ?[78] Nehru was also aware of the problem that his leadership may appear to be lacklustre if judged by his record of solving domestic problems rapidly and dramatically.[79] Leadership needs dramatic ability. How is that need to be met ? Ills of India's economy were no more tractable. When India emerged independent in 1947, her economic problems were the problems of underdevelopment ; average consumer expenditure being the poorest in the world, the bulk of the population continued to live below the breadlines ; India's yearly savings were too small to enable her to finance a selfsustaining economy. The situation necessitated more

---

[77] Devdutt, "Nonalignment and India," *Indian Journal of Political Science,* XXIII (1962), 390-397. Also, M. S. Rajan, "Indian Foreign Policy in Action, 1954-56, "*India Quarterly,* XVI (July-September, 1960), 203-236."

[78] Devdutt, "Nonalignment and India," 390-397.

[79] George Liska, "The Third Party," 90 ; also, Robert C. Good, "State-Building as a Determinant of Foreign Policy," in *Neutralism and Nonalignment,* 12.

money, more production, more skill, technical and managerial.[80] How are they going to come ?

In the matter of organization of the economy, both public and private sectors were playing their part, although the latter was undoubtedly dominant. The uneasy balance between the two sectors was not unlike that in the political field. How to maintain the balance, by freeing it of extradomestic concerns and/or frictions ? The imperative of the situation was : international political considerations which might outweigh economic considerations must not be allowed to prevail.[81] How to satisfy this imperative ?

But perhaps the most important element that tilted India's foreign policy in the direction of nonalignment/neutralism is, as has been pointed out by one keen student of India's foreign policy,[82] that of *ideological independence* [emphasis added]. That this factor played a decisive role is evident in this observation made by Nehru in the Indian Parliament in 1955 :

The world seems to be divided into two mighty camps, the Communist and the anti-Communist, and either party cannot understand how anyone can be foolish enough not to line up with itself. That just shows how little understanding these people have of *the mind of Asia* [emphasis added]. Talking of India only, and not of all Asia, we have fairly clear ideas about our political and economic structure. We function in this country under a constitution which may be described as a parliamentary democracy. It has not been imposed upon us. We propose to continue with it. We do not intend changing it. We intend to function on the economic plane, too, in our own way. With all respect to some Hon. Members opposite, we have no intention to turn communists. At

---

80 Devdutt, "Nonalignment and India," 393 ; also Devdutt, "A Reappraisal of Nonalignment," *United Asia,* XV (November, 1963), 766-768 ; and K. P. Karunakaran, "Domestic and Afro-Asian Requirements," in *India's Nonalignment Policy,* 60.

81 Devdutt, "Nonalignment and India," 393.

82 J. Bandyopadhyaya, *The Making of India's Foreign Policy,* p. 250.

the same time, we have no intention of being dragoon-
ed in any other direction.... We have chosen our path
and we propose to go along it, and to vary it as and
when we choose, not at somebody's dictate or pressure ; and we are not afraid of any other country
imposing its will upon us by military methods or any
other methods....Our thinking and our approach do
not fit in with this great crusade of communism or
crusade of anti-communism.[83]

If these were the requirements of the situation, if
these were related to the past thinking of India and the
conditioning of the Indian mind during the struggle for
freedom in India, and if these were the contemporary
circumstances of India, the resultant policy cannot be any
different from what it really became at the hands of
Nehru. Nehru himself believed that he did not originate
the policy ; he even thought that his being in charge of
external affairs of India after Independence had nothing to
do with the particular type of foreign policy followed by
India. In Nehru's words : "Looking back, India's policy
has not been some sudden bright inspiration of an individual, but a gradual growth evolving from even before
Independence. The inevitable line that we took subsequently has followed that thinking as a matter of
course."[84] As one student has said :

Nehru's view is correct in this sense that a policy of
nonalignment [sic] was logically indicated by the
basic determinants of India's foreign policy. But it
is wrong in the equally important sense that what was
logical was not inevitable ; it has never been so in the
history of international relations. It requires a rational statesman to see the logical implications of given
facts and situations for policy decisions and to act
upon them. History would not otherwise abound
with irrational decisions on the part of statesmen. In

---

[83] Jawaharlal Nehru, *India's Foreign Policy, Selected Speeches,* September, 1946 to April 1961, (Delhi : Publications Division, Government
of India, 1961), 68-69.
[84] *Ibid.,* p. 83.

this sense, Nehru was personally responsible for the policy of nonalignment [sic].[85]

So if these were the requirements of the situation, and if they were left to be interpreted and solved by a complex personality like Nehru, with his eclecticism, emotions and prejudices ; whose 'syncretic theory of democracy'[86] allowed him to combine in himself a strong dislike for colonialism-imperialism of the West with the love for the latter's liberal traditions—democracy, parliamentary system, individual liberties, and scientific outlook ; who had his distrust for dogmatic communism or for that matter any "ism"[87] but who thought highly of socialism in the Soviet Union and felt the need for the latter as a counterpoint to the West ;[88] who, as Foreign Minister thought more of the economic bases of politics ;[89] who accepted Gandhism as a technique but not as any Gospel-sermon ; and finally, whose internationalism was geared to making India a nation to reckon with in international politics ;[90] the result of such interpretation and effort to solve the problems noted above

85 *Ibid.*, p. 260.

86 A. P. Rana, "Intellectual Dimensions," 393.

87 Cf. "I am not enamoured of these 'isms' and my approach is, and I should like to say the country's approach should be, rather a pragmatic approach in considering the problem and I want to forget the 'ism' attached to it. Our problem today is to raise the standard of the masses, supply them with their needs, give them the wherewithal to lead a decent life, and help them to progress and advance in life . . . I should like to set them on the right road and I do not care what 'ism' it is that helps me to set them on that road, provided I do it." Nehru as quoted in A. Appadorai, *Indian Political Thinking* : From *Naoroji to Nehru* (London : Oxford University Press, 1971), p. 118.

88 A. P. Rana, "Intellectual Dimensions," 304 ; also, Jawaharlal Nehru, *A Bunch of Old Letters* (New York : Asia Publishing House, 1960), pp. 424-425.

89 Cf. this statement by Nehru : "Behind them (foreign policies) lie all manner of things. Ultimately foreign policy is the outcome of economic policy, and until India has properly evolved her economic policy, her foreign policy will be rather vague, rather inchoate, and will be groping." *India's Foreign Policy*, pp. 24-27.

90 Cf. this statement by Nehru : "A free India, with her vast resources, can be of great service to the world and to humanity. India will always make a difference to the world ; fate has marked us for big things. When we fall, we fall low ; when we rise, inevitably we play our part in the world drama." See *Unity of India : Collected Writings, 1937-1940* (London : Lindsay Drummond, 1948), p. 307.

cannot be but neutralism as a technique of foreign policy for India in the period under consideration.

Although, according to some, it is the philosophic bases that have provided the rationale of foreign policy, and therefore there is nothing accidental or casual about India's devising neutralism,[91] to a man of Nehru's temperament, it is the concrete situations that have given rise to the present requirements which directly affect the people while the abstract and non-material factors have undoubtedly helped in the matter of building the attitude that neutralism also connotes. The clinching proof of this point lies in the fact that with each major change in concrete situations, international as well as national, the contents of neturalism have changed, making the neutralism of India in some situations 'rightist,' in others 'middle-of-the-road,' and in still others 'leftists'. In the very first years of independence, India in spite of her expressed desire to steer clear of bloc politics in international affairs, did not follow a conspicuously neutralist course. For example, she decided to remain within the Commonwealth of Nations, headed still by Great Britain, a constitutional monarchy and an avowed member of the Western bloc, as typified by her membership of NATO, a rival alliance in the raging cold war politics of the era. Even Nehru himself had to admit :

India has to depend on the rest of the world for her trade, for her commerce and for many supplies that she needs, including very badly, food and military supplies. Due to past associations India has come to depend very largely for certain supplies from the United Kingdom and has built up commercial relations.[92]

Even if we are unable to deny it the appellation of neutralism or nonalignment, it could be stated without arousing undue controversy that this was rather vague,

---

[91] It was not only Krishnalal Shridharani who actually provided the words that we have used above ; U. R. Ehrenfels also tried to stress these philosophical-cultural bases. See, Ehrenfels, "The Culturological Approach to Nonalignment," 124-136.

[92] Quoted by Ramjana Sidhanta, "Indian Nonalignment," in J. W. Burton, *International Relations*, p. 30.

without precision and clarity and much content, at least in the beginning.

Section IV : Developing Contents of Neutralism

It has been suggested that neutralism is an evolutionary concept which has taken years to come to its present stage of development. So far as India herself is concerned, her neutralism initially was rather vague and imprecise, but with every passing year, it acquired a kind of definiteness. At first certain general propositions came to the surface : (i) Opposition to colonialism and racialism, as evidenced by her championship of the cause of Indonesian independence and that of Indians of South Africa ; (ii) organizing international assistance for economic development of the underdeveloped areas ; (iii) urge for peace and disarmament, and (iv) strong support to the United Nations, the world body which has succeeded the League of Nations. At first, at this first formative stage of neutralism, known as nonalignment, Indian neutralism was generally inclined toward the West—as has been point out before, she was the first Asian state to reconcile her independent status with membership in the Commonwealth of Nations. This was due to several factors, the most important amongst which were economics, history, education and language. But this initial leaning toward the West was very much short of alignment with the West. This refusal to be aligned signified that she would not remain indifferent or neutral or passive in regard to questions of colonialism, racialism or peace. It further signified that she would not remain indifferent to question of war and in the event of war breaking out, Nehru himself said : "We are going to join the side which is to our interest when the time comes to make the choice."

Yet there were certain lingering negative elements in her basic approach, and they were : aloofness from bloc alignments, power-politics of the two Super Powers, and from the struggle for supremacy between Capitalism and Communism. In this period therefore India hesitated to take a full plunge into world politics. Behind this hesitation, however, was her awareness of her own weakness, and therefore, the realization that any such plunge would not be practicable and may even be counter-productive. By 1961, however, India was sufficiently cured of this hesitation to be able to subscribe to the joint communique (India was a signatory to it) of the Belgrade Conference of the Nonaligned Countries which included the statement, requiring considerable modification of her previously known attitudes, to the effect that : "The participating countries consider it essential that the nonaligned countries should participate in solving outstanding international issues concerning peace and security in the world, as none of them can remain unaffected by or indifferent to those issues."[93]

As regards India's attitude toward the regional blocs, this showed some change. Initially, India did not particularly object to the military alliances ; her attitude was one of supreme unconcern. In fact, India did accept some alliance systems as contributing to world peace. For example, India agreed with the United Kingdom when the latter adhered to the Brussels Pact and the Western Union which she (India) held was in accordance with the interests of other members of the Commonwealth of Nations, the United Nations and the promotion of peace in general. India, however, changed her mind when NATO, which included some colonialist countries like Portugal, widened its scope and took upon itself the defense of the colonial possessions of the member nations of the alliance, which directly affected India. An attitude of unconcern was thus replaced by that of unconcealed antagonism.

From this changed attitude to the regional (especially) military pacts emerged a new enlargement of the concepts of neutralism, the idea of a "peace area," comparable to that of an "atom-free zone" as suggested by Poland's then Foreign Minister Adam Rapacki. This served notice

---

[93] For the original text of the communique, see G. H. Jansen, *Nonalignment and the Afro-Asian States* (New York : Praeger, 1966), Appendix A-5, 421-422.

in effect that India would not tolerate without resistance
any extension of regional pacts in certain parts of Asia
and Africa—for that would mean, as India feared, extension of cold war in an hitherto undisturbed area, an area
of comparative peace.

Later, in April 1954, when India signed a treaty with
the People's Republic of China over Tibet, now an accepted *region* of China after subjugation by the People's
Army of China, another dimension was added to neutralism in the shape of Panch Sheel or the Five Principles of
Peaceful Coexistence, the most important of which was
the Principle of Peaceful   Coexistence itself. With the
formulation of this principle, neutralism became more
positive in tone than it was ever before. Neutralism,.
which had simply opposed cold war before, now pointed
the way to its containment.

The above mentioned conceptual developments were
finally regularized to be following from neutralism itself
by the joint communique issued at the end of the Belgrade
Conference in September, 1961. Finally, another development took place after China invaded India in the closing
weeks of 1962. India, stunned by the invasion, sought
help from both the United States of America and the
Union of Soviet Socialist Republics in her effort to thwart
the Chinese, the erstwhile friends with whom ironically
enough India had signed the Panch Sheel Treaty. This
novel experiment by neutralist India of seeking help
from both the Super Powers against the People's Republic of
China added another dimension to India's neutralism, and
this stance of India, variously described as bialignment,
equidistance, or equal proximity, has not been held by those
who opposed neutralism as signifying any departure from
neutralism, and has been held by neutralists themselves,
including Indian policy-makers, to be actually in fulfillment of the purpose of neutralism, and therefore, its final
vindication.[94]

---

[94] In preparing this section, the writer has relied on N. Parameswaran
Nayar, "Growth of Nonalignment in World Affairs," *India Quarterly*,
XVII (January-March, 1962), 4-45.

Section V : Neutralism and the Balance of Power

It has been pointed out in previous section (Section 3) that neutralism means being uncommitted up to the time of committing itself. This suggests that there may be a "latent threat of alignment" in neutralism. So long as India remains nonaligned, rather neutralist, there is always the possibility of her aligning with one or the other bloc, and it is this possibility, as A.P. Rana for one suggests, that exerts pressure on the two contestants in the cold war. This is not unlike the policy Britain had followed with regard to the continent (of Europe) across the channel for the greater part of the nineteenth century, and the policy that she followed did include a threat of intervention, and later, even of alignments. The abstention that is implicit or inherent in this kind of policy is only tactical and temporary, not strategic and permanent ; and Nehru's policy was not much different from Britain's, and indeed, according to Rana, it was so remarkably similar that Nehru the diplomat could very well be considered "in line with the great incumbents of the British Foreign Office."[95]

That India's neutralism is not in any fundamental sense different from Britain's European policy in the nineteenth century is shown in the following facts : one, India refuses to be linked permanently to any other power or to any of the existing alliances ; two, at the same time her neutralism carries a latent possibility, if not an actual threat, of alignment ; and three, India does resist the power of both sides—she confronts their power with her own which, as could be pointed out, is highly artificial, and uni-

---

[95] A. P. Rana, "The Nature of India's Foreign Policy," *India Quarterly*, XXII (April-June, 1966), 125. The whole article is indeed valuable (pp. 101-139). Rana's ideas are not entirely original ; however, they are in elaboration of those of Girja Shankar Bajpai, who was independent India's first Secretary-General of the Ministry of External Affairs and as such one of Prime Minister Nehru's principal foreign policy consultants in earlier years. Bajpai suggested the use of neutralism in the direction of maintenance of a world balance of power in an article, "India and the Balance of Power," *Indian Yearbook of International affairs*, 1952, II (Madras : University of Madras, 1952), 1-8. And it could be said without fear of contradiction that Bajpai could not have published his article without Nehru's permission.

quely too, because it is derived from a *policy*, and not from the nation's tangible resources, and thereby helps to lessen or to divide their potential power *vis-a-vis* each side and the world. This policy therefore does not imply exact repudiation of power ; it may be repudiation of power conceived in naked terms, but it is not repudiation of power following from the *policy*, which is neither tangible nor natural, but intangible or artificial. Also, since the aim of India's foreign policy is to maintain her sovereign independence intact, to continue to be a sovereign power within a society of sovereign states, it is rather difficult to see how neutralism is in any way different from traditional balance of power.[96]

Feasibility of this balance of power however depends upon the realities of the world after World War II, which include, among other things, the novelty of nuclear technology with all that it means. That is to say, the effectiveness of neutralism depends among other things on the difficulty of the Super Powers in resolving their conflicts by an ultimate resort to war. Maintenance of the "Balance of Terror in a cold war situation of bipolarity thus is the guarantor of its workability."[97] As Coral Bell puts it : "The viability of nonalignment [sic] as a policy has been and is related to particular phases of the power balance."[98] Thus, the advocates of this view do not want to project neutralism as a policy of abstention from power-politics or as a refusal to follow the ages-old and questionable ways of the balance of power, for to do so would be to represent it falsely.

---

[96] A. P. Rana, "The Nature of India's Foreign Policy," 101-131. The thesis that India's neutralism carries a latent possibility, if not an actual threat, may however be contested on the ground that no proof has been adduced for its assumption that the threat of alignment with one side or the other was implicit in it. See G. L. Jain, "Indian Nonalignment and the Balance of Power," *India Quarterly*, XIII (April-June, 1966), 177.
[97] Georg Schwarzenberger, "Scope for Neutralism," 238-239.
[98] "Nonalignment and the Power Balance," *Australian Outlook*, XVII (August, 1965), 117. Cf. Nehru's statement : "When there is substantial difference in the strength of the two opposing forces, we in Asia, without limitations, will not be able to influence the issue. But where the two opposing forces are fairly evenly matched, then it is possible to make our weight felt in the balance." *Ibid.*, 118.

However, some scholars have tried to pick holes in the theory that neutralism is a twentieth century variation of the balancing process by referring to the other radical characteristic of the post-World War II era with its flaws. This radical nature consists in the existence in the international arena of a large number of new Asian and African states—of which India was only one but perhaps the most representative—all of which underscore the end of historic colonialism-imperialism. International politics has undergone a tremendous transformation beacuse of the attitude of these nations, or rather political entities, born as they are of common historical experience of military subjugation, economic exploitation and racial discrimination by the empire-minded nations of the West. They are all economically underdeveloped and therefore want economic development. They are also militarily weak, yet because of their nationalism that has won them their independence they want to play a role in international affairs. India shared their experiences and their objectives and thus quite naturally tried to organize and even consolidate the political bonds of the area of peace and to help create a third force in international politics. This third force, thought India, would prevent hot war and mitigate cold war, increase the 'area of peace' and control international conflict situations and the nations of the third force would by working together in international forums check imperialism and racialism and further security, national development and world order.[99] Michael Brecher, a well known student of neutralism, however, thought some years ago, even while conscious of the changes they represented that there was a flaw in them, that no state of the 'area of peace' individually measured up to play the role of the balancer ; neither was the area as a whole any better off. Brecher said :

> ...No state can be a balancer in the nineteenth century sense simply because the gap between the power of the two Super Powers and all others is such

---

[99] Jayantanuja Bandyopadhyaya, *The Making of India's Foreign Policy,* pp. 95-96.

that the addition of the powers of India or anybody else won't make any difference.[100]

Even so, Brecher admitted a stabilizing role for the neutralist, as typified by India, in international politics. Neutralists, he admitted, could help divert the surplus energies of the Super Powers from direct conflict to peaceful, time-consuming and very beneficial competition in the form of economic development and aid in the hope of getting support from the neutralists. And, as Brecher thought, it was in the interests of the Super Powers to have a zone of competition, and ultimately, cooperation for this zone, for the neutralist zone, 'the area of peace' in Nehru's language, seemed to offer a "tolerable alternative" to military warfare. Also, the neutralists promised to function as a cushioning agent, thereby bringing some sort of flexibility in a system that has been dominated by rigid bipolarity.[101]

There are however some obvious differences between neutralism as a variant of balance of power and balance of power itself. First, neutralism, in contrast, seeks to prevent any single coalition of states from threatening the peace and security of the rest by calling upon a central organization to prevent a dangerous concentration or misuse of power on the international scene. In other words, whereas neutralism's main thrust is toward providing balance overall in the whole international relations dominated by the two Super Powers, the traditional balance of power was interested in providing a balance in a small area or region of the world. Also, as regards methods employed to enforce the power equilibrium, neutralist methods are preeminently negotiations, arbitration, conciliation, peace observation commissions, peace keeping forces as opposed to military alliances and divide and rule tactics in the balance of power policies. Second, neutralism seeks revision of the status quo, preservation of which is the main motivation of balance of power. As a student of

---

100 Michael Brecher, *New States of Asia : A Political Analysis* (New York : Oxford University Press, 1966), pp. 121-122.
101 *Ibid.,* p. 122.

nonalignment/neutralism has put it : "Within the frame-work of the United Nations, the nonaligned nations/states seek to advance their economic, political, social development and hereby to redefine the power equilibrium without destroying it."[102]

Section VI :   **Neutralism as a Technique, an Aspect of India's Foreign Policy**

Many tend to identify neutralism with the whole of India's foreign policy, but this attempt seems to be wrong. There is no doubt that the principal feature of the international system in the period under consideration is the dominance of the two Super Powers, their cold war, and most of the issues around the world are in some way or another mixed up with this world situation. To the extent neutralism is a technique of meeting the problems arising out of this cold war, its scope is indeed all-pervasive, and one can say that India, which is a part of the 'dominant world system' and not simply of the 'subordinate South Asia system'[103] and therefore concerned with the problems arising throughout the globe, follows a policy or policies which is/are guided by the ideas, negative and positive, that are subsumed under neutralism. Even so, neutralism is not the whole of India's foreign policy—for, not only has India global interests ; she also has regional and local and bilateral interests,[104] and these latter may not all be mixed up always with cold war considerations. In the latter field or area, India may not and in many cases does not follow neutralism ; in fact, India's policy there may be entirely different from neutralism or may only be remotely connected with it. To give one or two examples : India's policy toward Pakistan is not neutralism, but something

---

102 For a fuller treatment of the differences, see May Coates King, "Nonalignment and the United Nations : The Congo Crisis" (Unpublished Ph.D. dissertation, University of Idaho, 1968), pp. 46-48.

103 For an acceptable definition of the two terms, see Michael Brecher, *New States of Asia,* Chapters 3 and 6.

104 For a discussion of what these global and regional/local interests were as conceived by her top policy-makers, see the following chapter in this current work.

else that can hardly be considered anything but pro-India, geared to serving India's national interests *per se.* . A particular stance that a country takes in a particular context would be decided by its definition of objectives, sometimes called primary or vital interests and sometimes secondary national interests, and neutralism is a technique for securing objectives in the global context of the cold war.   Thus viewed in the context of the global and total objectives or goals at all levels of India's multidimensional foreign policy, neutralism is only an aspect, and an instrument as opposed to the goal, of that policy. While this is such an important proposition, that, if we forget this we fail to grasp the whole significance of neutralism, we must not at the same time lose sight of the calculation of the neutralist, in our study, India, that the two Super Powers, because of the practice of neutralism in the cold war global context, would also fulfill the practitioner's requirements in the areas close to his vital national interests, that are conceived more narrowly. That is to say, the neutralist, by his pursuit of neutralism in the global context, tries to induce the Super Powers to behave in a certain way, preferably helpful, in areas of more immediate concern to the neutralist, in this case India.

Another thing that must be remembered in this connection is that there is a certain relationship between the context defined in a certain way and the policy. The type of context in which neutralism operates we have already described in a previous section (Section 3) ; if the nature of the context changes, neutralism would also change, from right neutralism to left neutralism or vice versa. If, however, the contextual change is radical, then of course, a mere change in the character of neutralism would not be enough, because that context may require the innovation of an entirely new technique, a radical remedy. It would also be imprudent to promote one that is only a technique, applicable in a certain context to the status of an objective or goal of foreign policy, that is at once permanent or immutable. Indian policymakers, especially the late Jawaharlal Nehru, in spite of their occasional lapses, were aware of this relationship between a technique of foreign policy and the goals of foreign policy, and they tried to use this neutralism as a means of realizing certain foreign policy goals.[105]

---

[105] Comparable ideas are expressed in N. R. Deshpande, "National Interests and India's Policy of Nonalignment," *Indian Journal of Political Science,* XXV (January-March, 1964), 68-75.

CHAPTER II

NATIONAL INTERESTS OF INDIA AS DEFINED
BY HER POLICYMAKERS

It has been pointed out already in our previous chapter that Jawaharlal Nehru's personality and his ideas have been one of the most important formative influences upon India's foreign policy—not only because he was independent India's first Prime Minister and External Affairs Minister. Even before the advent of independence, when the Indian National Congress, led by Mahatma Gandhi, was carrying on the battle for freedom unaided by any other organization ; when not many in the Congress Party itself cared anything if at all for its expression in the realm of external policies ; it was Nehru, who as the unofficial foreign affairs spokesman of the Congress Party began to formulate and draft foreign policy stances and resolutions, after persuading his colleagues "to realize that the Indian struggle for freedom was actually a part of a global struggle and that it could be made to succeed only if geared into the context of international developments".[1] Michael Brecher, a famous Nehru biographer, has seen his subject's role or service in this regard as consisting in preventing the movement from becoming narrowly egocentric.[2] It is this Nehru, who as his nation's first Prime Minister, assisted of course by a few able men,[3] the most outstanding among whom was V. K. Krishna Menon,[4]

---

[1] Willard Range, *Jawaharlal Nehru's World View* (Athens : University of Georgia Press, 1961), p. 42. For support of the same view see Frank Moraes, *Jawaharlal Nehru* (New York : Macmillan Co., 1958), pp. 177-178 ; B. S. N. Murti, *Nehru's Foreign Policy* (New Delhi : Beacon, 1953), pp. 7, 38-39 ; and N. V. Rajkumar (ed.), *The Background of India's Foreign Policy* (New Delhi : AICC, 1952), pp. 1-2.

[2] Michael Brecher, *Nehru : A Political Biography* (London : Oxford University Press, 1969), p. 616.

[3] For a discussion of the people around Nehru, see *ibid.*, pp. 569-575.

[4] Brecher described Menon as "the adjunct Minister of External Affairs", *ibid.*, p. 573, and Nehru's "deputy for all purposes", *ibid.*, p. 567. In a later work, Brecher says, "...Menon occupied a position second only to Nehru from 1953, some would say earlier, until 1962", *India and World Politics : Krishna Menon's View of the World* (New York : Praeger, 1968), p. 299.

formulated the essential ideas, general and specific, about India's national interests. But this he did not do in a hurry or a start, but gradually. In fact, his general ideas about nationalism and international.sm, that provided in a way the broad framework of more specific ideas, had all been developed long before he became Prime Minister and had a chance to say anything specific about India's more current and updated specific interests against the backdrop of international situation of the post-World War II period. But without an understanding of those general ideas regarding nationalism and internationalism, it would be difficult to grasp his ideas regarding general and specific vital interests of India. In the section following, an attempt will be made to gain familiarity with the general ideas in the realm of international affairs of Nehru, the architect, by common consensus, of India's foreign policy and the person mainly responsible for the definition of national interests, for the real.zation of which at least the specific technique of neutralism was designed.

Section I : General Ideas of Nehru in Regard to International Affairs

If any image of the world that Nehru cared about most, it was the image of a world with nations following foreign policies characterized by enlightened self-interest. The latter in Nehru's mind encompassed two things ; one, a certain dilution of nationalism with internationalism leading to a degree of international cooperation, and two, a prudent and careful conception of national interests which left scope for the latter's development in accordance with the interests of the international community.[5] In this conception of enlightened self-interest, the dream of nationalism was not abjured ; in fact, it was allowed to play a rather important part, for he, a keen student of modern history, was all too aware of the power and resilience of the phenomenon that is nationalism. Nehru articulated this awareness in this way :

---

[5] Willard Range, *Nehru's World View,* p. 42

...In a contest between nationalism and internationalism nationalism is bound to win. That has happened in every country and in every crisis ; in a country under foreign domination, with bitter memories of continuous struggle and suffering, that was an inevitable and unavoidable consequence.[6]

Nehru further realized that the strength of nationalism was such that it was the international interests that had to be in keeping with the national interests and not vice versa. For, he said :

Individuals and small groups may become internationally minded and may even be prepared to sacrifice personal and immediate national interests for a larger cause, but not so nations. It is only when international interests are believed to be in line with national interests that they arouse enthusiasm.[7]

Later, as Prime Minister of India, he voiced the same sentiment :

A movement must define itself in terms of nationalism if it has to become real to the people. In any Asian country a movement will succeed or fail in the measure that it associates itself with the deepseated urges of nationalism. No argument in Asia is going to carry weight if it goes counter to national aspirations.[8]

This apart, Nehru discerned certain virtues in nationalism. And, among the virtues he most cherished were "its abiding appeal to the spirit of man, giving unity and vitality to many people, contributing vigour, growth, unity, selfesteem to those who ever cared to be guided by it".[9] These were the virtues he would need as a leader of a people who badly lacked unity, vitality and selfesteem, all of which had been sapped after years of foreign occupation.

While Nehru was aware of the strength of nationalism, he was not however blind to its bad aspects. Although he did

---

[6] *Discovery of India* (London : Meridian Books, 1961), p. 395.
[7] *Ibid.*, p. 396.
[8] *Jawaharlal Nehru's Speeches* : 1949-1953, II (New Delhi : Ministry of Information and Broadcasting, Govt. of India, 1954), pp. 163-164.
[9] Range, *Nehru's World View*, p. 44.

not completely agree with Tagore who considered the idea of the nation and nationalism as an unmitigated evil,[10] he was aware of its potentiality for narrowness, fanaticism and irrationality leading people astray—sick with suspicion and fear about their neighbours, arousing in their mind a feeling of superiority complex and making them aggressive and expansionminded. Nehru once said :

I generally do not encourage the idea, which is a peculiar product of intensive nationalism, of each person thinking his country as a chosen country of God— normally the people of each country think that they are the chosen people ; whether it is in America or Europe or Asia we all tend to think that we are the chosen race—I do not wish to encourage the idea. I am proud enough of my people, my country, my heritage, but it is a narrow-minded view to think that we are the chosen people and all the others are outside the pale.[11]

So Nehru's prescription was to guard it from the narrowness of outlook, to keep it restrained, and one way of keeping it within bounds in colonial areas was to restore independence to their people, for he believed that "Nationalism tends to fade away after political freedom to some extent,"[12] although even after a country attains independence, Nehru recognized, any movement it launches will still depend for its success "in the measure that it associates itself with the deepseated urge of nationalism."[13]

Nationalism should then be rational, and attempts should be made to keep it within the bounds of rationality. And, this rational nationalism, as he hoped, would lead to national solidarity and national strength. He wanted his countrymen inspired by rational nationalism in seeking "to build up our strength on ourselves and not by dependence

---

[10] Rabindranath Tagore, *Nationalism* (London : Macmillan, 1920), pp. 3-46. Indeed, Tagore looked upon the 'nation' as the organized self-interest of the people "where it is least human and spiritual."

[11] India, Constituent Assembly, *Legislative Debates*, 1949, II, March 8, 1949.

[12] Range, *Nehru's World View*, p. 45.

[13] *Speeches*, 1949-1953, II, p. 163.

on others.   Nations, it is said, by themselves are made.   By
seifreliance, we shall command respect and we shall make
our country more and more our own, of each one of us".[14]

But nations and their nationalism are not ends in
themselves.   He wanted nations and individuals to grow
out of their narrow grooves of thought and action, and to
lay emphasis on a world synthesis.[15]

What then should one do when he has *in practice* to
choose between national interests and international interests ?   So far as Nehru was concerned, he would no doubt
give preference to national interests in their clash with
international interests.   In a statement in 1947, he said :

> Whatever policy you may lay down, the art of conduct-
> ing the foreign affairs of a country lies in finding out
> what is most advantageous to the country.   We may
> talk about international goodwill and mean what we
> say.   But in the ultimate analysis, a government func-
> tions for the good of the country it governs and no
> government dare anything which in the short or long
> run is manifestly to the disadvantage of the country.
> Therefore, whether a country is imperialistic or socia-
> list or communist, its foreign minister thinks primarily
> of the interests of that country.[16]

That is to say, he accepted the proposition that a
state's own interests have priority over international interests.   He confirmed this again in a speech in 1948 when
he revealed that he had asked the Indian diplomats in the
United Nations to consider each question on terms of
India's interests and then any other.[17]

Is this not an instance of the attitude of the *ver-
krampte*[18] and therefore selfish ?   Nehru thought not, for
as Willard Range interprets Nehru, "it is selfish only when
she thinks of herself alone and fails or refuses to consider

---

[14] Quoted in M. N. Das, *The Political Philosophy of Nehru* (London :
Allen and Unwin, 1961), p. 93.
[15] *Ibid.*
[16] India, Constituent Assembly, *Legislative Debates,* 1947, II, 5, 1263.
[17] *Independence and After,* p. 215.
[18] African word that describes the narrow, white racist attitude
and policy of the present South African government.

the effects of her policy on the other states in the international community"[19] especially as Nehru thought "when the world has indeed become one single inseparable whole, each part influencing and being influenced by the other".[20]

So giving primacy to national interests, broadly conceived, while "keeping in mind the interdependence of states and remembering that the welfare of one's own state is intertwined with and dependent on the welfare of the whole world community"[21] is not narrowness. Nehru said in 1947, the year of India's independence, "We propose to look after India's interests in the context of world cooperation and world peace, in so far as world peace is concerned",[22] and, two years later, he reaffirmed the same thing in terms of his performance as the Prime Minister of India in this way : "I have naturally looked to the interests of India, for that is my first duty. But I have always conceived that duty in terms of the larger good of the world".[23]

Opposed as he was to national irrationalism which may lead each people to think their country as a chosen country of God, he thought that pursuit of enlightened selfinterest, that is to say, of rational nationalism bereft of jingoism, would keep within manageable limits, if not cure, many of our problems in the international arena.

Nehru also believed that a policy of enlightened self-interest should be free from its dependence on traditional conception of powerpolitics. Nehru thought that a policy that "relegated morality and justice" in its pursuit of naked power as major objective would not be in tune with his definition of enlightened selfinterest. This kind of policy only bred an atmosphere of rivalry which can be put an end to by friendly international cooperation. The masses wanted freedom and social and economic justice, and the only policy that could best secure these wants was the policy of enlightened selfinterest freed from the mad

[19] Range, *Nehru's World View*, p. 47.
[20] Quoted in M. N. Das, *Philosophy of Nehru*, p. 195.
[21] Range, *Nehru's World View*, p. 47.
[22] Das, *Philosophy of Nehru*, p. 200.
[23] Range, *Nehru's World View*, p. 47.

striving for power leading to war and conflict. As Willard Range so succinctly sums up Nehru's thinking in this regard : "The only sensible alternative was the elimination of the whole atmosphere of rivalry and the substitution of friendly cooperation to build a new and better world—a new civilization in which nations had no reason to fear or encircle each other".[24]

This, Nehru believed, could only be done through an achievement of balance between nationalism and internationalism—"Whatever line of thought you follow, you arrive at the conclusion that some kind of balance must be found."[25]

Thus in the "theoretical consciousness" of Nehru in regard to international affairs there is this "primacy of the nationstate as a unit for development and for relating one people to another"[26] but there is nothing there that leads the nationstate to cut itself adrift from the mainstream of human civilization that encompasses not just one country, India, but all the countries of the world, in all the five continents.[27]

With this general discussion of Nehru's views on nationalism and internationalism, we can now proceed to analyze the specific ideas of Nehru in regard to national interests of India, general as well as specific.

Section II :   A Study of National Interests of India[28]

Our problem in this section is the analysis of the national interests of India as conceived by India's policymakers,

---

[24] *Ibid.*, p. 50.

[25] *Speeches,* 1949-1953, II (made April 9, 1950), p. 361.

[26] Warren F. Ilchman, "Political Development and Foreign Policy : The Case of India", *Journal of Commonwealth Political Studies,* IV (November 1966), 219.

[27] Nehru specifically advocated harmonization of national interests with the needs of international community as a whole 'in a temper of peace', in a broadcast from London (BBC), January 12, 1951. Cited in A. Appadorai, *Indian Political Thinking : From Noorji to Nehru* (Madras : Oxford University Press, 1971), p. 169.

[28] The author in writing this section is indebted to Paul B. Parham, *The Content Analysis* (Unpublished Master's thesis in Journalism, University of Missouri, Columbia, 1970). He has also consulted Harold Lasswell, Daniel Lerner and Ethiel de Sola Pool, *The Comparative Study of Symbols* (Stanford :   Stanford University Press, 1952), esp. pp. 31-33.

especially by Nehru. The study would analyze the national interests of India as they are contained in the speeches actually delivered by Nehru *et al* in the context of world events and in response to happenings around the globe. Thus the theoretical orientation of this research is an historical survey of the Nehru speeches during the period of his stewardship of the Government of India from 1947 to 1964. This survey hopefully will contribute to the state of knowledge in this regard, for there appears to have been no identical study related to the problem under our consideration here. There have been some studies on Nehru's world view, which included his views on nationalism and internationalism to which reference has been made in the foregoing pages. There is a study by Arora and Lasswell which includes an analysis, empirically arrived at, of the public language of the political *elite* in India, which included in its turn both official and unofficial spokesmen.[29] There is also a study by Brecher of Krishna Menon's perception of India's national interests.[30] But there is no study yet on Nehru's views on the specific national interests as such. To the extent therefore this is a study of the definition of national interests, a claim could be made that this research is an exploration of an hitherto untrodden field, in the manner of content analysis conceived liberally and with the same purposes in view—objectivity, precision and generality.

As regards methodology, an attempt will be made to use basic quantification to determine descriptive statistics. An attempt will also be made to develop appropriate, mutually exclusive, and exhaustive categories which would enable us to get "a more exact summary of the situation than would be possible if only general impressions and memory were relied upon".[31] Sampling will not be used, for in the

---

[29] Satish K. Arora and Harold Lasswell, *Political Communication* : *The Public Language of Political Elites in India and the USA* (New York : Holt, Rinehart and Winston, 1969), pp. 282-284.

[30] Michael Brecher, *Krishna Menon's World View.*

[31] Claire Selltiz *et al, Research Method in Social Relations* (New York : Holt, Rinehart and Winston, 1967), as quoted in Lasswell, Lerner, and de Sola Pool, *Study of Symbols,* pp. 31-33.

absence of all the speeches of the policymaker in question it is really useless and somehting of a misnomer to call the deliberate choice of the speeches as sampling. This research does not, as has been indicated already, use samples and then project its findings to a much larger universe, as Lasswell *et al* suggests a truly well-conceived content analysis should do.[32]

Research Design

We have deliberately chosen generally the most comprehensive *two* of the several foreign policy speeches of the Prime Minister delivered each year beginning with 1949 and ending in 1964, on May 25 of which Mr. Nehru died. Despite the fact that India became independent on August 15, 1947, the choice of 1949 as the starting point of our study is not exactly arbitrary. It is due to the paucity of foreign policy speeches before that and to the nonavailability of even those that were made, beacuse the documents that contain them could not be located. We have chosen only such speeches as were delivered before national audience, especially Members of the Lok Sabha or House of People, the lower house of India's national Parliament, because the speeches delivered before such an audience are expected to be rather "clean", relatively freed of those elements of idealism and unreality, in other words, of emotional subjectivism that a speaker before a foreign and international audience would like to indulge in for the sake of producing drama and maximum impact. Speeches chosen each year are separated by some months, the longest difference being ten (10) months in 1950, and the shortest difference about one and a half (1½) months in 1951 ; the speeches in the other years are separated by periods ranging from two months in 1952, 1962, 1964 ; three months in 1949 ; four months 1956 and 1958, five and a half months in 1957 and 1963, six in 1955 and 1960, six and a half in 1954, eight in 1961 and finally nine in 1953. In 1959, there was only one speech that could be available. All the speech-

---

[32] *Study of Symbols,* p. 34.

es that we have sampled were delivered in the Indian Parliament, before the House of the People in most cases and the Council of States (Rajya Sabha) in some or in the Constituent Assembly (legislative) before the new Parliament under the new Constitution came into being. Only in one case, there has been some kind of departure from this pattern or rule ; the speech on March 22 that we have considered was addressed to the Indian Council of World Affairs which is an autonomous body enjoying the confidence of the Government of India ; and, this speech, like all the others, was deliberately chosen because of the contents of the speech, which were undoubtedly very rich concerning mostly specific abstract and general interests as well as geographical interests of India. The source of the last-mentioned speech is *not* an official document put out by the Government of India ; it is a work in two volumes edited by Dorothy Norman, entitled *Nehru : The First Sixty Years* (New York : The John Day Company, 1965) the authenticity of which can hardly be questioned because, as the editor mentions in her preface, it was shown to, and checked by Nehru before it was allowed to see the light of the day. All the other speeches have been taken from the official sources. For the speeches delivered between 1949 through 1954, primary reliance has been placed upon the *Official Reports of the Indian Constituent (Legislative) Assembly* and the *Parliamentary (House of the People) Debates ;* and for the speeches of a later period, from 1955 through 1964, due to the nonavailability of these official reports here in the United States so far as we are concerned, on *Foreign Affairs Record,* a publication, unlike the first two, of the Ministry of External Affairs, Government of India, which is none the less accorded the status of government documents.

In the speeches, we have looked for both abstract and general national interests and specific geographical interests. The most difficult problem encountered in arranging these interests, general as well as specific geographical, in order of priority, has been the question : What is the indication of the degree of importance attached to each of these interests ? In seeking an answer to the question we have been constrained to depend upon the different adjectives and phrases used by the policymaker in question ; sometimes when no such adjectives or epithets have been used, we have depended upon the expression of emotion and sentiment in judging the relative importance attached to the interests ; for, although a realistic policymaker should as much as possible eschew emotionalism in the calculation of national interests, and every worthy policymaker knows that he should, Jawaharlal Nehru, a worthy Foreign Minister and a great champion of rationalism that he was, could not entirely succeed in rising above emotional considerations in evaluating his country's national interests. However, it has been possible to develop three codes : 1 for the most, 2 for the more, and 3 for the least important compared to the other two, but not entirely negligible, for the purposes of categorization of specific national interests.[33] The following are the words and phrases used by the policymakers[34] in conjunction with their expressions involving national interests which from our observation appear to indicate to us the three codes :

1.   List of words/phrases indicating priority code 1

Indivisible, basic matter, the whole world wants, should aim primarily at, want at least 10-15 years of..., special interest, inevitably think, inevitable to have close relations,

---

[33] In a doctoral dissertation, hitherto unpublished, "The National Interests as Perceived by U. S. Policymakers" (The American University, 1964), David C. Holly first attempted such codification. Compare the priority as developed by Holly :

Priority	Words
1	vital, fear danger, imperative, necessity, national security
2	serious, dominant, necessity, all-important, essential
3	cornerstone, foundation, important, constant concern (or specifically in he national interest)
4	long-term concern, interest to the nation
5	desirable to the nation, general interest, for the public good

Ibid., p. 217.

[34] For sentences from which such words and phrases have been taken/ abstracted, see the Appendix.

cannot be indifferent, a most vital problem affecting the whole of Australia, Asia and perhaps America, of vital significance to the world, fundamental problem, so terrible to contemplate, a matter of greatest import and consequence, vital matter, a symbol of incarnate evil, important subject of primary importance, vital issues, cannot risk our own security, chief need, the most important, most terrible of disasters, should strain every nerve to prevent it, most immediate issue, we would have given up everything that has made life worthwhile for us, crisis, danger, unalterably opposed, a very serious matter, one of the outstanding problems, we passionately seek it, it is essential, one of the subjects of high importance, of great interest and concern, will react strongly against it, unthinkable, an emergent necessity, a very important event, fate of Asia depends upon a good deal, one of the major issues before the world, unless something is *done* to it, it will become more and more harmful to the interests..., one of the biggest factors, a most extraordinary situation, a very dangerous situation, all I want, we cannot escape the consequences, more dangerous than any other problem, immediate problems, a very big question with a soul of its own, deepest sympathy, occupy our minds more than these world problems, can't be the slightest slackening, basic aims, imperative, good deal of importance, a very explosive region of the world, wrong, dangerous and harmful, even if...it had not acceded to India then too it would be our duty to defend it..., without this there would be utter disaster, a very difficult situation, the most difficult, affect us much more intimately and directly, live and vital issue, has an immediate direct effect and adverse effect upon us, where India's interests are directly threatened, the most important thing, affect us tremendously, at least as much important as any other matter, questions of most immediate concern, the biggest problem, most deplorable, there is an emotional feeling, a most terrible catastrophe, they bring insecurity, the most significant feature, a measure of anxiety, a direct interest, of most urgent consequence, a matter of tremendous significance, this very important issue, our nearest neighbours, a very important post for our foreign service, a very big matter, of the most profound importance to us, constantly thinking about it, the most important thing, utter absence of prudence, part of our struggle for independence, no country with any selfrespect can ignore such a problem, a very big step will have been taken, tremendously disastrous affair, a vital approach, according to our honour, integrity and all that, death of India and ruin of Kashmir, largely affected by, matter of world importance, we must prepare ourselves with all our strength to meet such contingencies as might arise, our chief concern.

2. List of words/phrases indicating priority code 2

Fairly intimately connected, more important than many, a huge problem, ought to be our positive policy, big questions on which we have strong feelings, not an immediate issue that it must be settled immediately, we did not allow that to affect our policy, a matter of concern, deeply interested, real importance of this is in relation to..., important, dark spots, a serious situation, we can view distantly, dangerous and explosive, element of danger, symbol of disturbance, of the international questions that affect us, not an easy matter, not good for us, of local importance, not so important, partially a threat to us, not a basic policy but a reaction to events.

3. List of words/phrases indicating priority code 3

Not my concern, has not been functioning very much. [Observation : Because there has not been much emphasis on these interests, there has not been much phrase mongering, and so far as we are concerned, therefore, the general rule to follow in determining code 3 has been the mere mention of an interest unaccompanied by phrase of the type of those mentioned in the lists 1 and 2.]

Each of these codes stands for a certain number of

points. In calculating the importance attached to various national interests over a period of time, we have added the points scored by each. Relative consistency of occurrence has also not been forgotten in our evaluation of the national interests.

With the above observations to guide us, let us now see how the various national interests, general (abstract) and specific (geographical) fare in the perceptions of India's policymakers, particularly Nehru.

Section III : **General National Interests of India as Viewed by Indian Policymakers**

It is interesting to find that Peace and Prevention of War occupies the most important place in the calculations of the Indian policymaker (Vide Tables I, II, III, IV given below). This is evident not only from the total points scored (81) by this general national interest over the whole period of sixteen years (1949-64) (Vide Table IV). It is also underscored by two other points : one, only in one out of sixteen years under reference it fails to be mentioned, that is to say, the consistency with which the Indian policymaker/s regarded Peace and Prevention of War as an important interest was remarkable ; two, most of the time it was mentioned it was regarded as no. 1 priority (twenty-two times compared to just once for no. 2, and thirteen times for no. 3—Vide Table IV). The second place went to Disarmament and related questions, the score for the entire period (1949-64) being 42. One thing however needs to be emphasized—Disarmament came to be accorded this importance only after 1955 (compare the Tables I, II, III). This fact together with the consideration that from 1956 onward peace failed to be accorded as much importance as it enjoyed in the earlier period (1949-1955)—most of the points were scored in this period—points perhaps to the conclusion that Disarmament became more important to peace than the simple talk of peace itself. The third place went to economic progress as a national interest, the importance given to it being at best spotty (Vide Tables I, II, III). Racial Equality was an ideal and an interest that greatly exercised the mind of the policymaker in India, and this seems to be clear from its score, 11 points over a period of 16 years. This fact should be considered in conjunction with the importance or priority attached to South Africa, a geographical interest, which was however an embodiment of racialism, so far as India was concerned. (Vide Tables V, VI, VII, VIII dealing with geographical priorities). Imperialism-Colonialism was another matter that exercised the Indians a great deal, its share of points being 10. This anticolonialism is in many instances another name of antiracialism, because in most cases the colonial regimes were involved in suppressing coloured people either African or Asian. These two together scored some 21 points, thus tending to prove that India's interest in these two matters was more than peripheral. Toward the last third of the entire period, nonalignment/neutralism, which, to us, the students and the policymaker, was a means to pursue foreign policy goals, assumed the proportions of an interest. Preservation of freedom as a separate interest is expected to be an important interest to a newly independent nation, but in the speeches of the Indian policymaker we have sampled, this was not very much articulated, its score of 8 points in our Table confirming it. This was probably because of the realization on the part of Nehru that since the entire thrust of India's policy was towards independence of thought, policy and action, geared to judging every issue on its merits, a particular articulation of it as a separate national interest was rather necessary. Maintance of Democracy or anti-Communism or nonaggression of one against the other India was perceived to be concerned with, but, in the perception of her policymaker/s, she was not unduly perturbed by them.

It seems rather curious that, in the speeches considered, national security as a general interest *never* figured at all, not to speak of prominently. This stands out rather prominently in comparison with the fact that in the context of certain geographical territories India's policymakers did indeed think seriously and hard about national security. India's *Panch Sheel* (Five Principles of Peaceful Coexistence) Pact with People's Republic of China as early as in 1954 (April) over Tibet was a proof of India's preoccupation with this problem of national security. Why then is this discrepancy between articulation and action ? This may be due to the realization on the part of Nehru and his advisers that national security was a problem too concrete and specific to be talked in terms of mere abstraction. Also, although it may be traditional for most of the nations, especially of the West, to think that the road to peace may lie through security, in the case of India emerging into a world radically transformed with her particular brand of nationalism profoundly influenced by Gandhian pacifism and Tagorean internationalism,[35] the road to security lies through peace (the doctrine of security through peace), and that, as one remarks, "to this extent, India's foreign policy is not only grounded in national interests, but it is also firmly guided by a philosophy which explains the richly conceptual interpretation of international relations by India's leaders".[36]

The Tables (I, II, III, and IV) dealing with general and abstract national interests of India as perceived by Indian policymaker/s follow. The first table (T. I) deals with the period from 1949 to 1955 ; the second (T. II) deals with the period from 1956 to 1960 ; the third (T. III) deals with the period from 1961 to 1964, the year Mr. Nehru died ; while the fourth (T. IV) deals with the total picture of India's general interests from 1949 to 1964. A further note may be added in regard to the time periods that the Tables are concerned with. The first period ended before the onset of the Suez Crisis ; the second started

---

[35] Tagore, India's Nobel Prize-winning poet and one of her foremost thinkers, who along with Gandhi exercised the greatest influence on Nehru's thinking, wrote in his *Gitanjali* about his fondest wish that his country would awake into a "heaven of freedom" where "the world has not been broken up into fragments by narrow domestic walls".

[36] C. K., "Review of Ross N. Berkes and Mohinder S. Bedi, ,*The Diplomacy of India*", in *India Quarterly*, XVI (April-June, 1960), p. 184.

4

with Suez and Hungary, and the third ended with the death of Nehru. From the point of view of India and from the point of definition of her national interests, the germinal period was the period as dealt with in Table I, for, as one shrewd observer of Indian foreign policy processes remarks :

India's moment of impact in world affairs took place during the six years between 1949 and 1955. This is to suggest at least that most Indian causes in foreign relations were during that period the most freely joined, the most vigorously pursued, the most dramatically registered, and for that matter the most excitingly won or disconsolately lost....

...The major lines of Indian foreign policy were thus cast at a time when India stood forward and somewhat alone as the voice of seething nationalisms.[37]

Besides, all the periods are significant from another standpoint. As one points out, in the first period of our study the Great Powers generally enjoyed some success in applying the bipolar idea to the operation of the world political system. In this period the Great Powers wielded maximum domination of events. The second period saw the gradual liquidation of the bipolar idea. And, in the third period of our study one can notice a growing acceptance by both Great Powers of the fact that their scope of dominion has been sharply decreased, and consequently greater willingness to deal bilaterally with one another.[38] That is to say, in all the periods one can detect a certain change in the behaviour pattern of the two most significant Powers on the world scene.

Section IV : **Geographical Priorities of India as Perceived by her Policymaker/s**

Now in regard to the geographical interests of India

---

[37] Ross N. Berkes, "India and the Communist World", *Current History*, XXXVI (March 1959), 146-52.
[38] See Charles O. Lerche, *The Cold War and After,* Spectrum Book (Englewood Cliffs, New Jersey : Prentice-Hall Inc., 1965), pp. 95-96.

as perceived by her policymaker or makers, a look at Tables V, VI VII, and VIII, especially the last one, immediately brings home the conclusion that even though India is supposed to be one of the bigger powers (at least potentially so), yet so far as her geographical interests are concerned, she does not seem to have had very many global interests, in the sense that the areas in which she seems to be interested most of the time are not scattered or spread over all the six continents. Rather, her geographical interests seem to be more or less confined to her own region, Asia in general and the neighbouring countries of South Asia in particular. This is rather conspicuously evident from the fact that the Asian countries together score some 331 points, while the other two continents catching some attention come poor second and third with scores of 50 and 44 respectively. The Americas and Australia do not even find any mention. A much closer look at the Tables further reveals that it is the neighbours of India that receive the greatest attention, their combined score being 171. If however one adds to this the score of China, which after her absorption of Tibet, did indeed become a close neighbour, then one indeed gets the impression that India cared a great deal for her immediate neighbours.

Again, of all the neighbours, it is Pakistan and issues concerning Pakistan which seem to compel most of Indian policymaker's attention, as evidenced from the score of 51. If, however, one adds to this score that of Kashmir, which is the crux of the India-Pakistan relations, then it becomes apparent why one cannot but consider Pakistan as India's geographical priority no. 1. The remnants of foreign control or colonialism in India, as typified especially by Goa (at that time under Portuguese colonialism), weighed rather heavily in the conscience and calculations of the Indian policymaker, its score being 51. (People's Republic of) China obviously occupies a very important position as a priority interest, its score being 52, which is among the highest. If the score of Tibet is added to it, then one could reasonably conclude that India indeed accorded the most

TABLE I : GENERAL INTERESTS, 1949–1955

Interests	1949	1950	1951	1952	1953	1954	1955	Total	Points	
War and Peace	5a	2a	1a	3a	1a	2a	4a	18a	54	
	1b							1b	2	
	1c						2c	5c	5	61
One World U.N.	2c			2c				4c	4	4
Economics	3a							3a	9	
						1b		1b	2	
	1c							1c	1	12
Freedom		1a		1a				2a	6	
	2c							2c	2	8
Racial Equality		1a		1a				2a	6	
						2c	2c	4c	4	10
Disarmament/ Rearmament			1a					1a	3	
	2c					2c		5c	5	8
Non-Alignment	1c		1c					2c	2	2
Imperialism				2a				2a	6	
						2c		2c	2	8
Non-aggression etc., Panchshila					1c	1c	1c	3c	3	3
Communism/ Anti-Communism							1b	1b	2	2

Legend: a=code 1 ; b=code 2 ; c=code 3

Figures in front of the symbols signify the number of times such symbols occur.

TABLE II : GENERAL INTERESTS, 1956–1960

Interests	1956	1957	1958	1959	1960	Total	Points
War and Peace	1a					1a	3
	2c	1c	1c	2c	1c	7c	7 (10)
One World U.N.						—	—
Economics	1a					1a	3
	2c					2c	2 (5)
Racial Equality			1a			1a	3
Disarmament/ Rearmament		1a	1a		3a	5a	15
	3c	1c				4c	4 (19)
Non-Alignment						—	—
Imperialism/ Anti-Colonialism		1c				1c	1
Non-aggression/ Panchshila			1c			1c	1
Communism/ Anti-Communism						—	—
Democracy/ Parliamentarianism	1c					1c	1
Summit Conference				1c		1c	1

Legend : The same as in Table I.

TABLE III

GENERAL INTERESTS, 1961-1964

Interests	1961	1962	1963	1964	Total	Points	
War and Peace		2a	1a	1c	3a 1c	9 1	10
Disarmament		1a 1c	2a 1c	1a 1c	4a 3c	12 3	15
Non-Alignment			2a	1b	2a 1b	6 2	8
Colonialism			1c		1c	1	1
Communism/ Anti-Communism			1b		1b	2	2

Legend : The same as in previous Tables.

TABLE IV

GENERAL INTERESTS TOTAL FOR THE ENTIRE PERIOD, 1949-1964

Interests	1949-55	1956-60	1961-64	Total	Points
War and Peace	18a 1b 5c	1a 7c	3a 1c	22a 1b 13c	81
One World U.N.	2c			2c	2
Economics	3a 1b 1c	1a 2c		4a 1b 3c	17
Freedom	2a 2c			2a 2c	8
Racial Equality	2a 4c	1c	4a 3c	2a 5c	11
Disarmament	1a 5c	5a 4c		10a 12c	42

TABLE IV (*Continued*)

Interests	1949-55	1956-60	1961-64	Total	Points
Non-Alignment	2c		2a 1b	2a 1b 2c	10
Imperialism/ Colonialism	2a 2c	1c	1c	2a 4c	10
Non-aggression Panchshila	3c	1c		4c	4
Communism/ Anti-Communism	1b		1b	2b	4
Democracy/ Parliamentarianism		1c		1c	1
Summit Conference		1c		1c	1

Legend : The same as in previous Tables.

importance to her neighbour in the north, befitting her challenge as an ideological, military, political, and economic rival. Three other neighbours who received considerable attention are Nepal, Burma, and Ceylon. As a region, Southeast Asia might be considered to be important so far as India's policymaker is concerned—its total score of 60 rather unmistakably confirming that. But individual countries of the region do not seem to carry much weight ; India, curiously enough, does not seem to care much about Indo-China, even though during the time under consideration, the region already became the center of a bitter international conflict, tending to engulf the rest of the world.

The Middle East as a region is not unimportant to the Indian policymaker, but no individual country is singled out as deserving of special attention. But, it is the Suez region, falling under Egypt, that caught some attention.

Of the African scene, the Union of South Africa is the focus of most of her attention, obviously because of her racist policy of *Apartheid* that did not spare the residents of Indian origin. This emphasis on the South African question can be taken as a confirmation of her obvious preoccupation with anti-racialism as an abstract general interest which has been alluded to already.

The European theater of the world does appear to be rather far from India. But some European questions are indeed treated by India as important world problems brooking no aggravation. Berlin and the rearmament of Germany received top priority consideration. NATO as European, rather trans-Atlantic alliance, system was not frowned upon, but as a protective umbrella sheltering distant colonies like Goa (Portugal), it seemed to draw strident criticism. Hungary, in spite of its being a focus of global interest in 1956 and for right reasons did not seem to overly perturb the Indian policymaker.

As regards the other questions, the speeches sampled do not reveal much, and for the purpose of this study must be considered to be relatively unimportant.

Curiously enough, a study[39] made of the foreign policy questions asked of the External Affairs Ministry by Indian MPs (Members of Parliament) reveals the same emphasis (given by the MPs) to various geographical regions as revealed in our study. This study seems to indicate that the Indian legislators who do not have much clout in decisionmaking in regard to foreign policy matters yet reflected the Indian policymaker's interest in such countries as Nepal, Burma, Ceylon, East Africa and Southeast Asia as well as such obvious concern about China and Pakistan than "with the more spectacular but more remote events in the developed Western world".[40] The same study seems to further confirm the same conclusion by analyzing the content of questions asked of the External Affairs Ministry on a randomly selected day during the seventh session of the Fourth Lok Sabha (House of the People) and points out that of the thirteen questions asked...one dealt with the Indo-Burma Border demarcation ; four were concerned with rebellion in Nagaland ; two dealt with relations in Nepal ; one asked about the Indo-Pakistan agreement on division of river waters ; a demonstration by Tibetan refugees at the Chinese Embassy in New Delhi was questioned ; one concerned Indians residing in African countries ; another related to the capture of foreign shipping vessels and one asked the Government to respond to remarks about the role of India in Southeast Asia ; the thirteenth asked about the Israeli attack on Beirut airport and whether India was trying to ease the situation in the Middle East.[41] There seems to be another way in which the findings of our study are confirmed by the study under reference—it is where it makes the point that the interest of the Parliament is "naturally the greatest in those areas of policy

---

[39] Judith Brown, "Foreign Policy Decisionmaking and the Indian Parliament", *Journal of Constitutional and Parliamentary Studies*, III (April-June, 1969), 15-52.

[40] *Ibid.*, p. 37.

[41] *Ibid.*, pp. 37-38.

which are the most relevant to India's security and national development".[42]

Shifts in Emphasis

There are certain geographical interests that remain constant in intensity. Examples of these area : Pakistan, Kashmir, Goa or the foreign possessions in India. But there are certain others which while remaining strong over the entire period do however show some fluctuation from being accorded less interest to greater interest and from greater interest to less interest. China's is a case of fluctuation from less interest to more interest—for example, in the period 1949-55, China's score was 12 points ; in the next period there was some tapering off of India's interest in Chaina, but in the last period of our study, India's interest in China seemed to intensify five-fold over that of the period immediately preceding (1956-60) and threefold over that of the very first period (1949-55). Middle East is another instance where we see another intensification of the interests of India, from a previous low of 3 in 1949-1955 to 19 in the next period (1956-60), but in the last period one witnesses a sort of complete disappearance of India's interests, as one can judge from these Tables. Interests in South Africa, on the other hand, seemed to evaporate as the years rolled by. Indo-China, Indonesia, Formosa-Quemoy, and Korea are the other examples of evaporation of India's interests, in so far as our analysis of the speeches enables us to make any evaluation. A look at the following Tables[43] will, it is hoped, bear out the observations made above.

Section V : A Summary

From a perusal of the above sections of our chapter, the following observations seem not to be quite out of

---

[42] *Ibid.*, p. 38.
[43] The same observations as have been made in reference to the periods of the first four Tables given in this chapter will apply to the Tables V through VII (dealing with the geographical interests of India).

TABLE V : GEOGRAPHICAL PRIORITIES, 1949-1955

	1949	1950	1951	1952	1953	1954	1955	Total	Points
Asia : Neighbors									
Pakistan	2a	1a	1a	1c	1a 1c		1a	6a 3c	21
Kashmir					1c		1a	1a 3c	6
Foreign Poss. in India		1b				2a 3c	3a	7a 1b 4c	27
Afghanistan	1a	1a						2a	3
Nepal	1a	1a						2a	6
Tibet	1a		1b	1c		1a		2a 1b 1c	9
Ceylon	1a				1a	2c	2a	4a 2c	14
Southeast Asia									
Burma	1a				1a			2a	6
Indo-China						2a	1a 1c	3a 1c	10
Malaya	1a							1a	3
Indonesia	4a							4a	13
SEATO						1a		1a 1c	3
Bandung Conf.							1c	1c	1
Geneva Conf.							1c	1c	1
Far East									
China	1a 1b		1a	1b	1a	1a	1a	3a 1b 1c	12
Formosa-Quemoy		1b				1a	1a	2a 1b 1c	9
Korea			1c	1b	1a	2a 1c		3a 1b 2c	13

TABLE V (*Continued*)

	1949	1950	1951	1952	1953	1954	1955	Total	Points
Middle East									
Egypt, Syria, Lebanon, Israel	1b						1c	1b 1c	3
Baghdad Pact									0
Africa									
South Africa	1a	1c 1a		1c	1c		1a	4a 3c	15
Tunisia				1c		1c		2c	2
Algeria							1b	1b	2
Kenya				1c				1c	1
Sudan				1c				1c	1
Morocco						1c	1b	1b 1c	3
Europe									
Berlin	1b		1a 1c					1a 1b 1c	6
Germany						1a	1c	1c	1
Austria						1c	1c	1c	4
NATO				1c 1a		1a	2a	1c	7
Sov-Yugo									0
Rapprochement							1c	1c	1

Legend : a=code 1 ; b=code 2 ; c=code 3
Figures in front of the symbols signify the number of times such symbols occur.

TABLE VI
GEOGRAPHICAL PRIORITIES, 1956-1960

	1956	1957	1958	1959	1960	Total	Points
Asia : Neighbors	1c					1c	1
Pakistan	1a	1a	1a	1a	1c	4a 1c	13
Kashmir	1a	1c				1a 1c	4
Foreign Poss. in India		2a	1a		1a	4a	12
Afghanistan							0
Nepal							0
Tibet				1c	1b	1b 1c	3
Ceylon							0
Southeast Asia							
Burma							0
Indo-China	1c	1c				2c	2
Malaya							0
Indonesia							0
SEATO	1a	1a		1c		2a 1c	7
Bandung Conf.						--	0
Far East	1c					1c	1
China	1a				1a 1b	2a 1b	7
Formosa-Quemoy						--	0
Korea							0

TABLE VI (*Continued*)

	1956	1957	1958	1959	1960	Total	Points
Middle East	1a	1c 2a 1b	2b	1a		4a 3b 1c	19
Egypt, Syria							
Lebanon, Israel							0
Baghdad Pact	1a	1a		1b	2a	2a 1b	8
Africa						3a	9
South Africa			1a	1a		2a	6
Algeria	1c				1c	2c	2
Ghana		1c				1c	1
Congo					1c	1c	1
Europe							
Berlin				1a		1a	3
Germany				1a		1a	3
Austria							0
NATO		1b				1b	2
Poland			1c		1c		1
Hungary		1b				1b	2
Warsaw Pact		1b				1b	2
Commonwealth	1c		1c			2c	2

Legend : The same as in Table V.

Table VII

GEOGRAPHICAL PRIORITIES, 1961-1964

	1961	1962	1963	1964	Total	Points
Asia : Neighbors						
Pakistan	2a		2a	1a 2c	5a 2c	17
Kashmir			1a	1c	1a 1c	4
Foreign Poss. in India	2a 1b	1a 1c			3a 1b 1c	12
Afghanistan	1a				1a	3
Nepal	2a		1a		3a	9
Tibet		1c	1b		1b 1c	3
Ceylon	1a				1a	3
Seventh Fleet in Indian Ocean				1c	1c	1
Southeast Asia						
Burma	3a				3a	9
Indo-China			1b		1b	2
Malaya	1a				1a	3

TABLE VII (*Continued*)

	1961	1962	1963	1964	Total	Points
Far East						
China	2a	2a 1b 1c	5a	1a 1c	10a 1b 1c	33
Middle East						0
Europe						
Berlin		1a			1a	3
EEC		1b			1b	2
Africa						
South Africa				1c	1c	1
Algeria	1a	2c			3c	3
Congo			1c		1a	3
Commonwealth			1a		1c	1
Sino-Soviet Schism		1a			2a	6

Legend : The same as in previous Tables.

5

TABLE VIII

GEOGRAPHICAL INTERESTS IN THE PERIOD, 1949–64

	1949-55	1956-60	1961-64	Total Points
Asia : Neighbors	0	1	0	1
Pakistan	21	13	17	51
Kashmir	6	4	4	14
Foreign Possessions in India	27	12	12	51
Afghanistan	3	0	3	6
Nepal	6	0	9	15
Tibet	9	3	3	15
Ceylon	14	0	3	17
Seventh Fleet in Indian Ocean		0	1	1
Southeast Asia				
Burma	6	0	9	15
Indo-China	10	2	2	14
Malaya	3	0	3	6
Indonesia	13	0	0	13
SEATO	3	7	0	10
Bandung Conf.	1	0	0	1
Geneva Conf.	1	0	0	1
Far East	3	1	0	4
China	12	7	33	52
Formosa-Quemoy	9	0	0	9
Korea	13	0	0	13
Middle East	3	19	0	22
Egypt, Syria, Lebanon, Israel	0	0	0	0
Baghdad Pact	0	8	0	8
Africa	0	9	0	9
South Africa	15	6	1	22

TABLE VIII *(Continued)*

	1949-55	1956-60	1961-64	Total Points
Algeria	2	2	3	7
Tunisia	2	0	0	2
Kenya	1	0	0	1
Sudan	1	0	0	1
Morocco	3	0	0	3
Ghana	0	1	0	1
Congo	0	1	3	4
Europe	6	0	0	6
Berlin	1	3	3	7
Germany	4	3	0	7
Austria	1	0	0	1
NATO	7	2	0	9
Poland	0	1	0	1
Hungary	0	2	0	2
Warsaw Pact	0	2	0	2
EEC	0	0	2	2
Soviet-Yugoslav	0	0	0	0
Rapprochement	1	0	0	1
Sino-Soviet Schism	0	0	6	6
Commonwealth	0	2	1	3

order. There is a kind of correspondence between what
Nehru thought about the world and India's role in it before he became free India's first Prime Minister and the
way he, assisted by a few trusted aides, articulated (his
perceptions of) India's national interests in the context of
floating world and domestic events after he became responsible for the conduct of her foreign policy in the post-indepen-
dence period. It is, however, possible to detect in his articulations a kind of shift toward national interests more
narrowly conceived as the end of his regime approached.
The shift could be detected in two ways : One, by his

greater reluctance to talk about interests that did not directly impinge upon India's present and future ; and, two, by his more direct and explicit concerns for those problems intimately affecting her, those that touched upon her national borders. Geoffrey Tyson, one of the select band of Nehru's political biographers, has pointed out that there are, analytically speaking, three sectors in India's external relations : there are those relations which "oblige her to have a view about or to take some action concerning the great global issues which affect all" ; and this he calls the first sector ; there are those "with contiguous areas in which India claims a special interest : the Indian Ocean and the states along the country's frontiers", and these fall into the second sector ; and there are those relations involving the Asian and African where "both history and geography induce India to lend a sympathetic, understanding ear to the demands of their group for a larger voice in world affairs", and these can be categorized as falling under the third sector.[44] It appears that India's interests and moves in the first and third sectors tended to evaporate as years rolled by, while those in the second tended to be more and more stressed, and to the exclusion of others, by her policymakers. This would strengthen our understanding that India's foreign policy moves were profoundly motivated by a desire to further her national interests more narrowly conceived, that those moves were not exactly ulterior in design or essentially altruistic in inspiration. On the other hand, it would be hard to conclude that in the shaping of her moves and national interests Machiavellian considerations of *realpolitik* were the *only* considerations. As India's innocence in world affairs gradually wore off in face of profoundly unsettling, almost traumatic, practical (as opposed to purely intellectual) experiences, India seemed simply to try to trim her interests to include those that she could consider quintessential of her sovereignty, independence,

---

[44] See Geoffrey Tyson, *Nehru : The Years of Power* (London : Pall Mall, 1966), p. 69.

security, and economic wellbeing, that she thought she can secure even further on the basis of her diplomacy and military strength. In the process perhaps her national interests became more manageable, but did not go essentially against the theoretical consciousness of India's role as a participant in world's affairs, as revealed in the writings of Nehru before India's independence.

CHAPTER III

INDIAN NEUTRALISM IN ACTION : CASES OF CHINESE RECOGNITION, KOREA, SUEZ, HUNGARY AND THE CONGO

In our first chapter we have had occasion to make a point that neutralism (which includes non-alingnment) refers to a policy that is usually resorted to in a certain situation prevailing in the international arena. Usually this situation is described as the cold war, a *status mixtus* of war and peace. This situation is further characterized by the dominance of the two Super Powers, the United States of America and the Union of Soviet Socialist Republics ; so that we can say that the era of the cold war, which includes the period of Indian foreign policy that we are studying, has, as its organizing construct, the phenomenon known as "bipolarity". The intensity of bipolarity, that is to say, the extent to which the relationship between the two power centers, Washington and Moscow, dominated all other issues at the global level, has, however, varied, and this variation enables us to look upon the era of cold war as falling into four major periods. The first period began with the end of World War II and ended with the outbreak of the cold war, formally ushered into being by Churchill's Fulton Speech of 1946 and followed by the establishment of rival alliance systems. This was undoubtedly a period of almost total dominance of the two Powers. The second period stretched from 1950 through 1954, which included several wars, all limited and conventional, the outstanding amongst which was the one in Korea. In this period, the Super Powers were still in a position to freeze the affairs of the world in their problems without necessarily fashioning any solutions themselves. The third period began immediately after the previous period and ended with the abortive Paris Summit Conference of 1960, and this period witnessed the gradual disappearance or weakening of the socalled bipolar world. The fourth and the last period began where the third ended and is continuing and is characterized by a growing conciousness on the part of the Super Powers that there are limits even to their powers and therefore by their willingness to deal bilaterally with one another.[1]

Charles O. Lerche, a well-known student of the cold war period of international relations whom we have followed in dividing the era into the four periods, isolates a single crisis, or at most two, in each of these periods, that accurately epitomizes the period and that may be thought of as a micro-cosmic portrait of the period. These are the Berlin Blockade of 1948 (in the first period), the Korean War of 1950 (in the second period), Hungary and Suez of 1956 (in the third period), the Berlin and Cuban Missiles Crises of 1960-61 (in the fourth period)[2].

India, whose foreign policy we are studying, however, came into existence in 1947, and as such she was relatively unprepared as a new nation in world affairs to take any stand in regard to the earlier world problems. The Indian policymakers, whose perceptions of specific national priorities we have studied in the preceding chapter, did not, for reasons that are quite obvious, care much about the world outside her immediate periphery, and Berlin, for example, was definitely considered outside her immediate periphery and even peripheral. In regard to Korea, however, India took very deliberate and even determined stands, inasmuch as India was better prepared by then to take initiatives in defence of interests, as symbolized by and inherent in the outbreak of the war in Korea, which she considered vital (see Table V on geographical priorities in Chapter II). In regard to the crisis in Suez, her stances were no less determined, and this was because the central theme in this crisis was colonialism or its attempted resurrection that touched a very sensitive spot in the mental make-up of her policymakers which was to a large

---

[1] For the division of the periods, see Lerche, *The Cold War and After*, pp. 95-96.

[2] *Ibid.*, pp. 96-113.

extent moulded by their experience with colonialism. Happening almost simultaneously were the events in Hungary, where India had perforce to take some stand if only because she had set some traditions of participation in the solution of international crises that tended to engulf the whole world. Then came the Congo, throwing into relief the problems that newly independent states faced in being masters of their destiny in a complex modern world, and this was not where India with her emotional involvement in anything concerning anti-colonialism could possibly remain absolutely indifferent when others especially former colonialists threatened intervention and actually did so. In regard to the other crises that followed, as for example in Berlin and Cuba, they were so very far away that she did not consider them worthy of her attention. In the ones that India intervended cold war considerations prevailed fully ; they were also those in which to a considerable extent India's own particular concerns were fully reflected. We are going to discuss these cases from the point of view of the cold war and from the point of view of India's national interests and analyze India's neutralism as reflected in her positions concerning the cases. It is rather interesting to note that, with the progressive erosion of bipolarity in world affairs, India's participation in global matters also diminished, with corresponding increase in her participation in those affairs where the two Super Powers were not very much visible and also where she was particularly and immediately affected. In addition to the cases mentioned by Lerche we have chosen another that is global in character yet at the same time important from the point of view of India's national interests. This is the question of China's recognition, which loomed rather large in world affairs in the very first phase of the cold war. In the pages following it will be our endeavour to discuss India's neutralist posture in the cases just referred to. Each case will be discussed together with India's policy in the chronological order in which it occurred.

Section I : **Case studies of India's Neutralism**

A. *Recognition of Communist China*

In the very first period of the cold war, we see the world seized with a very important problem—the problem of coming to terms with an emergent reality—the fact of a newly installed People's Republic of China. The United States of America, as the avowed foe of the international communist movement directed from Moscow, was understandably and predictably chary of recognizing this reality which she thought might lead to the strengthening of the Communist bloc. The U.S. reluctance to come to terms with the reality in the East Asia manifested in several ways : one, her refusal to recognize the People's Republic of China (hereafter mentioned simply as PRC) ; two, her continued recognition and military protection of the rump regime of Gen. Chiang Kai-Shek which found refuge in Taiwan, which at the time was still legally a part of the Jananese Empire[3] ; three, her efforts, largely successful, to prevent the PRC from occupying the United Nations General Assembly and Security Council seats. By not allowing the PRC to enter the United Nations, the US for the time being at least, wanted for one thing, not to jeopardize or limit her opportunities of using the United Nations, with its non-Communist majority then prevailing in the United Nations General Assembly, as a weapon of US diplomacy.[4] The USSR equally understandably and predictably took the opposite stand which led her, first, to accord recognition to the newly formed fraternal Communist regime as the only legitimate government of not only mainland China but also Taiwan, which, if not legally at the time, at least historically, formed part of China ; and two, to espouse the cause of the PRC in the counsels of the world, including the United Nations.

---

[3] This is true in spite of the fact that Japan renounced her claim to Formosa (Taiwan) by accepting the Potsdam Declaration of 1945. The legal transfer of the island to China did not take place before the Japanese Peace Treaty of 1952.

[4] P. R. Sarbadhikari, *India and the Great Powers*, p. 47.

What position did India take in regard to this problem of China ? How did it differ from the positions taken by the cold war adversaries ? What particular characteristics, if any, her neutralist posture took ?

Almost immediately after becoming independent, India was called upon to consider the problem of China. In the month of October, 1949, the newly established PRC sent a communication to some important governments in the world which the regime thought friendly expressing the desire "to enter into diplomatic relations. . .on the basis of the principles of equality, mutual interest and mutual respect for sovereign and territorial rights".[5]

The Government of India had no difficulty in deciding the course of action to take. From the beginning, its policy, based as it was upon unanimous support of various elements composing the government, was unambiguously clear.[6] It favoured recognition of the PRC, and the decision to establish diplomatic relations was conveyed to the government of the PRC in December, 1949, after seeing that the Kuo-Min-Tang was finally out and the PRC firmly in power.[7] India thus became "virtually, though not technically, the first country outside the Russian bloc and certainly the first in the Commonwealth to accord recognition to China".[8]

---

[5] Reference to this communication from the PRC was first made in the press communique issued by the External Affairs Ministry of the Government of India on Dec. 30, 1949. See *Hindustan Times,* New Delhi, Dec. 31, 1949, as cited by K. P. Misra, "India's Policy of Recognition of States and Governments", *American Journal of International Law,* IV (April, 1961), 399.

[6] See K. M. Panikkar, *In Two Chinas* (London : Allen and Unwin, 1955), p. 67.

[7] Misra, "India's Policy of Recognition," pp. 399-400.

[8] *Ibid.,* p. 400. Burma was the first country, technically, to recognize the PRC. As regards India's being the first Commonwealth country to recognize the PRC, it must be pointed out that India did not want to recognize the regime alone. Mr. Menon, India's High Commissioner, had many meetings with the late Ernest Bevin, Labour Foreign Secretary, regarding recognition immediately after the PRC was established in October, 1949. But the British frustrated this attempt of the Indian Government to have a joint policy. Menon says of this : ". . . I went day after day, week after week, to see Ernest Bevin. I had long talks with him on the recognition of China. Each time he would say, 'tomorrow, tomorrow' meaning soon. He gave me a date in October and then again in November (1949). These did not come off. Ultimately I had to tell him, 'We cannot wait any longer and we are going to recognize China' . . ." See Brecher, *Menon's View of the World,* p. 136.

The decision of the Government of India was not exactly a "matter of choice", but was almost automatic. As Nehru explained in the Indian Parliament about two months later :

> It is a question of recognizing a major event in history and of appreciating it and dealing with it. . . . When it was clear that the new Chinese Government was in possession of practically the entire mainland of China. . . that the govt. was stable and that there was no force which was likely to supplant it or push it away, we offered recognition to this new government and suggested that we might exchange diplomatic missions.[9]

Thus the permanence of the regime which Nehru emphasized and the "habitual obedience of the bulk of the population" which was to be considered as a separate factor in a separate speech at the UN by B. N. Rau, then India's chief UN delegate,—the two factors together constituting the principle of effectiveness[10]—played an important part in India's policy of recognition of the PRC.

And to the fleeing KMT regime, now settled in Taiwan, the Indian Government refused to give any recognition, not the least because of the legal point involved, which was put this way by K. M. Panikkar, India's first ambassador to PRC (who before his appointment had been India's ambassador in Nanking, capital of KMT China before Communist success), "Taiwan was not even technically a part of China, because it was juridically a part of the Japanese Empire, since the Treaty transferring it to the allies had not been signed".[11]

Later, in regard to the question who should represent China in the United Nations, India's stance was quite in keeping with her policy of according diplomatic recognition to her regime, the PRC.

---

[9] India, Parliament, *Parliamentary Debates,* III, Pt. 2, (March 17, 1950), col. 1699.

[10] India was in fact following the prescription of such well-known experts on International Law as Oppenheim. See Rau's speech, United Nations, General Assembly, *Official Records,* (UNGAOR), Fifth Session, 277th Plenary Mtg. (September 19, 1950), p. 9.

[11] *In Two Chinas,* p. 68.

India's advocacy of the regime's right to represent China in the UN could be traced as early as to 1950. She felt then, and her feeling was well articulated later by Nehru in 1953, that :

... the UN is incomplete without China. If China is not there, then from the point of view of population, nearly a quarter of the world is not there. It is not a question of anybody liking it or not.... You have to suffer the consequences of ignoring something which is there and which you don't recognize.[12]

This was therefore a very clear enunciation of the policy of recognition of a reality that needed to be treated "on its merits". India's policy here appeared to be in sharp opposition to that of the United States in the defence of which the latter was ready to use her ultimate power in the United Nations—the use or the threat of the use of veto in the Security Council. At the opening meeting (277th) of the fifth session of the UN General Assembly in 1950, the Indian delegation moved a resolution[13] to seat the PRC only to see it defeated and the United States promptly evaluated the defeat as "overwhelming". The chief of the Indian delegation B. N. Rau did not concur : He reasoned :

...The adverse votes included that of Nationalist China. Leaving that vote out of account as being the very vote whose validity was at issue, I find the total population of the countries that voted for it was 809 millions, the abstention accounting for 117 millions.

---

12 Cited by P. R. Sarbadhikari, *India and the Great Powers*, p. 48.
13 U. N. Document A/1365, Sept. 19, 1950. The Indian resolution ran as follows : "The resolution, noting that the Republic of China was a member of the UN and of its various organs, considering that the obligations of member under the charter of the UN could not be carried out except by a government which, with a reasonable expectancy of permanence, actually exercises control over the territory of that member and commands the obedience of its people, recognizing that the Central Government of the PRC is the only such government functioning in the Republic of China as now constituted, would have the G.A. decide that the aforesaid Central Government should be entitled to represent the Rep. of China in the GA ; further, the draft resolution would have the Assembly recommend that the other organs of the UN adopt similar resolutions". UNGAOR, Fifth Session, 277th Plenary Mtg., Sept. 19, 1950, p. 2,

Lest anybody should imagine that the supporters were
mainly Communist countries, I have separately com-
puted the figures of the indisputably Communist countries that voted for the draft resolution. These add up
to 527 millions as compared with 282 millions of the
Communist countries. Thus on a population basis and
even taking into account only non-communist countries, the draft resolution, far from being defeated by
an overwhelming majority, may be said to have been
carried.[14]

Six sessions later (1955-56), when another effort to
seat the PRC came to nought, V. K. Krishna Menon, leader
of the Indian delegation, reminded the august body that :
There are 582 million people of China and their voice
must be heard...24 members voted in favour...
these members represent 1036 million people ... the
members that voted against the inscription of the item
represent 585 million in the world.[15]

Thus, in this phase of India's external relations her
neutralist policy was clearly not marked by any concern for
equidistance from the two cold war adversaries, the USA
and the USSR. It is quite clear that she repudiated the
American policy and her criteria of determining the recognition policy clearly led her to concur with the Soviet Union.
As it has been already indicated before, the criteria that
she depended upon followed the prescriptions of authorities on International Law and could be considered to be
highly objective and free from any obvious political bias.
Neutralism in this case did indeed mean deciding questions
"on merits."

But behind this obvious objectivity were considerations
that were political, and they pertained to perceptions of
her national interest. The PRC did indeed command the
allegiance of the bulk of its people and was sufficiently
secure and looked reasonably permanent. More fundamen-
tally however the security-conscious Indian Government
could not overlook the fact that the PRC was a neighbour-

---

14 Cited by Sarbadhikari, *India and the Great Powers*, p. 48.
15 *Ibid.*, p. 49.

ing regime ; that the regime, which symbolized the victory of the Maoist revolution, also indicated the collapse of Western colonialism-imperialism that backed the discredited KMT and the victory of the nascent forces of Asian nationalism. The Government of India was further aware that India was not prepared to meet China militarily that any non-recognition, an almost belligerent act, would require it to do. Later, Menon justified the recognition of China in very blunt terms, in terms of benefit—"that cooperation and harmony was for our benefit as well as for others."[16]

These were the calculations, at once shrewd and enlightened, that dominated the Indian policymakers. The enlightened part lay in the realization that shrewd calculations could be given an objective facade. The objective conditions surrounding the recognition of the PRC allowed the Indian policymaker not to talk about national interests, which may appear in the eyes of foreigners purely selfish. This reliance or emphasis on the objective factors in the matter of Chinese recognition indeed allowed the policymakers to hide the grand strategy of India's China policy (as it prevailed then) : loosening the ties between the USSR and the PRC and the contingency, if ties were indeed loosened, of forming an Asian bloc led by China and India which could be an effective third bloc in the world. Friendship with China that recognition of the regime would entail tied with the basic mediatory role between the USA and USSR that India envisaged for herself. This calculation about China was not remote from the hopes of a future Titoist trend of Chinese policy which were entertained by influential circles in London and Washington, as reported by a competent observer.[17]

B. War in Korea

The war in Korea broke out on June 25, 1950 when

---

[16] Brecher, *Menon's View of the World*, p. 141.
[17] The observer in question is G. F. Hudson, a reputed British Sinologist. His remarks are cited by Sarbadhikari, *India and the Great Powers*, p. 46.

the North Korea forces, as reported and confirmed by the United Nations Mission on Korea (UNCOK), crossed the Thirty-Eighth Parallel that separated their country from the South. This touched off a very grave international crisis threatening to draw into direct conflict the two Super Powers and their allies. The situation prior to the invasion of Korea was as follows.

The United States and the Soviet Union, while still formally allies, agreed at the end of World War II that so far as the Korean Peninsula was concerned the former would accept the surrender of the Japanese in the South and the latter in the North. This agreement clearly led to the de facto partition of the country at the Thirty-Eighth Parallel. The parallel thus became the battleline in Asia of that struggle in the world that had already been launched in the name of containment of Communism. Each power by considering its half of the country (Korea) as falling within its sphere of influence failed to agree about the final disposition of the question of unification of Korea. From 1947 through 1949 various attempts were made by the United States to dispose of the problem through the United Nations, where the former hoped to outmaneuver the Soviets because of the numerical superiority America enjoyed at the time. On November 14, 1947, the United Nations General Assembly seemed indeed to fulfill the US hopes when it recommended, among other things, elections throughout Korea which would be supervised by the UN Temporary Commission on Korea intended to establish a national assembly with the power to establish a security force, dissolve all other military formations, take over administration of both the halves of the country and arrange for withdrawal of all foreign forces. But the regime in the North of Kim Il Sung and the USSR dashed all US hopes for unification. However, elections were held on May 10 in the Southern part of the country which resulted in the victory of an anti-Communist regime headed by Syngman Rhee, "a valid expression of the free will of the electorate" as certified by the UNTCOK. Following this, a republican constitution was promulagated,

Rhee was formally elected President, and the Republic of Korea was finally recognized on December 12, 1948 by a bloc of nations led by the United States in the General Assembly (comprizing a majority at the time) as "the only lawful government" of Korea, the fact of establishment of a People's Republic in the North notwithstanding. At this stage another attempt was made, this time under the auspices of the UNCOK (a new commission on Korea, established by the General Assembly) to unify Korea. But the Commission, not unexpectedly, was boycotted by N. Korea and her mentor, the USSR, and hence nothing came out of it. However, consequent upon the holding of another election (May 30, 1950) in South the results of which were not very promising for the Rhee regime, the North Koreans proposed on August 5 the holding of fresh nationwide elections and followed this up by sending representatives to S. Korea with the plea for peace and unification. The Rhee regime's response was quite belligerent : arrest of the N. Korean emissaries and the threat of forcible unification of Korea.[18] Thus, as one observer has remarked : "The impasse was obviously incapable of resolution through any recourse to the United Nations, since the Super Powers had already irrevocably taken sides in the controversy".[19]

From the very beginning of the conflict and even before that as the brief narrative above shows, Americans wanted to contain international communism, feared as a monolithic and satanic movement under the overall direction of Moscow. The main thrust of American policy was directed toward containing communism in Europe, so that there would not be any more communist states outside Eastern Europe, which had already been communized, and this policy was showing every promise of success. But there was Asia resurgent, where the USA saw

---

[18] For basic data on Korea, see Soon Sung Cho, *Korea and World Politics* (Berkeley : University of Calif., 1965), pp. 121-38 : Frederick L. Schuman, *International Politics,* Seventh Ed., (New York : McGraw-Hill, 1969), pp. 239-40 ; B. Shiva Rao and C. K. Kondapi, "India and the Korean Crisis", *India Quarterly,* VII (Oct.-Dec., 1951), 295-315.
[19] Schuman, *International Politics,* p. 240.

the rise of PRC in the mainland as a further mani-
festation of increasing strength of the Communist bloc,
led by the same satanic band in Moscow. The USSR,
on the other hand, thwarted in Europe, but certainly
comforted and even elated by the rise of the Red Star
over China, looked for an opportunity to test the firmness
of the US policy of containment, by then operational in Asia
also. This opportunity presented itself in Korea[20] where the
battle had been going on for some time only in an attenuated
form. The Soviets, who already had a sphere of influence
in Korea, now saw a chance for them and their portégé North
Korea to salvage S. Korea, which was to them the remainder
of the prize of the cold war.[21]

From the very beginning of the conflict the Indian
position was quite distinct from those of the two Super
Powers, which were for most purposes dictated by cold war
considerations. First, India did not agree to the US position that the North Korean aggression if not repelled
posed an ultimate threat to the whole of Asia and that it
represented a chapter of a worldwide communist plan for
expansion.[22] Secondly, she felt that China, although a

---

20 Nikita S. Khrushchev, who became USSR's no. 1 political leader
after the death of Stalin, says however in his memoirs that although
Stalin and Mao had blessed the idea of the Korean adventure they had
reservations about it. It was Kim Il Sung of N. Korea who had master-
minded it. In Khrushchev's words : "I must strees that the war wasn't
Stalin's idea, but Kim Il Sung's. Kim was the initiator. Stalin, of
course, didn't try to dissuade him. In my opinion, no real Communist
would have tried to dissuade Kim Il Sung from his compelling desire to
liberate S. Korea from Syngman Rhee and from reactionary American
influence. To have done so would have contradicted the Communist
view of the world . . . Stalin persuaded Kim that he should think it
over, make some calculations, and then come back with a concrete plan
. . . I remember Stalin had his doubts. He was worried that Americans
would jump in, but we were inclined to think that if the war were fought
swiftly—then intervention by the USA could be avoided." Later on
Khrushchev points out that Stalin removed some Soviet advisers at the
first discomfiture of N. Korean forces in S. Korea ; this point he offers
in corroboration of his contention that Stalin did not indeed approve of
the idea of reuniting Korea through force. See *Khrushchev Remembers*
(Boston : Little Brown & Co., 1970), pp. 368, 370.
21 For a better philosophical understanding of the views and motivations of the two sides in the conflict, see Louis J. Halle, *The Cold War
as History* (New York : Harper and Row, 1967), pp. 413-418.
22 S. L. Poplai and Philip Talbot, *India and America : A Study of
their Relations* (New York : Published for Council on Foreign Relations
by Harper and Bros., 1958), p. 117.

6

Communist power, was *not* acting as a mere agent of the Soviet Union and that in general the revolution that just toppled the *ancien regime* in China was not so much a victory of Soviet Communism as it was a victory of the forces of nationalism against imperialistic exploitation to which some of her traitorous countrymen led by KMT had played a subservient and collaborationist role ; indeed, India felt that by treating the new regime as an independent agent it might be possible to help it free itself from whatever feeling of dependence it had toward Moscow.[23] And, as regards Korea, she was in favor of treating the country as an integral whole ; while she felt the necessity of recognizing the division of Korea temporarily, she felt impelled toward according the two parts every opportunity to compose their differences with a view to eventual unification through peaceful means, under the UN auspices, and *not* under the dictates of the occupying powers, the US and the USSR. Her interest in peace and the prevention of war was very strong (see the Tables in the preceding chapter) from the very beginning, and by trying to free the Korean problem from cold war politics of the two Super Powers, she was indeed trying to localize the conflict thereby, according to her perceptions, also making it easier to save.

An analysis now of the policy of India concerning the problem after the outbreak of the war reveals the following stances. India accepted the first resolution of the Security Council of June 25, 1950 condemning the North Koreans (making it clear herself at the same time that she did not condemn the whole Communist bloc) and asking them to withdraw behind the Thirty-Eighth Parallel and to cease hostilities.[24] She also accepted (somewhat later,

[23] Sarbadhikari, *India and the Great Powers,* p. 32.

[24] UN Doc. A/1501, June 25, 1950. Also, United Nations, Security Council, *Official Records* (UNSCOR), Fifth Year, 473rd Mtg. June 25, 1950, 7-8, 13-14.

presumably for purposes of mediation),[25] the United States inspired second Security Council resolution of June 27 asking the UN members to furnish such assistance to the Republic of Korea (South Korea) as may be necessary to repel the armed attack and to restore international peace in the area.[26] India however never participated militarily in the Korean venture of the United Nations—her acceptance of the June 27 resolution took the shape of an offer, made not immediately but on July 29, to send a small surgical unit from her regular defense forces—presumably because she wanted to save herself from future embarrassments and to keep her opitons open. As one observe has put it : "India from the very beginning wanted to localize the conflict and that in case of its spread she wanted to be out of it".[27] Thus despite India's public condemnation of the aggression by North Korea, she stood outside the American camp, and this fact, together with the other moves that she initiated, it would be seen later on, enabled her to carry on dialogue with the other bloc.[28]

A major declaration of her aloofness from the Western position regarding the conflict came by way of her withdrawal from the sponsorship of the Eight Power Resolution[29] of the General Assembly which established the UN Commission for the Unification and Rehabilitation

---

[25] The Government of India while explaining the delay expressed the hope "that even at this stage it may be possible to put an end to fighting and settle the dispute by mediation". See K. P. Karunakaran, *India in World Affairs : Feb. 1950-Dec. 1953* (London : OUP, 1958), p. 102.

[26] UN Doc. S/1511, June 27, 1950.

[27] J. S. Kundra, *Indian Foreign Policy, 1947-1954* (Groningen : J. B. Wolters, 1955), p. 128.

[28] At the time these things were happening, India was taking certain diplomatic moves, such as, suggesting admission of the PRC to the Security Council and terminating Soviet boycott of it as ways to solve the Korean question. These moves were significant, because, first, they tended to legitimize Peking's interests in the Korean War, and, second, challenged "the Communist image of a world neatly divided into two warring camps with no neutral nations occupying a third position". See Allen Whiting, *China Crosses the Yalu* (Stanford : Stanford University Press, 1960), pp. 61-62.

[29] It was carried Oct. 7, 1950 as Resolution 376(V). For the stands taken by the different powers, see UNGAOR, Fifth Session, 294th Plenary Mtg., Oct. 7, 1950, 230 et seq.

advocating unification by force, if necessary. India which abstained from voting on the resolution that carried had earlier introduced her own resolution aimed at creating a special subcommittee for the examination of all draft resolutions.[30] This was defeated in spite of the reluctant acceptance by the USA and moderately warm support of the USSR, whose delegate the M. Andrei Vishinsky had commented on the Indian move in this way : "a new situation had been created by the submission of the Indian proposal (A/c. 1. 572) which deserved support as did all efforts at conciliation."[31]

After abstaining from voting on the Eight Power Resolution, India opposed the crossing of the Thirty-Eighth parallel by the United Nations forces. Her opposition was based upon her belief that "faith in the United Nations might be impaired if the UN were even to appear to authorize unification of Korea by the use of force against N. Korea, especially after the UN resistance to the North Korean attempt to unify the country by force against South Korea".[32] She was influenced in her behavior by the information that China might intervene if the UN forces did indeed cross the Yalu[33] and this she believed would result in an extension of the conflict in an area which, although conventionally called the Far East (now East Asia), was in fact "very near East" to India.[34] Even so, India was careful not to preempt the UN forces from crossing the Parallel until all other possibilities had been exhausted.

After the UN forces had indeed crossed the Thirty-Eighth Parallel and the Chinese had responded by crossing the Yalu as had been warned by India, India tried her best

---

30 UN Doc., A/c. 1. 572, Oct. 4, 1950.

31 UNGAOR, Fifth Session, Fifty-first Commission, 353rd Mtg., Oct. 4, 1950, pp. 55-56.

32 Rao and Kondapi, "India and the Korean Crisis", 306.

33 Panikkar, then Indian Ambassador, had been called to the Chinese Foreign Office by Chou En-Lai to be told that China will intervene. See Panikkar, In Two Chinas, p. 77.

34 B. N. Rau used this phrase, see Rao and Kondapi, "India and the Korean Crisis", p. 301.

to arrange for a "ceasefire", without trying to "condemn" China's "aggression", as January 29 resolution did. Before that, she had submitted on Dec. 12 a draft resolution, with twelve other Asian nations, for constituting a ceasefire group to the UN First Committee, to which reference has already been made.[35] India also had appealed to the Chinese and the North Koreans to declare that they had no intention to cross the Parallel into South Korea, only to be rebuffed by the Chinese and the Russians (and their bloc) in the UN. The Indian supported resolution, presented to General Assembly's First (Political) Committee on January 11, 1951 and which embraced five principles[36] was finally adopted 50 to 7 by the General Assembly two days later. Nothing came out of this since Peking rejected these principles, and its rejection was considered as "total defiance of the United Nations" by the United States.[37]

Anyway, the United Nations, led by the USA, branded China an aggressor on February 1, 1951[38] in the teeth of strong opposition from India,[39] Burma and the Communist bloc. Acts of omission and commisson on the part of the United Nations having achieved nothing, it was the sheer

---

[35] UN Doc. A/c. 1/641. Dec. 12, 1950.

[36] Resolution 384 (V) of Dec. 14, 1950. Also UNGAOR, Fifth Session, 324th Plenary Mtg., Dec. 14, 1950, p. 660. Five principles included : (i) An immediate ceasefire with safeguards against use of truce "as a screen for mounting a new offensive", (ii) action during truce on a permanent Korean peace, (iii) exit of all non-Korean forces "by appropriate stages", (iv) UN approved administration of Korea during the truce, (v) creation of UN agency including US, USSR, Britain and PRC to settle Far Eastern issues. For text see UN, *Yearbook of the United Nations,* 1956 (New York : Columbia University Press, 1952), 209-210.

[37] United States, Department of State, *Bulletin,* XXIV (Jan. 29, 1951), 165-166.

[38] Resolution 498 (V), February 1, 1951.

[39] India's UN delegate Rau had said earlier (Jan. 18, 1951) why India opposed branding China aggressor : "it would serve no useful purpose. If such a step were taken, it would hardly increase the prestige of the UN unless it were intended to be followed by other steps ; since the feasibility of further steps had not yet been examined, the only result of such a resolution would be not only to leave all Far Eastern problems unsolved, but also to make them insoluble". UNGAOR, Fifth Session, 426th Mtg., Jan. 18, 1951, 523-524.

It could be added here that, when another resolution recommended an embargo on goods to the PRC, India abstained while explaining that she did export any goods to PRC.

physical and spiritual exhaustion of the antagonists that finally brought about the ceasefire.

The most important issue concerning the ceasefire was that of Prisoners of War. The negotiations for the ceasefire started in July, 1951 and were stalled by the seemingly insuperable differences between the US and the USSR. The Americans were of the view that any plan concerning the POWs would have to eliminate the possibility of forced repatriation or forced detention and set up workable machinery to handle repatriation, provided no humanitarian consideration came in the way. The Soviets, on the other hand, called for an examination of the problem, morally, politically and legally ; and that morally, they agreed, the consideration was that one should be guided by the principle that POWs must freely express their wishes, but in actual practice, they emphasized a defenseless person did not have much freedom of choice because propaganda, pressure and even violence may alter his views.[40]

Here again India came forward with a proposal to solve the deadlock. The Indian proposal originally expressed on Nov. 19 was modified on Nov. 26 and finally adopted on Dec. 3, 1952.[41] The proposal aiming at reconciling the two views comprized the following points, among others (in a list of 17 points) : One, POWs would be released into the temporary jurisdiction of the Neutral Nations Repatriation Commission—so that there would not be any forcible detention ; two, after release of the POWs both parties would have the opportunity to explain to their prisoners the rights and conditions prevailing in their homelands.[42] The first point, it could be seen, tended to meet the American objection, while the second at removing the Soviet objections. The Indian resolution, initially rejected by the Soviet bloc and approved with some reservations by the United

---

40 *Facts on File*, XII (1952), 369 A-E, 377. Also, Sarbadhikari, *India and the Great Powers*, p. 35.

41 GA Resolution 610 (VII), Dec. 3, 1952.

42 For the entire text of the resolution, see UN, *Yearbook of the United Nations*, 1952 (New York : Columbia University Press, 1953), 201-202.

States and her allies, was finally accepted by both the sides, and the NNRC was finally ushered into being with the following members : Sweden and Switzerland (for the West), Poland and Czechoslovakia (for the Soviets), with India (non-aligned/neutralist) in the Chair.[43]

As chairman, India's General Thimayya showed great independence in discharging his duties. While there was some difficulty in regard to methods of disposing of those anti-Communist North Korean POWs who refused to be interviewed by the official North Korean interrogators, he (Thimayya) was finally successful in persuading them to listen to interviews and in rejecting the use of force to bring them to the interviews. The success of the Indian chairman was attested to by one objective student of world affairs in this way:

> On four of the major issues facing the Commission, the break-up of POW organizations, the use of force, the extension of the explanation period, and the final disposition of the prisoners—Indian sympathies were with the Polish and Czechoslovak delegates ; however, on no one of those issues was this sympathy translated into action. For one reason or another, the chairman ended by supporting the Swedish and Swiss position. However, neither side challenged India's actions as being biased in favour of its opponents.[44]

Thus, from an analysis of the stances taken by India it appears that India never gave support to just one side and opposed the other side for ever. As Blema Steinberg observes :

> India voted for the UN condemnation of North Korea, yet felt that she should have a chance to be heard in the Security Council. She opposed the crossing of the

---

43 The final agreement on the exchange of prisoners was signed in Panmunjon, June 3, 1953, and this was incorporated as Art. III in the Armistice Agreement, July 27, 1953. For the text of the agreement see UN, *Yearbook of the United Nations*, 1953 (New York : Columbia University Press 1954), pp. 136-146.

44 Blema S. Steinberg, "The Korean War : A Case Study in Indian Neutralism", *Orbis*, VIII (Winter 1965), 953-54.

38th Parallel, yet was willing in the face of bitter Chinese protests to support a UN advance across it after all possible steps taken to reach a settlement with the North Koreans had failed. She refused to condemn China as an aggressor in 1951, yet left her ambulance unit to help the UN command. On the prisoner repatriation question, India drafted a resolution that largely followed the UN command's stand, but included enough modifying clauses to save the face of the Chinese.[45]

All this suggests perhaps that India tried to follow an independent policy that was by and large independent of the decisions of the other powers, including the two Super Powers. This "independent" policy, (Nehru preferred this description to neutralism/non-alignment) consisted in, as Nehru himself said, "taking decisions on merits". But the merits in question were not the merits of a narrow issue taken without consideration of the larger goals with which it is mixed up. Or, in other words, the implication in Nehru's mind, as suggested by Steinberg, was that "the merits of an issue must be considered with the larger goals in order to arrive at a wise solution".[46]

She was indeed in the eastern flank of the Western bloc of nations, but she set herself above everything else the mission of never losing contact with the aggressor on the diplomatic front and of maintaining the contact between the two forces, as another observer remarks.[47] And she did indeed succeed in fulfilling her mission of not losing contact with either of the two contending blocs. The success of India's policy, howsoever it may be called, should be judged by this criterion and no other.

---

45 *Ibid.*, p. 953.
46 *Ibid.*, p. 954.
47 The observer here is Marc Frankenstein, a French political commentator. Cf. ; "Range ur le flanc Est du bloc occidental, l'Inde s'assignait avant tout pour mission de ne jamais perdre contact avec l'agresseur sur le front diplomatique et de maintenir ce contact entre les deux forces en presence". See "Les Initiatives de l'Inde pour le Reglement du Conflit Coreen", *Revue Politique et Parlementaire*, CCIII-CCV (1951), 56.

C. *The Crisis in Suez*

In June, 1956 the crisis in Suez broke out in its full fury. An understanding of the Crisis requires first a discussion of its historical background.

The Suez Canal, a 101-mile long Canal extending from Port Said to Port Suez, owed its origin to Ferdinand de Lesseps, a Frenchman who obtained, November 30, 1854, from the then Khedive (Viceroy) of Egypt a concession enabling him to establish an international company, to be known as the Universal Company of the Maritime Canal of Suez (UCMCS) to build a canal and some months later it was further agreed that the concession was to last for ninety-nine years after which the Canal would be handed over to Egypt. The construction of the canal that started in April, 1859 took more than ten years to complete and was formally opened to international traffic in November, 1869.

The Suez Canal that fell wholly within Egyptian territory was nevertheless recognized as an international waterway built and owned by an international company and therefore made subject, with Egyptian acquiescence, to international regulation and administration. The Constantinople Convention of October 29, 1888 stipulated in Article I that the waterway was "always to be free and open, in time of war as in time of peace, to every vessel of commerce, without distinction of flag". The Convention further stipulated, in Art. X, rather inconsistently, that this obligation "shall not interfere with the measures which the Khedive might find necessary to take for securing by their own forces the defense of Egypt and the maintenance of public order".

However, in course of time, the British came to hold the dominant position in the region. In 1875, the Khedive, faced with bankruptcy, sold his shares in the company, amounting to 44 per cent, to Britain. In 1882, Britain 'temporarily' occupied Egypt in order to ensure 'stability and peace' in the region and to protect her share in the company. But what was intended to be a temporary occupation proved to be semi-permanent, continuing as it did until 1922, when Egypt was granted its independence. But even then Britain hardly withdrew from the area. In fact, as late as in 1936 Britain imposed upon Egypt a treaty that gave the former the right to defend the Suez Canal and to jointly rule the Sudan. This treaty came to an end in October, 1951, when Egypt abrogated it. It was followed by some great changes in Egyptian politics. An army junta, led by Gen. Neguib, captured power and abolished monarchy. It also tried to solve the differences with Britain over the abrogation of the 1936 treaty by signing on February 12, 1953, an agreement with Britain that provided for self-government, international supervision and eventual self-determination for the Sudan. The new regime also succeeded in getting Britain to agree to military withdrawal from the area by 1956. But soon Neguib fell from power, and his place was taken by Col. Gamal Abdel Nasser, who, like Neguib, was anti-monarchist, yet unlike him was young with heady passions of anti-colonialism and pan-Arabism with neutralist overtones. By mid-June the British did finally withdraw from the area. Nasser followed this up with his nationalization of the canal, with the declared objective of finding new sources of revenue to finance the ambitious Aswan dam, necessitated by the Americans and the British withdrawing their offer of aid for the project. Nasser's nationalization measure did not envisage outright expropriation of the shareholders, for it did not rule out compensation; nor did it threaten the rights of the users (with the exception of Israel) under the Constantionple Convention. The main purpose of nationalization was indeed to find money for the dam. But, nonetheless, it did affect the power equations in the area, and the world.

Of the many affected by the decision, two NATO members, Britain and France, figured most prominently, for between them they had the control of the company. The threat posed by the nationalization decision, some others imagined, was unacceptable not only because of the nature of threat, but also because of the source of threat, that is, Col. Nasser, who fared no better than another Hitler in their perception. Thus, they were determined to prevent such a person from gaining absolute control of the canal. After their initial attempts through multilateral conferences to keep international control of the canal had failed, the two Western powers (Britain and France) decided to use the strategem of egging Israel on to attack Egypt, so that they would be able to use the ensuing unsettled conditions in the area as an excuse to intervene in the Canal zone to protect the waterway for international use.[48] And this started the crisis finally involving the Super Powers and the international organization in which India's participation was so active and extensive.

In the period immediately after the nationalization of the canal, the interests of the various powers involved in the crisis started to assume shape, and the differences in their interests suggested the different policies and methods that they wanted to pursue in the resolution of the problem.

The most directly involved parties in the crisis as has been indicated already were undoubtedly Egypt on the one hand and Britain and France (and Israel by association) on the other. Since Nasser considered that the Canal lay in the Egyptian territory, his nationalization primarily was an assertion of Egypt's sovereignty and freedom from colonialism-imperialism of the former colonial masters, the British and their associates. He also attempted to unify all Arab nationalists—against all their enemies, imagined and real. He also wanted to raise new revenues for Egypt, geared to making life for the fedayeen better. To Britain and France the same act tended to violate certain legal and political rights in the area which permitted them to claim the status of World Powers. And, since much of their commerce and supplies passed through the Canal, the loss of its control that nationalization made inevitable threa-

---

[48] For a competent discussion of the background, see the following : F. L. Schuman, *International Politics*, pp. 362-370 ; *Asian Recorder*, I (1956), 963-65 ; and E. G. Mezerik (ed.), "Suez Canal" (A. Chronology) *International Review Service*, III, 28-32.

tened their economy and standard of living. The French, in addition, put off as they were by Egyptian support of Algerian rebels, took this as another unacceptable rebuff. Furthermore, the Western powers (Britain and France) found it emotionally unacceptable, since they sensed high stakes in the matter—victory or defeat of their brand of imperialism vis-a-vis Nasser and his insolent nationalism.[49]

The United States, the leader of the West, was not directly involved in the crisis and her economic wellbeing did not in any significant way, at least in the short term period, depend upon her access to the Canal. But her withdrawal of economic aid from Egypt led the latter not only to seek nationalization as a source of revenues but also to turn away from, even to reject the US-inspired alliance system in the region (e.g., MEDO or the Middle East Defence Organization) which has one of the main props of the worldwide containment program of the US.[50] And, since her allies in NATO, Britain and France, were affected by the said move of Egypt, this must have caused her additional concern. Thus, the initial reactions of the United States to the crisis in Suez were favorable to her allies, although she was not at the same time overly eager to see force used for the protection of their rights. This caution on her part might have been due to the concern she felt for her image of a power with relatively little colonial traditions.

The USSR, on the other hand, saw the crisis as a rare opportunity for advancing her interests. From the very beginning she espoused the Arab nationalist cause against the colonialist-imperialists and the Zionists who were bent upon expanding at the expense of the Arabs. By appealing to Arab nationalism, essentially anti-Western in character, the USSR expected to eject Western influence from, and also gain a foot-hold of her own in, a strategically important area contiguous to herself—its strategic importance

---

[49] For an analysis of the policies of the directly involved powers, see John Stoessinger, *The United Nations and the Super Powers*, Second Ed. (New York : Random House, 1970), pp. 63 et seq.

[50] Sarbadhikari, *India and the Great Powers*, p. 40.

coming from its containing the important water-way and the important mineral resources of the area. These last factors are indeed very important in her cold war confrontation with the Western bloc, led by the US.[51]

The Indian position in regard to the crisis in Suez was to a certain extent dictated by her basic attitudes and interests. She was against colonialism—and Suez was a reminder of Western dominance and colonialism in Asia. The strength of her feeling against colonialism could be gauged from Mr. Nehru's denunciation of Franco-British-Israeli adventure in Suez—"this record of unabashed aggression and deception".[52] Moreover India was determined to support a sister neutralist nation in ridding the area of any foreign interference that smacked of cold war struggle of the giant powers. India was also interested in "supporting progressive Arab nationalism as practised by Egypt as a means of minimizing the danger of unqualified Muslim support for Pakistan and an anti-Indian course".[53] And, perhaps the most important single factor attributable to India's stand in regard to Suez, as pointed out by an Egyptian student of Indian foreign policy, was "the inclusion of Pakistan in the Baghdad Pact, which aroused the fear that the cold war had been brought close to her door".[54] India was further interested in seeing that the control of the Suez Canal lay in friendly hands, or else, India would stand to lose a great deal economically speaking. Mr. V. K. Krishna Menon explained this concern thus :

---

[51] Stoessinger, *UN and Super Powers,* pp. 68-69. Stoessinger rightly saw in the crisis three "different yet interrelated struggles in one : the hostility between Israel and the Arab states ; the nationalism of Egypt vs. Colonialism-imperialism of the British and the French, and the struggle for the allegiance of the Arabs between the Americans and the Russians". *Ibid.,* pp. 78 et seq.

[52] India, Parliament, *Lok Sabha Debates,* Vol. 9, Part II, No. 3, Cols. 260-267.

[53] W. F. Van Eekelen, *Indian Foreign Policy and the Border Dispute with China* (The Hague : Martinus Nijhoff, 1964), p. 71.

[54] Bahman Amini, "Indian Foreign Policy with Particular Reference to Asia and Africa", (Unpublished Ph.D. Dissertation, University of Maryland, 1959), p. 188.

India was concerned in the Suez Canal as a lifeline of her economy...76% of her imports and 70% of her exports pass through the Canal. The fulfillment of India's Five Year Plans depended upon traffic through it. India did not approach the problem in a legalistic way but with a full sense of reality of the importance of the Canal for the many countries of the world who [sic] used it.[55]

Given the interests of the Powers that were to play some role in the solution of the problem, let us now see what actions they took.

The Western nations first tried to compel Egypt to back down from her policy of unilateral control of the Canal, and this they did in many ways. One way was to have agreement among the three Powers, Britain, France, and the USA, reached in London in August, that the Suez Canal should be administered by an international authority to be discussed at the Twenty-four Nation Conference beginning August 16. Egypt and Greece having refused to attend, only twenty-two nations finally attended, and the conference heard several proposals including one from the Indian delegation. The Indian proposal included among other things the acceptance of the following points :

1. Consideration be given, without prejudice to Egyptian ownership and operation, to the association of international user interests with the Egyptian Corporation for the Suez Canal.

2. A Consultative body of user interests be set up to help the Egyptian Corporation for the Suez Canal.

3. Government of Egypt should transmit to the UN the annual report of the Egyptian Corporation for the Suez Canal.[56]

Neither the Indian plan as outlined above nor a Soviet plan that went a little bit further in accommodating Egyptian demand for complete sovereignty in regard to the

---

[55] *Asian Recorder,* I (1956), 994-995.
[56] For further details, see *ibid.*

Canal was accepted. Instead, the Conference accepted with some modifications the US proposal (known as "Dulles Plan") which proposed that the Canal be operated by an international board established within the UN and that the latter be guided by the principle that the canal should be operated without prejudice to anyone's rights.[57] This and other subsequent efforts to prevent Egypt from gaining absolute control over an internationally managed canal however came to nought, because of Egypt's unwillingness to part with her sovereign rights. Finally an attempt was made to resolve the crisis through direct talks among Mahmood Fawzi (Egypt), Selwyn Lloyd (Britain) and Christian Pinay (France), who agreed on certain principles without resolving whether the Canal was to remain under exclusive Egyptian control.[58]

Thus thwarted to get Egypt to agree to re-internationalization of the canal, the two Western Powers, Britain and France, decided to intervene militarily in the region. They decided to use Israel, alarmed at the emergence of Pan-Arabism and Egypt's exclusive control of the waterway and also by Egypt's denial of any user right to Israel, to attack Egypt so that the troubled situation around the region, consequent upon the attack, would offer the Anglo-French conspirators ample excuse to intervene militarily in order to protect the waterway which was their lifeline. Thus, on October 29, 1956, Israel attacked Egypt and marched along toward the Canal, and on the following day, the Anglo-French alliance, after issuing a meaningless ultimatum which it knew would be rejected by the Egyptians, moved its armed forces into the area on October 31, 1956. Thus what started as a military conflict between Egypt and Israel degenerated, as the Anglo-French alliance wanted it to, into a confrontation between Arab nationalism

---

[57] *Ibid.*

[58] For actual wording of the resolution see UN. Doc. S/3675, Oct. 13, 1956. For a detailed chronology of the period since the Indian resolution until the last S.C. resolution before the outbreak of the armed conflict, see *Asian Recorder,* I (1956), 1087-1089.

and the forces of Western imperialism.

Thus, the United States, thoroughly shocked by the events, called on October 30 for a Security Council meeting to discuss the issue and take appropriate measures to restore peace in the area. In this she received cooperation from the USSR, each nation sponsoring a resolution in the Security Council with a view to putting an end to the crisis in the area. The US resolution, introduced on Oct. 30, called upon Israel to leave the area without dealy and asked all members to "refrain from the use of force or threat of force", but was vetoed by Britain and France. The Soviet resolution, introduced the following day (in the drafting of which Iran and KMT China participated), incorporated quite a number of points of the rejected US draft resolution, but met with no greater success, being similarly vetoed by the same two countries.[59]   Later, on November 5, the Soviet Union introduced a resolution proposing under Art. 42 that a joint US-USSR force be established to keep peace in the region, but by this time the United States had already changed her mind regarding cooperation with the USSR, and so nothing came of it.[60]

Even without the US-Soviet differences, the Security Council had earlier found itself stymied. Thus, Yugoslavia suggested convening the Emergency Special Session under the 'Uniting for Peace' Formula, and it met on November 1, the Anglo-French opposition to it notwithstanding. After the US and USSR had tried in separate ways to condemn and stop the Anglo-French-Israeli action in Egypt,[61] they jointly sponsored a Compromise plan which urged ceasefire and withdrawal of all forces behind the armistice lines.[62] But Canada, which had abstained on the

---

[59] UNSCOR, Eleventh year, 749th and 750th Mtgs. (October 30 and 31, 1956).

[60] *Ibid.*, 755th Mtg., Nov. 5, 1956.

[61] UNGAOR, First Emergency Session (Special), 562nd Mtg., (Nov. 1, 1956,) p. 18.

[62] It was adopted 64-5 with 6 abstentions.   See *Ibid.*, First Emergency (Special) Session, 562nd Mtg. Nov. 1, 1956, p. 36.   The text of the resolution was adopted by the GA at its 563rd Mtg. (Plenary) on Nov. 2, 1956, UN Doc. A/3256 [A/Res/390].

Compromise plan, tried to remove a key defect by proposing on Nov. 3, a draft resolution requesting the Secretary General of the UN to submit a plan within forty
hours for the creation with the consent of the nations concerned of an Emergency International Force to secure and
supervise the cessation of hostilities. It is at this point
that India came to play a role in the UN for the first time
in regard to the issue. India supported the Canadian proposal. Indeed India had been thinking along the same line
for some time ; in fact, Mr. Krishna Menon had suggested
a "boundary force" even before the Canadians, but had
somehow refrained from introducing any resolution.[63]
Thus, when the issue came to be discussed in the Emergency Session of the General Assembly, India supported
Canada when the latter proposed the establishment of the
International Force. The resolution embodying the proposal was finally adopted on November 5.[64] The Emergency
International Force was eventually made up of contingents
from ten small countries, including a contingent from India.
However, the adoption of the resolution on Nov. 5 was
followed immediately (on Nov. 6) by the British declaration that they would be willing to order a ceasefire from the
midnight. It must be mentioned in this connection that
even outside the UN India had tried, after the outbreak
of armed hostilities in the Suez area, to take a position
on the crisis. In concert with other Asian countries
(Burma, Ceylon and Indonesia) she had stressed "concern"
at the development and had expressed "strong disapproval"
of the aggression by greater powers against weaker
countries.[65]

From the above it appears that the two Super Powers
and India (and Canada) did agree on the question of ceasefire, and it is precisely because of that that the resolution
referred to above was finally adopted. But this agreement

63 Brecher, *India and World Politics*, p. 75.

64 UNGAOR, Emergency Session, I, 563rd Mtg., Nov. 4-5, 1956. (UN
Doc. A/3290 and A/Res/394.)

65 Cited by Sarbadhikari, *India and the Great Powers*, p. 44.

7

seemed to hide more than it revealed. For, in terms of motivations, the US differed from the USSR ; while India (also Canada) differed from the two Super Powers. The US purposes included : (1) regard for the principles of the UN and world opinion, (2) prevention of a war that spurred Russian support for Egypt, (3) desire not to forfeit the goodwill of Afro-Asian states.[66] The Soviet purposes, on other hand, were mainly to clear the strategic region of the Mid-East of the colonialist-imperialists (Britain and France in particular) and to move into the resulting power vacuum in the area. The USSR underscored this last purpose by her readiness to be part even of a force that comprised contingents from the US.

India and Canada, both suspicious of the motives of the two Super Powers and fearful that simple ceasefire may not be enough, proposed that there be an international Emergrency Force under the UN auspices which would not include any contingent other than that from such small states as will be willing to contribute any to the said force. Thus the ceasefire proposal was finally adopted because it was equally unacceptable to both sides. But since it put an end to Anglo-French imperialism-colonialism, it marked a great victory for Arab nationalism.

Thus the Indian stand in this case was a novel kind of neutralism the precise application of which did not help one side or the other ; in fact, it checked both to a degree, and of course helped end colonialism and its revival, encouraged Afro-Asian nations to pursue neutralism unmolested, and perhaps won India the friendship of *at least* one Moslem state in a future conflict, where India might be pitted against another Moslem country, Pakistan. As on observer has put it :

India's stand during the crisis therefore measured up with the principles guiding her foreign policy in that area. Her efforts towards the withdrawal of foreign troops stemmed both from her anti-colonial policy and

---

[66] *Ibid.,* p. 43.

the fear that the intervention of the Great Powers which was in the logic of events would spark off a major war. The impact of the crisis in strengthening the nonaligned policies of some Arab governments, such as Egypt, and paving the way for others to follow suit, such as Iraq, was a success for India's rationale, that neutralism was the most logical policy for the developing states. Moreover, the support of a secular India for a Muslim state on the basis of colonial intrusion was an acute embarrassment for Pakistan, wedded as she was to Western alignments ; it revealed that diplomacy on the basis of religion was unsuited to modern relations of states.[67]

D. *Civil War in Hungary*

At about the same time the Middle East was in turmoil, another country in Eastern Europe was going through a period of political fermentation and violence which became a subject of cold controversy in the United Nations and outside. This country was Hungary, a part of the so-called Soviet satellite system, where a group of reform-minded Communists encouraged by Premier Khruschev's attempted de-Stalinization of the Soviet society sought to liberalize their own communist system. As part of their reforms they demanded the withdrawal of the Soviet Union's Warsaw Pact forces from their territory. They were supported (politically) by a medley group of international sympathizers which brought about a number of developments that invited cold war confrontation between the two Super Powers.

In the latter part of October, 1956, in the wake of widespread demonstrations by students, workers, soldiers leading to the appearance of Soviet tanks in Budapest, Imre Nagy formed a new government composed of Communists and some non-Communists. The demonstrations in the course of which many persons lost their lives became the

---

[67] *Ibid.*, p. 44.

subject matter of particular concern in the West. The United States and her allies tried on October 27 to bring the matter to the Security Council. But the Security Council action on Hungary could not be taken until a few new developments took place ; such as the entry of Soviet troops into Budapest, the fall of Imre Nagy's government, and its replacement by a more conservative, orthodox communist regime of Janos Kadar— all of which took place on November 4, 1956.[68]

It is in the circumstances surrounding the events of Nov. 4, 1956 that the Security Council was finally summoned to an urgent meeting to consider the Hungarian situation. The Security Council heard a United States resolution calling on the USSR not to introduce additional armed forces into Hungary and to withdraw without delay all her forces from that country, but it was not passed because of Soviet objections. Thus frustrated, the United States brought in a resolution in the Security Council for an emergency special session of the General Assembly, as provided for in "Uniting for Peace" formula, to consider the situation in Hungary which was adopted.[69] The Emergency special session of General Assembly meeting on November 4 adopted the United States resolution which called on the USSR to stop armed attack on Hungary, to withdraw her forces from Hungary without delay ; the resolution further asked the USSR and Hungary to admit UN observers.[70] It is interesting to note that India, having had no role to play directly in the United Nations (because she was not a member of the Security Council)

[68] For background happenings in Hungary, see E. G. Mezerik (ed.), "Hungary and the United Nations", International Review Service, IV, 1-21. Also UNGAOR, Eleventh Session, "Report of the Special Committee on the Problem of Hungary", Supplement No. 18 (UN Doc. A/3592), esp. Ch. II.

[69] UNSCOR, Eleventh Year, 752nd Mtg., Nov. 2, 1956, UN Doc. S/PV 752.

[70] Verbatim Record of the 564th Mtg. of the General Assembly, Nov. 4, 1956. UN Doc. S/PV 754.
On Nov. 9, the special Assembly further reaffirmed the Nov. 4 resolution by calling for cooperation by Hungary with UN observers.

so far,[71] now got her chance to take a stand and along with fourteen other African-Asian nations she abstained on the US resolution.[72] The Indian stand in this case reflected her basic attitude which was : it is better to confine discussions to practicable matters and to avoid actions that would aggravate situations. Krishna Menon, India's UN delegate at the time, later reminiscing about India's stand, pointed out that :

> ...the Hungarian uprising in the beginning was natio-
> nal in character...should not be allowed to lead to the
> outbreak of a world war...the way to deal with it was
> not to isolate the Hungary question in respect of the
> use of foreign forces and to point your finger of scorn
> but to demand that all foreign occupying forces should
> be withdrawn from Europe...they were primarily
> there as part of the forces (Soviet and Western) after
> the World War and were a component of the cold war
> complex...and finally, since Hungary was a member
> state of the UN, she had a voice there, and one could
> not talk of her as a colony.[73]

Menon, however, believed that India was not neutral where human freedom was concerned, and India in fact endorsed the right of the Hungarian people to choose the form of government they desired and held force and violence by governments or peoples inside a country or against it "as reprehensible and contrary to the outlook and approach of my government and country...."[74]

---

[71] Outside the United Nations, however, India began reacting to events in Hungary much earlier. Nehru made a statement in a press conference in New Delhi on 25 October to the effect that "this is what might be called a nationalist upsurge...it is affecting their (Hungarians) independence...Anyhow, it is not for us to interfere in anyway, even by expressing opinion on the internal affairs of those countries". Also, on Nov. 5 Nehru bracketed Hungary with Egypt in pointing to "outrage on human dignity and freedom". Cited by D. N. Mallik, *The Development of Nonalignment in India's Foreign Policy,* (Allahabad : Chaitanya Publishing Houes, 1967), pp. 179-180

[72] Again, when on Nov. 9 Special assembly adopted the US resolution calling for cooperation by Hungary with UN observers, India abstained —Verbatim Record of 761st Mtg. of the General Assembly, Nov. 9, 1956. UN Doc. A/PV 571.

[73] Michael Brecher, *Menon's View of the World,* pp. 85, 87-89.

[74] UNGAOR, Eleventh Session, Nov. 4-10, 1956, p. 44.

This was not the only instance where India stood to differ from the entire Western bloc. In answer to the socalled Five-Power (Cuba, Ireland, Italy, Peru, Pakistan— the last with an eye to its value as a precedent for Pakistan itself) Resolution in the Special Assembly on Nov. 9 asking for, inter alia, free elections in Hungary,[75] India took a position that was *not* one of abstention, but outright opposition to the wishes of the majority that included the United States and Britain[76] and, India, as Berkes and Bedi pointed out, "found itself in the singular position of being the only non-Communist Power to vote in the negative."[77] India based her stand on the ground of Hungarian sovereignty and the view that :

> ...the UN is unfortunately not an organization which can hold plebiscites in different parts of the world. There are a lot of members of the UN, very respectable, some of them members of the free world, which I am sure would hate to hold plebiscites in their own countries or in various territories under the control.[78]

The same view was expressed a little differently by Menon himself thus :

> My delegation cannot subscribe at any time to phraseology or proposals before the Assembly which disregard the sovereignty of states represented here. For example, we cannot say that a sovereign member of the Assembly can be called upon to submit its elections and everything else to the UN without its agreement. Therefore any approach we make as though this were a colonial country which is not represented here at the UN is not in accordance with the facts or law of the position.[79]

[75] UN Doc. A/RES/397.
[76] UNGAOR, Eleventh Session (ES-II), 571st Mtg., Nov. 9, 1956.
[77] Berkes and Bedi, *Diplomacy of India,* p. 51.
[78] This view was expressed by A. K. Mitra, political adviser to the Indian delegation to the UN. Cited by Sarbadhikari, *India and the Great Powers,* p. 38.
[79] UNGAOR, Eleventh Session (ES-II), p. 68.

Later on Nov. 19, however, India along with Ceylon and Indonesia co-sponsored a resolution in the eleventh Session of the General Assembly urging Hungary to allow observers designated by the UN Secretary General to enter that country[80] which was adopted with some minor modifications in the teeth of Soviet bloc opposition[81] but when the Fourteen Power resolution supported by the Western bloc insisted on setting a time limit as to when the observers had to be received by the Hungarians, the Indian delegation abstained.[82]

It must be pointed out however that on questions that are humanitarian, not patently political, capable of isolation from cold war questions, India's stances were positive (as opposed to abstentive or obstructive) and tended to side with the Western bloc. For example, the Special Assembly had adopted earlier (67 for, 0 against, 9 abstentions) an Austrian resolution requesting "immediate aid" for Hungarian refugees with India's support.[83]   And this aid was continued with continuing support from India.[84] In the final stages, India's initial position on the political questions (including the question of accepting the Hungarian contention that the "UN cannot intervene in her domestic jurisdiction") was reaffirmed when she made the following moves : She abstained on Dec. 12, 1956, on the Twenty Power resolution (co-sponsored by the US and nineteen others and approved 55 for, 8 against, 13 abstentions) condemning violation of the UN charter by the USSR and Hungary ;[85] and also, in September, 1957, she felt disinclined to go along with the setting up of the special com-

---

[80] Ceylon, India and Indonesia, revised Draft Resolution, Nov. 19, 1956. UN Doc. A/3368.
[81] Verbatim Record of the 576th Mtg. of the General Assembly, Nov. 21, 1956.
[82] Verbatim Record of the 608th Mtg. of the General Assembly, Dec. 4, 1956. UN Doc. A/PV 608.
[83] Verbatim Record of the 577th Mtg. of the General Assembly, Nov. 15, 1956.
[84] Verbatim Record of the 587th Mtg. of the General Assembly, Nov. 21, 1956.
[85] Verbatim Record of the 618th Mtg. of the General Assembly, Dec. 12, 1956. UN Doc. A/PV 618.

mittee on Hungary because the existing circumstances did not warrant any hope for the success of such a step.[86]
In sum it can be stated that, throughout its second special Emergency Session and its twelfth regular session following it, India's overall position comprised the following moves : one, urging withdrawal of the Soviet Forces from Hungary ; two, recognition of Hungarian sovereignty ; three, urging cooperation by Hungary with the United Nations in the verification of charges of deportation of its citizens ; and four, supporting relief measures of humanitarian character isolated from cold war considerations. However, India would not have anything to do with any of these following moves : one, outright condemnation of the USSR ; two, denigrating the Hungarian regime as less than free ; three, free elections in Hungary under UN auspices, or other methods that smacked of outright intervention by other powers. No wonder, she voted against some resolutions, abstained on many others, and suggested amendments to some, and initiated some others. In short, she could not be identified with any one side ; sometimes she favoured one side and opposed the other. And, this she did not for the sake of favouring and opposing one or the other side, but because such stances were dictated by her own reading of the situation in Hungary and the world from her own viewpoints.

E.   *Turmoil in the Congo*

On June 30, 1960, the Belgians relinquished their political control of the Congo, and the Congo thus became a sovereign nation. A republican regime, headed by Joseph Kasavubu (President) and Patrice Lumumba (Prime Minister) took over from the Belgians. These two men, although members of the same nationalist movement in the Congo, harboured different political beliefs and attitudes ; the former a moderate Conservative with

---

[86] UNGAOR, Twelfth Session, 677th Plenary Mtg., Sept. 13, 1957, pp. 1428-29.

mildly pro-Western, and the latter a fiery leftist with strong anti-Belgian, feelings functioned very uneasily from the very start. Their problem was further complicated by the immediate challenge they faced from Moise Tshombe, a wealthy, decidedly pro-Belgian and conservative Premier of Katanga, a constituent part of the new republic which happened to be at the same time its richest part. Thus, as Stoessinger observes, "the new Congolese leadership held political views along the entire political spectrum—from Lumumba's uncompromising anticolonialism to Tshombe's pro-Belgian and rightist sentiments."[87]

This very divided and therefore shaky political leadership was confronted with a developing political crisis in the Congolese army (Armée Nationale Congolaise) when enlisted African soldiers demanded that Belgian officers quit and their own pay be increased. A mutiny, later joined by other disgruntled elements in the Congo, finally broke out and spread all over the country resulting in mass departure of Belgians, civilian and military, from the country. The crisis assumed critical proportions when Moise Tshombe declared Katanga's secession on July 11, asked for Belgian military help to crush the mutiny, and the Belgians, in their turn, using the pretext that the new government of Lumumba had in effect been unable to protect Belgian lives and property, intervened militarily and finally marched into Leopoldville, sparking off extensive riots between the marching Belgians and the Congolese. Lumumba accused Belgium of aggression and conspiracy with Tshombe to reimpose colonialism. The stage was thus set for a conflict between nationalism (of the Congo) and imperialism-colonialism of the Belgians.[88]

87| John Stoessinger, *UN and Super Powers*, p. 82.

88 For a fuller treatment of the background, see James L. Ballard III, "The United Nations in the Congo Crisis," Austin : The University of Texas, 1962, (Unpublished Master's thesis), pp. 1-46 ; Catherine Hoskyns, *The Congo Since Independence, January 1960-December 1961* (Oxford : RIIA, Oxford University Press, 1965), 1-104 ; Ernest E. Lefever, *Crisis in the Congo : A United Nations Force in Action* (Washington D.C., : Bookings Instn., 1965), 3-16 ; and Stoessinger, *UN and Super Powers,* pp. 81-93.

Patrice Lumumba, the Congolese Premier, tried to involve the United Nations in his country's affairs, when he in fact cabled the United States for aid on July 13, 1960. Nikita Khrushchev, then Soviet Premier, complicated matters by saying that the Congolese mutiny was right and that the USA and others in the NATO had conspired to reimpose colonialism in the Congo. Under the circumstances, Dag Hammarskjoeld, the UN Secretary General, called on July 13, 1960, an Emergency Session of the Security Council when he requested authority to send a United Nations military force to the Congo for containing the crisis. The Security Council, in spite of mutual US-USSR recriminations, adopted on July 14 a Tunisian resolution, by 8 to 0 vote including the votes of the USA and the USSR ; this called on Belgium to withdraw her troops from the Republic of Congo and authorized the Secretary General to provide the Government of Congo "with such military assistance as may be necessary...in the opinion of the government to meet fully their tasks".[89]   The American and the Soviet national interests in the Congo were mutually contradictory ; the US sought interposition of the authority of the United Nations between the East and West to prevent the Congo from becoming another battlefield in the cold war, and the USSR wanted a speedy withdrawal of Western colonialism from a vital area of the world. But somehow there emerged in the beginning of the crisis a temporary and tenuous US-Soviet consensus regarding the crisis. In spite of Soviet intentions and Lumumba's wishes to the contrary,[90] the Security Council on July 22, 1960 through a resolution adopted unanimously, requested, among other things, all states 'to refrain from any action which might tend to impede the restoration of law and order and the exercise by the Government of the Congo of its

---

[89] UN Doc. S/4387, July 14, 1960. Another resolution to the same effect sponsored by Ceylon and Tunisia was passed July 22, 1960 after it was felt necessary that operations may be needed in Katanga and Kasai the two secessionist provinces (see UN Doc. S/4405). Unlike the previous resolution this was passed, unanimously

[90] See Stoessinger, *UN and Super Powers*, p. 84.

authority and also to refrain from any action which might
undermine the territorial integrity and the political independence of the Congo",[91] another resolution of August
9 (adopted 9 to 0, the US and USSR agreeing once again)
authorized the UN Secretary General to do the same thing
in regard to Katanga, hitherto untouched by UN action.[92]
This paved the way for the establishment of a United
Nations Force, ONUC (which was composed of 20,000
troops including those from India, Ireland, Sweden all flying the UN flag) geared to building of a responsible and
viable Congolese government[93] to which apparently the
two Super Powers, in spite of their difference agreed.
India did not at this stage play any direct part, simply
because she was not a member of the Security Council, but
she thoroughly subscribed to the Ceylon-Tunisia resolution
which had been adopted by the Security Council.

The Congolese imbroglio acquired new dimensions when
the Government of the Congo split, with Kasavubu and
Lumumba firing each other from their respective positions ;
at this stage, pro-Western Colonel Joseph Mobutu took
command of the armed forces through a coup, thus making
it possible for the Belgians (mostly administrators) to
return to the Congo as unofficial advisers. These developments elicited mutually opposite reactions from the two
Super Powers. The United States definitely welcomed the
emergence of Kasavubu-Mobutu as the dominant faction
and therefore the legitimate government. On the other
hand, the USSR, whose representatives were expelled by
Mobutu, fearing that Lumumba's eclipse might endanger
their chance of gaining foothold in the Congo and Africa,
began supplying material to the hardpressed Lumumba
forces. But Andrew Cordier, Executive Assistant to the
Secretary General, took an action of effectively preventing
Soviet supplies from reaching Lumumba, thereby destroy-

---

[91] UN Doc. S/4405, July 22, 1960.
[92] UN Doc. S/4426, Aug. 9, 1960.
[93] See Stoessinger, *UN and Super Powers*, pp. 84-85.

ing his (latter's) chances of remaining in power.[94] The Soviets were profoundly frustrated by this Cordier action and accused the UN of acting as the stalking horse of neo-colonialist Western powers ; they then submitted a draft resolution directing the UN to cease operating in or interfering with the internal affairs of the Congo. Upon the rejection of the Soviet resolution, a substitute resolution by Tunisia and Ceylon (having the support of the USA) was submitted that endorsed the policies of the Secretary General, but this was also vetoed. This stymied the Security Council, necessitating the convening of the special session of the General Assembly. The Super Powers in this special session showed the same attitudes as exhibited before ; the USA continued to support the continuation of the mandate already given to the Secretary General by the Security Council ; and, the USSR presisted in her demand for the cancellation of the mandate because of the Secretary General's already tarnished role as an alleged supporter of the colonialists.[95] This helplessness was mitigated to a degree by the action in the emergency session that followed it of an overwhelming majority, including India, which supported the US position and therefore the Secretary General's position ; the session through the action of the majority created a conciliation commission made up of Afro-Asian representatives in order to pacify the internal dissensions in the Congolese Government.[96]

Since the Congolese Government had already split, the question of proper representation of the Government in the UN became important in the regular session of the General Assembly that followed the Emergency Session (Special). In the former, Guinea proposed that until the decision of the Credentials Committee was made, it was Lumumba, not Kasavubu-Mobutu who should represent the Congo, and

94 *Ibid.*, p. 86.
95 UNGAOR, Sixteenth Session, 858th Plenary Mtg. September 17, 1960 (ES-IV).
96 UN Doc. A/1474 (ES-IV), Sept. 20, 1960.

this had the support and blessings of India and other Afro-Asian nations and the USSR, but unfortunately nothing came of it. Finally, the Credentials Committee, dominated by Western nations, having ruled the Kasavubu delegation as the legitimate delegation, the Lumumba delegation invoked the General Assembly where the US side prevailed over the Soviet bloc countries that challenged them (voting being 53-24-19). Here, India, opposing acceptance of the Kasavubu delegation, voted with the USSR.

Be that as it may, despite Soviet Union's withdrawal of support (She had earlier vetoed it in the Security Council), the Secretary General persevered with the UN operations as intended by the previous resolutions. This frustrated the purposes of the USSR, and Khrushchev brought in the Fifteenth General Assembly his famous *Troika* proposal, which suggested that, instead of one Secretary General, there should be a three-man committee representing the West, the East and the developing countries of the world that professed neutralism. But Secretary General Hammarskjoeld refused to knuckle under Soviet blandishments ; his position was finally approved and he was given a fresh mandate by the General Assembly[97] by an overwhelming majority that included India, whose representative Mr. Krishna Menon said on December 10 in the Security Council as if in answer to the Soviet demand that "the withdrawal of the UN forces in Congo would be a calamity" and "we yield to none in our respect for the sovereignty of other countries, but if all this is entirely a domestic matter, why did the UN go there at all ?"[98] In regard to the *Troika* proposal, the Indian position, not unlike most other members' was negative, although India had proposed (one of her own) by way of reforming the Secretariat, an advisory committee from different geographical areas, "a sort of inner cabinet whose views and perhaps even approval would have

---

[97] UN Doc. A/4510, Sept. 20, 1960.
[98] *Asian Recorder,* VI (February 12-18, 1961), 3795.

to be sought on any important matter".[99] Late in December, two very important draft resolutions were sought to be adopted by the General Assembly. The first was proposed by India and seven other non-aligned countries ; it asked for "immediate convening of the Parliament of the Congo". In the debate on this resolution, Mr. Krishna Menon of India revealed that his government considered the regime of Kasavubu-Mobutu as 'unvarnished', 'unashamed', and 'unconstitutional' dictatorship. The other resolution of Dec. 18, jointly proposed by the USA and UK, called on the Secretary General to "do everything possible to assist the chief of State of the Republic of the Congo in establishing conditions in which Parliament can meet and function in security and freedom from outside interference". Although each of the two rival resolutions failed to pass the General Assembly because of lack of affirmative 2/3rds majority, they were important in revealing widening differences between India (leading a number of other non-aligned-neutralist nations) and the bloc led by the USA.[100]

A new phase opened with the death in February 1961 of Patrice Lumumba. This phase of the crisis saw at least a partial restoration of the US-Soviet consensus that previously existed. After another Soviet demand for Secretary General's resignation and insistence that Gizenga was the lawful head of the Congolese Government (which was an attempt to get the support of the neutralist bloc in the United Nations), the Soviet Union came finally to support a strong United Nations stand, despite her strong misgivings. It has been suggested that Mr. Nehru's categorical rejection of Mr. Khruschev's February 25 appeal for India's support to the USSR position in the Congo might have been a clinching factor in getting the Russians to revise their position in regard to the strong UN role in the Congo.[101] Thus when the Security Council on February 21

---

99 John Stoessinger, *The Might of Nations,* Third Ed. (New York : Random House, 1969), p. 285.

100 *Asian Recorder,* VI, 3795-3796.

101 See Ernest Lefever, *Crisis in Congo,* 57.

adopted a resolution (9-0 with Soviet Union and France abstaining) urging the UN to take *immediately* all measures to prevent the occurrence of civil war in the Congo, including those involving use of force if necessary, in the last resort, the USSR merely abstained.[102]

In the spring and summer of 1961, the Congo was in utter confusion. Cyrille Adoula, the newly appointed Prime Minister of Joseph Kasavubu, was finding it increasingly difficult to control the entire country in the face of Vice-Premier of Lumumba Antoine Gizenga's assertions of the legitimacy of his government that operated from Stanleyville. Besides, there were many mercenaries,—French, Belgian and South Africans in Moise Tshombe's Katanga, which was opposing the UN forces. Once again, a group of Afro-Asian powers, including India, took the initiative in passing a resolution calling upon Belgium "to accept its responsibilities as member of the United Nations..." and wanted 'all Belgian and other foreign military and paramilitary personnel and political advisers and mercenaries to be withdrawn" ;[103] and they also took a number of other positions that tried to solve the budgetary problem of the United Nations brought about by its Congo operations.[104]

A final vigorous action to tackle the problem of secession was taken by the Security Council when it rejected the claim that Katanga is "a sovereign independent nation" and authorized the Secretary General to take vigorous action, which would not shrink from the use of force, if necessary, for the immediate apprehension, detention pending legal action, and/or deportation of all foreign military

---

[102] UN Doc. S/4741, February 21, 1961. Both tne USA and the USSR had misgivings about one or the other part of the resolution but both had to act clearly on it (either supporting or abstaining) because of fear of alienating the Afro-Asian countries. See Stoessinger *UN and Super Powers,* p. 89.

[103] UN Doc. A/Res/1599 (adopted by the Gen. Assembly, April, 1961).

[104] UN Doc. A/Res/1619. UNGA 995th Plenary Mtg., April 21, 1961. India did not sponsor it, but she voted on it favourably along with Western powers with the Soviet bloc nations voting against.

and paramilitary personnel and political advisers not under the UN command, and mercenaries as laid down in para A-2 of the Security Council resolution of Feb. 21, 1961.[105] With the passing of the resolution, as Stoessinger observes, "the United Nations was now clearly committed to support Adoula's Central Government against the secessionist attempts of Tshombe and Gizenga".[106] And, finally, after final United Nations military thrusts, this time under the direction of the new Secretary General U. Thant, the Katangan Premier Tshombe found it impossible to continue his secessionist activity any more and thus felt constrained to sign the Kitona Agreement acknowledging the authority of the Central Government, emerging ironically as the next Prime Minister of the Congo.

Apart from the way India voted one way or the other, she contributed a great deal by way of material contribution. Out of about 20,000 troops from about 30 countries, India's share was about 5,600 ; India's pledge to the United Nations Fund for the Congo, although not very large, was to the tune of $ 105,000 ; [107] it was an Indian national, Rajeswar Dayal, Secretary General Hammarskjoeld's personal representative in the Congo, who paved the way through his reports on the Congo to eventual strong action by the United Nations. The Indian military contribution particularly was politically important for the United Nations. For, as one student of UN's Congo operation observes :

> ...Hammarskjoeld chafed under the Communist charge that the Congo operation was a tool of the western "colonialist". Support from a leading neutralist government helped to blunt this attack. It also helped the Secretary General to improve his relations with

---

105 UN Doc. S/5002 was adopted by 9 to 0, Nov. 24, 1961. There were two abstentions—France and Britain.

106 Stoessinger, *UN and Super Powers*, p. 89.

107 Ballard, *UN in Congo*, App. I, 175.

some African states.[108]

The same observer goes so far as to say that the success-ful conclusion of the UN operation in the Congo depended to a large extent on two powers, India and USA.   To quote him :

> In a real sense India and the United States were the two countries the UN operation most depended upon, both for political support in New York and for mili-tary in the Congo. Despite some differences in inter-preting the mandate, the United States-India partner-ship remained solid throughout the Congo drama. The Congo operation would probably have collapsed if either New Delhi or Washington had withdrawn its support before the integration of Katanga in January 1963.[109]

In a real sense, the   operation would have remained incomplete without the use of force and the use of force was necessitated by certain accidental factors with which India was associated. For, as the same observer says :

> ...the disposition of the Indian officers to finish what in their view was the unfinished tasks of Rounds One and Two, the expected withdrawal of the large Indian brigade in early 1963 because of Red China's attack on India's northern border, and the financial plight of the United Nations—all these factors pointed toward one end, the final solution of the Katanga problem by force.[110]

Section II :   A Summary

What kind of neutralism did India show in these cases ? Did India lean toward the United States bloc or

---

108 Lefever, *Crisis in Congo*, p. 61. Lefever says elsewhere (p. 70). "India by virtue of its heavy contribution of troops became chief partner along with the United States."
109 *Ibid.*, p. 107.
110 *Ibid.*

8

toward the Soviet bloc ? Or did she follow a policy of equidistance or equal proximity in regard to them ?

In the case of Korea, India did not side permanently with any nation or bloc of nations. She was determined from the very beginning to play a mediatory role which required her to avoid taking any overtly partisan stances. As it has been shown before, India favoured the United States position on some occasions ; and on other occassions, she sided with the Soviet Union. But even when she did that, her behavior was governed more by her own reading of the situation than by any purely opportunistic policy of satis-fying one bloc or the other. The only thing she cared about in following the policy she did was to secure peace in the area (which happened to be quite close to her) and the world. And following the particular policy of recog-nizing China (People's Republic), which was part of her overall policy toward the Korean imbroglio, she was not so much supporting the Soviet Union (or the bloc countries), as she was trying to secure the victory of nationalism (even though that was directed by communist ideologies and totalitarian methods) in Asia, to establish relations with a powerful neighbour on a friendly basis, even to wean her away from the clutches of Moscow-directed Communism.

In the case of Suez, India's stances were greatly in-fluenced by her feeling toward colonialism of the West of which she herself was freed only a few years ago. She was scared of the attempted revival of colonialism in an area very close to her, an area of great strategic importance and abounding in great natural resources. In this case the United States initially appeared to be on the side of the United Kingdom and France in their (latter's) fight against nationalization of the international waterway and the Rus-sians appeared to be on the side of the Egyptians. Yet, in the crucial period following the military intervention of her allies, the United States decided to go against colonialism, even when that was being perpetrated by her allies, so that the US stand did not differ outwardly at least from that of the USSR (although the motivations were entirely different). In this instance, the Indian stand did not diverge from that of two Super Powers. Thus, India was not so much non-aligned with the two Super Powers as she was aligned with Egypt, a sister nonaligned nation, against the colonialist bloc of Britain and France. It is possible to think that, because of the strong determined stand taken by some of the Afro-Asian states that included India, it was possible for the United States to refuse to support her Western allies even at the cost of causing the whole Western system of alliance a tremendous jolt. It is also possible to think that such determination of Afro-Asian nations (including India) perhaps prevented the USSR from taking a more interventionist line not only in favor of the Egyptians but also for the sake of her own interests—securing a foothold in the region being one of them. India and the other Afro-Asian countries were determined to prevent *any* outsider from getting any military foothold in the area, and this is why they were so willing to have an Emergency Force, composed of smaller nations, under the overall direction of the United Nations, to police the ceasefire. In this way, they prevented any accretion of military strength to either of the two blocs ; and, in this sense, perhaps this stance was equally anti-USSR and anti-US or anti-West. By helping rid the area of colonialism or neocolonialism and by coming to the aid of a sister neutralist country she strengthened the world movement toward neutralism and the concept of the "peace area" in the world.

In the Hungarian case, on the other hand, India's position, although favoring the Soviets and Hungarians politically as evidenced from her refusal to condemn the USSR and Hungary and to have the UN intervene in domestic affairs of Hungary directly, yet could not be considered to be entirely in their favor ; that is to say, she was not against the United State bloc either, for she was willing to support the United States when she really wanted to help the people of Hungary in distress. One thing stands out in India's position regarding the crisis in Hungary : she was clearly opposed to any intervention in Hungary's domestic jurisdiction without her government's consent. This was a legalistic position, but it had strong political implications. India was determined to prevent the United Nations from taking a decision that could serve as a precedent for UN intervention in other cases, such as Kashmir, which she deemed as falling within her domestic jurisdiction. Also, India continued to support the special position of the USSR in Eastern Europe following from the tacit agreement between the Great Powers at the end of World War II, and she was of the opinion that this could not be changed singly but only if all other problems involving both the Super Powers are settled as part of a general world-wide settlement.

Many Western critics have accused India of double standards in her role in Suez and Hungary, the cases, which to the critics, were similar. India, while acknowledging certain similarities, was of the opinion that the two cases were in some important respects different. For, according to India, Egypt was within legal competence when she nationalized the canal ; Israel was an aggressor ; the Anglo-French military intervention was a clear violation of the charter. On the other hand, in Hungary, the point of law was not clear. Information available was scant. Hungary was indeed a member of the United Nations, and hence juridically speaking was sovereign. Thus one student of Indian foreign policy observes concerning the two cases :

> The application of India's nonalignment [sic], as it obtained in one question in comparison with the other disappointed those who had ignored the norms of India's foreign policy attitudes and behavior, as they had been coming from the very beginning, in expecting that she would call a spade a spade and react absolutely identically to the errors of both the power blocs. But contrary to their misguided expectations, India's nonalignment [sic] reflected as in the past, an independence of judgment and action, within her own perception of the factors and circumstances obtaining, which, as usual, was oriented to minimizing cold war tensions and preserving and promoting world peace. Skepticism in regard to it resulted largely from the fact

that India refused to partake of the cold war suscep-
tibilities of the socalled free world in a highly volatile
situation. But she could not act otherwise under the
premises of her nonalignment [sic].ᴵᴵᴵ

In the Congo, India's position was anti-colonialist,
anti-Belgian ; she was for the integrity of the Congo.
Although she was for Lumumba and against Kasavubu-
Mobutu, yet after the death of Lumumba she did not
support the Gizenga (Vice-Premier of Lumumba) faction
which drew support from the USSR, in order that there
may be in fact the emergence of an integrated Congo.
She thus remained a strong supporter of ONUC (the UN
operation in the Congo), even though that might have gone
against the interests of one of the Super Powers, in this
case the USSR. And as pointed out by Lefever, India
and the United States were the pillars of the United Nations
efforts in the Congo.

From the above analysis of India's neutralist postures, it seems obvious that neutralism did not mean equidistance from the blocs—India did indeed come closer to
one bloc or the other on some occasions, while on rare occasions maintained a posture of equidistance. The particular postures were determined by particular circumstances
of the cases and by her own reading of her interests and
situations. India's was thus a balanced and moderate
neutralism that could very well be considered the hallmark
of a pragmatic and independent policy.

The different stances taken by India show that neutralism has in fact meant the pursuit of different objectives, and these objectives may be pursued separately at
separate times. India's policy in Korea meant in fact "an
active role in promoting the cause of peace through mediation". In the case of Suez it meant opposition to "colonialist" and "racialist" policies. In Hungary it meant "a
code of international behavior on the lines of the Five
Principles of Panch Shila proclaimed at the 1954 Agree-

ᴵᴵᴵ Dev Narayan Mallik, *Non-alignment in India's Foreign Policy,*
pp. 182-183.

ment between India and China. In the Congo again her basic stand was against colonialism and for strengthening the integrity of an ex-colony through strengthening of the United Nations.

These objectives are the ideological bases of her non-alignment-cum-neutralism,[112] but the methods of pursuing them have varied over the years. In the first three cases (especially in regard to Korea and Suez), India took the initiative and was outspoken in explaining her stances ; in the latter cases, she became more circumspect, less outspoken ; in Hungary her reluctance to condemn any party in international forum was quite pronounced. Also, in the Congo, while India was chary of supporting a regime headed by Kasavubu-Mobutu, she was unwilling to support Antoine Gizenga, the deputy to the deceased Patrice Lumumba.

---

112 For a summary of India's basic objectives irrespective of any case or problem, see P. J. Eldridge, "India's Nonalignment Policy Reviewed", *International Politics of Asia : Readings,* edited by George P. Jan (Belmont, Calif. : Wadsworth, 1969), p. 135.

CHAPTER IV

OBJECTIVES OF INDIA'S FOREIGN POLICY : THEIR DEFINITION AS GIVEN BY INDIA'S POLICYMAKERS

In one of our previous chapters it was averred that neutralism is a means of pursuing and furthering national interests,[1] and the success of neutralism, it could be reasonably concluded, should be determined by the degree of furtherance of those objectives. Two important things thus remain to be done. First, the areas of national interests that have already been identified on the basis of empirical study in Chapter II could further be explored, and this exploration should take the shape of outline of contents of those national interests, as given by the policymakers themselves. Second, an attempt should be made to discuss the consequences of neutralism, which is pointed out to be, a tactic or instrument of foreign policy goals ; that is to say, it should be our endeavour to see whether or not neutralism has indeed led to the realization or furtherance of the objectives of foreign policy we call national interests. The first task, that of outlining the contents of national interests as given by the policymakers themselves, is relatively easy. The second task as seen by this author is not easy, and in fact is admittedly fraught with grave difficulties. The consequences of one's (an individual or a state—an actor in international politics) action in international politics are so inextricably and unavoidably mixed up with those because of the complexity of international politics—the number of nations involved and multiplicity of interrelationships thus established—it indeed would be difficult to scientifically establish a causal relationship between India's actions, either committed or omitted, and the subsequent sequence of events in the cases cited in the previous chapters. But,, it may not be as difficult to identify some of the pressures

---

[1] See Section 6 of Chapter I, pp. 31-33.

or tilts caused by the action of one, in our case India's, in a particular case or over a whole period of time. Indeed, the consequences, understood in the sense of pressures or tilts in one direction or another, could be viewed from two perspectives that are at once separate and related : One, —the consequences from each stance in terms of the national interests involved in each of the cases ; and two, —the consequences over the entire period of time of our study in terms of the *entire* gamut of India's national interests, not simply those that were involved in those particular cases. It must be remembered that neutralism was primarily an instrument of furthering the interests of India in global disputes, affecting third parties that included the Super Powers at least indirectly. For tackling such intimate territorial questions as Kashmir, Goa, or India's northern boundaries, India did not intend to depend upon neutralism or the principle of it : India was clearly anti-Pakistan in defense of her interests in Kashmir ; India was clearly anti-Portuguese while she wanted the return of Goa to her control ; India was clearly anti-Chinese when she resisted the latter's invasion of her northern regions. India's neutralism in global questions, however, was modified—one can even say inhibited—by her awareness of what the Super Powers might or might not do in reaction to her policy of neutralism that affected them more intimately, in matters that affected her most immediately but which the Super Powers in their global strategic thinking were hardly able to separate from their own. To the extent that there was this awareness or even inhibition, neutralism was indeed an instrument of pursuing national interests even in her politics of bilateralism, in which she herself figured as a party. Additionally, she also felt that some domestic matters could also be furthered by her stances relating to global matters that tended to concern the Super Powers, that is to say, stances that are subsumed under neutralism. So, our study should discover whether or not all these various kinds of national interests were indeed helped.

It is now proposed that this chapter will try to deal

with the first task—that of outlining the contents of the
national interests the areas of which have already been
identified. And the chapter following will deal with the more
difficult task of gauging the consequences in terms of the
national interests.

Section I :   An Overview of India's National Interests

Chapter II contains a list of national interests in terms
of their priority. Only some of these interests were involved
in the cases which, as it has been seen already, came to be of
such global importance as to affect the interests of the two
Super Powers—the USA and the USSR—and which necessitated nonalignment-cum-neutralism of powers such as
India. Apart from the interests of India that were directly
involved in these cases which her neutralism tended to
protect and further, there were certain other interests
which, although vital, yet to less discerning eyes, cannot
easily be associated with cases like Korea, Suez, Hungary,
Congo. However to the policymakers of India, even when
they were fashioning India's neutralist role in the cases
referred to, they were among the most important. Mr.
Nehru's speech in the Constituent Assembly of India, on
March 8, 1948, contains fairly copious references to those.
The speech deserves quotation *in extenso* :

> I do not think that anything could be more injurious to
> us from any point of view—certainly from an idea-
> listic and high moral point of view but equally so
> from the point of view of opportunism and national
> interest in the narrowest sense of the word—than for
> us to give up those policies that we have pursued,
> namely of standing up for certain ideals in regard to
> oppressed nations and trying to align ourselves with
> this great power or that or becoming its camp fol-
> lower in the hope that some crumbs might fall from
> their table.

> It is certainly true that our instructions to our dele-
> gates have always been obviously and firstly to con-

sider each question in terms of India's interests, secondly on the merits—I mean to say that if it did not affect India, naturally on the merits and not merely to do something or give a vote just to please this Power or that Power, though of course it is perfectly natural that in our desire to have friendship with other Powers, we avoid doing anything which might irritate.

We have to look after ourselves [emphasis added]. That is why, I am, if I may say so, in spite of being minister in charge of External Affairs, not interested in external affairs so much as *internal affairs* at the present moment because external affairs will follow internal affairs, but there is no basis of external affairs if internal affairs go wrong.

...Nothing is more important in the opinion of this government than to make *Indian economy strong*, and *militarily*—not strong in the Big Power sense, because that is beyond our capacity, but *as strong as we can to defend ourselves if anybody attacks*.

We want to do that. We want the help of other countries ; we are going to have it and we are going to get it too in a measure .... Even in taking that help, economic or other, or even in getting political help, *it is not a wise policy to put all your eggs in one basket*, if I may say so, that one should get help and more especially at the cost of one's self-respect.

We stand in this country for *democracy*, we stand for an *independent sovereign* India. Now obviously anything that is opposed to the democratic concept ...we ought to be opposed to .... It may be that sometimes we have to side with this Power or that Power. I can conceive of our siding ʻeven with an imperialist Power—in a certain set of circumstances that may be the lesser of the two evils. But nevertheless, as a general policy, *it is not a worthy policy or a worthwhile policy* [emphasis added].[2]

---

2 India, Constitutent Assembly, *Legislative Debates,* III (March 5-18, 1948), p. 1766-1769.

From an analysis of the above statement, it should appear obvious that apart from fulfilling certain idealistic interests in foreign affairs, India's main interests to be pursued through foreign policies lay in the direction of maintenance of independence, sovereignty, safety, security, democracy (all the above being political in nature) and economic well-being. These, together with a number of territorial concerns which have been identified previously as vital, formed the *strategic* interests of India. But there were other interests, like peace, disarmament, anti-colonialism that were related tactically to the main strategic interests. And nonalignment-cum-neutralism, a foreign policy weapon, postulating no military alliance with the Super Powers but geared to the development of friendly contacts with both the Super Powers even to the extent of making India emerge as the 'area of agreement' in their calculations, this tended to complete the circle of tactical interests which Indian policymakers were to constantly define, improve upon, pursue and further in India's external environment where she came in contact with a great many nations, including the Super Powers. In the sections following, an attempt will be made to outline the contents of national interests, with strategic interests being taken up first, and then tactical and instrumental. Of the strategic interests again, the most concrete are the territorial interests and these will be delineated first.

Section II : Strategic Interests of India

A. *Territorial or Geographic*

India is strategically situated in Asia. It appears obvious that this strategic situation leads India to develop her range of interests not only in South Asia, but in regions beyond the region. Guy Wint, one of Britain's most perceptive students of the area, said as early as 1947 that independent India's principal foreign policy interests as determined by her geography would be :

1. The integrity, neutrality and possibly, alliance of all the border states from which India might
be attacked—Persia, Iraq, Afghanistan, Nepal,
Burma, Ceylon, Malaya, Indo-China, Siam, Netherlands East Indies (Indonesia) ;

2. Access to the oil of the Middle East, Burma,
at the Netherlands East Indies ;

3. Welfare of Indian communities in these border countries and the promotion of Indian trades ;

·   4. Safety of sea and air-routes in the Indian
Ocean on which the security and commerce of India
depend ;

5. The desire to play a great part in the external world in the affairs of the family of sovereign
powers which is fitting to its own status, culture and
past history.[3]

When Wint made the above prognosis, Great Britain
was still in control of India, India was still united (Pakistan was yet unborn), there was even the possibility that
even if India and Pakistan came into existence, they would
still be dominions with the willingness to coordinate their
policies with the rest of the Commonwealth (where the
Queen of Great Britain still remained a meaningful link
between the nations). But the assumptions upon which
the prognosis rested changed ; India and Pakistan did
become two separate states with contrasting *weltanschau-
ungs,* secularism for the former and theocracy for the
latter ; Pakistan invaded (or abetted the invasion of)
Kashmir in 1947 ; and India after the partition continued
to nurse the wounds inflicted by the events surrounding
the partition. These factors seemed to curtail or modify
the territorial interests as outlined by Wint above. From
the very first Kashmir became the symbol of India's vital

---

[3] Guy Wint, *The British in Asia* (London : Faber and Faber, 1947),
pp. 198-199, as cited by Satyapalan, "India's China Policy", (Unpublished
Ph.D. Dissertation, University of Pennsylvania, 1964), pp. 647-648.

interests.   On October 25, 1947, more than two months after the transfer of power and one day before the Maharaja of Kashmir's accession to India, the Indian Foreign Department advised, in a telegram to the British Government, that the Maharaja be supported against the invading tribesmen (aided by Pakistan) on the following grounds :

> Kashmir's northern forntiers, as you are aware, run in common with those of three other countries, Afghanistan, the USSR and China.   Security of Kashmir, which must depend upon internal tranquillity and existence of stable government, is vital to the *security* of India, especially since part of the Southern boundary of Kashmir and India are common.   Helping Kashmir, therefore, is an *obligation of national interest to India* [emphasis added].[4]

Later on, Nehru himself articulated India's interests in Kashmir in this way :

> Kashmir, because of her geographical position, with her forntiers marching with three countries, namely, the Soviet Union, China and Afghanistan, is connected with the security and international contacts of India. Economically also, Kashmir is intimately related with India.   The caravan trade routes from Central Asia to India pass through Kashmir state.[5]

Another interest that India has in Kashmir relates to secularism, which happened to be one of the important principles that inspired India's fight for independence and which happens presently to be one of the guiding principles of the present Constitution of India.   Nehru was referring to this, among others, when he said :

---

4 Government of India, *White Paper on Jammu and Kashmir* (New Delhi : the author, 1948), p. 45 as cited by Alastair Lamb, *The Kashmir Problem* (New York : Praeger, 1966), p. 40.

5 Made on Nov. 25, 1947 in the Constituent Assembly. See S. L. Poplai (ed.) *Select Documents on Asian Affairs : India* 1947-50, (Bombay : Oxford University Press), 389.

The State of Jammu and Kashmir has been to us not merely a piece of territory which acceded to India five and quarter years ago but a symbol representing certain ideals and principles for which our national movement always stood and which have been enshrined in our Constitution.[6]

The Indian leadership felt, even after partition, that all the inhabitants of India, Muslims not excepted, formed *one* nation and Kashmir's continuing a part of India would offer clinching proof of it, and they felt that if Kashmir is allowed to get away solely on grounds of religion it would surely mark the disintegration of India as is presently composed. Josef Korbel called it the "real issue".[7] And, Sisir Gupta, one of the most perceptive students of the whole gamut of Indo-Pakistani relations, agrees. He says :

While Kashmir's accession to India would be an important gain in the pursuit of her goal of a strong, unified secular state, its accession to Pakistan would strengthen the latter's claim to be the guardian of Muslims in the subcontinent. Thus the most important stake of India in Kashmir was political.[8]

Krishna Menon said in 1957 in the course of a Security Council debate, and this aptly summarizes India's interests in Kashmir, that Kashmir "concerns our sovereignty, our honour, our integrity, our vital interests".[9]

Kashmir became indeed the symbol of India's continuing integrity and security ; and, as later events in 1965 and 1971 were to prove, Kashmir would not ever be sacrificed for any other interest, big or small. The uniqueness of India's position in regard to Kashmir is best understood

---

6 Indira Rothermund, *The Philosophy of Restraint* (Bombay : Popular Prakashan, 1963), pp. 118-119.

7 Josef Korbel, "Danger in Kashmir", *Foreign Affairs,* XXXII (April, 1954), 486.

8 Sisir Gupta, *Kashmir—A Study in India-Pakistan Relations* (Bombay : Asia Publishing House for ICWA, 1966), p. 442.

9 Cited by *ibid.,* p. 328.

in the context of Pakistan's understanding of the problem, comprising both intangible and tangible aspects. Mr. Zulfiqar Ali Bhutto said in 1964 expressing the intangible aspect most typically that "Kashmir must be liberated if Pakistan is to have its full meaning".[10] The security aspect (which included the problem of water) comprising the tangible aspect of the problem was put in this way by Liaquat Ali Khan, the first Prime Minister of Pakistan : "Kashmir is...like a cap on the head of Pakistan. If I allow India to have this cap on our head, then I am always at the mercy of India." He continued : "The strategic position of Kashmir is such that without it Pakistan cannot defend herself against an unscrupulous government that might come in India."[11]

Goa was another area to which Indian spokesmen attached the greatest importance. Goa was the symbol of colonialism (it was a colony of Portugal), and the Government of India repeatedly declared that "so long as Portugal continued to rule over the smallest part of Indian territory, India could not be considered to be wholly free."[12] That is to say, India considered the continuation of the Portuguese rule in Goa a blot on her independence ; it also challenged India's great interest in the elimination of colonialism not only from her own territory but from Asia and Africa. Portugal's control of the enclaves in India did not pose, initially, in the perception of the policy-makers of India, any military threat to the security of India ; its major significance was assessed in terms of *national selfrespect*. Also, as Nehru once remarked : "The issue is a touchstone by which peoples and professions will be tested."[13] This point was more tersely put

---

10 Zulfiqar Ali Bhutto, *Foreign Policy of Pakistan* (Karachi : Pakistan Institute of International Affairs, 1964), p. 13.

11 Cited by Latif Ahmed Sherwani, *India, China and Pakistan* (Karachi : Council for Pakistan Studies, 1967), p. 26. See also, Norman D. Palmer, *South Asia and United States Policy* (*Boston* : Houghton, Mifflin and Co., 1966), pp. 228-229.

12 *India,* 1961 : *Annual Review* (London : Information Service of India n.y.), p. 4.

13 *Times of India,* Dec. 1, 1955.

by Rikhi Jaipal, then Indian representative on the United Nations Trusteeship Council : "As far as we are concerned, Goa is a Portuguese colony established by force, initially by conspiracy, and later by conquest."[14] This argument of course ran counter to the Portuguese conception of their right in Goa : the Portuguese seemed to say that their effective occupation of Goa for several hundred years created a legal right in Portugal's favour ;[15] that Goa was part of "foreign sovereignty"—that is to say—that the overseas territories are an integral part of metropolitan Portugal and hence outside the purview of Chapter XI of the United Nations Charter.[16] But later on however with the Portuguese trying to invoke NATO protection over Goa, India became seriously concerned from the point of view of *security,* and as soon as that kind of perception dawned, Goa became the subject of India's police action in 1961. This last signified the final eradication of foreign rule in India and the completion of the hitherto incomplete independence of India. And thus the pledge that Nehru gave to the people of India, "We are prepared to wait a little, because inevitably the end must be the one we aim at. Our objectives must be realized"[17] was redeemed.

Another important area in India's psyche was the Indian Ocean. One of the early articulations on the subject was by K. M. Panikkar, a close adviser of Nehru in the early years of independence, who said :

> While to other countries the Indian Ocean is only one of the important oceanic areas, to India it is the vital sea. Her lines are concentrated in that area. Her future is dependent on the freedom of that vast water surface. No industrial development, no commercial growth, no stable political structure is possible for her,

---

14 *Ibid.,* Feb. 1, 1957.

15 See Oliveira Salazar, *Goa and the Indian Union* : *Legal Aspects* (Lisbon, 1954) as cited by J. S. Bains, *India's International Disputes* (Bombay : Asia Publishing House, 1962), p. 199.

16 This view is taken by Alberto Xavier, *The Rights of Portuguese India* (*Lisbon,* 1950) as cited by *ibid.,* p. 233.

17 *Asian Recorder,* I (1955), 139.

unless the Indian Ocean is free and her own shores fully protected.   The Indian Ocean must remain therefore truly Indian.[18]

In a later work, he added :

If the mastery of the Indian seas is established by a hostile power, its pressure would be relentless, since India's economic life is dependent on maritime trade ...Attack from the sea is more dangerous to the freedom of India than any threat from across her land frontier.[19]

The above two statements reveal very clearly the awareness of the policymakers of India of the Indian Ocean area. India is indeed determined to keep the Indian Ocean free from the clutches of any hostile power, and preferably to keep it under her own control—for the purposes of her own political stability and economic wellbeing. Defense and security interests that were there from the very beginning assumed greater importance when the Pourtuguese in an attempt to keep Goa tried to invoke NATO's military protection, and that apparently, aided by other factors, led the Government of India to decide in favour of military action to free it. It was in a sense a reassertion of their interest in the Indian Ocean.

One of the most important territorial interests of India lay in the entire Himalayan region of North India that was contiguous to China. Generally speaking, the entire Himalayan region figured very prominently in the consciousness of Indians ; indeed it formed part of the psyche of every Indian, from the earliest times to the present. Nehru expressed this emotional involvement in this way :

There is one aspect of the question which I wish the Chinese Government and indeed other countries would

---

18 K. M. Panikkar, *India and the Indian Ocean* (London : Allen and Unwin, 1945), p. 83.

19 Idem, *The Problems of Indian Defence* (Bombay : Asia Publishing House, 1960), pp. 130-131.

9

try to understand. The Himalayas are high mountains, of course, but they are something much more to us and more intimately tied up with India's history, tradition, faith, religion, beliefs, literature, and culture than, to my knowledge, any other mountain anywhere. The Himalayas are something much more than mountains to us ; they are part of ourselves. And I want the other people to realize how intimately this question affects our innermost being.[20]

Thus the Himalayan region in general attracted a high degree of attention of the Indian policymakers. But, some sectors of it enjoyed, within the framework of this general interest, a greater degree of interest than others. Among the sectors enjoying relatively high degree of interest, Kashmir, which includes Ladakh, has been seen already to be a priority interest vis-a-vis Pakistan. It is so vis-a-vis China also. Indeed Kashmir's integrity, nay that of India as a whole, cannot be safeguarded if India cannot protect the part known as Ladakh. The Chinese point of view seemed to run counter to India's claim to this portion. Chou En-Lai, Premier of China, wrote to Nehru on January 23, 1959, regarding India's claim in this way :

As a matter of fact, our people have also expressed surprise at the way the Sino-Indian boundary *particularly* its Western sector, is drawn on maps published in India.... China's main concern was with an area in the Southern part of China's Sinkiang-Uighur Autonomous region, which has always been under Chinese jurisdiction.... And the Sinkiang-Tibet highway built by our country in 1956 runs through that area.[21]

In regard to the eastern sector of India's northern boundary known generally as the MacMahon line, the

---

20 Cited by Shanti Prasad Verma, *Struggle for the Himalayas* (Jullundur, Ambala, Delhi : University Publishers, 1968), p. 156.

21 For the text of Chou's letter deated January 23, 1959, see *The Documents on the Sino-Indian Boundary Question* (Peking : Foreign Language Press, 1960).

Indians felt that this was absolutely sacrosanct. Nehru in a speech in the Indian Parliament (House of the People) in late 1950 (November 20) expressed the priority in this way : "It is our boundary, map or no map. We will not allow anybody to come across that boundary".[22] However, here again, the Chinese view seemed to oppose the Indian claim. The Chinese viewpoint was expressed by Chou En-Lai himself in this way :

> How can the Indian Government claim the boundary line which Britain unlawfully created through aggression against Tibet and which even includes areas to which British authority had not extended as the traditional customary boundary line... ? If this assertion is maintained, the inevitable conclusion to be derived would be that the British colonialists were most fairminded while oppressed China was full of undisguised ambitions....The Chinese Government believes that no one would accept this conclusion.[23]

In regard to the middle sectors that covered the Punjab, Himachal Pradesh and Uttar Pradesh boundaries there was relatively little controversy between the Indians and the Chinese. But there was the other part that included three principalities, Nepal, Sikkim and Bhutan. In the midst of the Tibetan crisis of 1949-50, Nehru declared that "the principal barrier to India lies on the other side of Nepal and we are not going to *tolerate* any person coming over that barrier". He continued :

> Therefore, much as we can appreciate the independence of Nepal, we cannot risk our own security by anything not done in Nepal which permits either that barrier to be crossed or otherwise leads to the weakening of our frontiers.[24]

---

22 Cited by J. C. Kundra, *Indian Foreign Policy*, p. 7.

23 Chou's letter to Nehru, December 26, 1959. See *Documents on the Sino-Indian Boundary Question*, p. 2.

24 India, Parliament, *Parliamentary Debates*, VI (17) (December 6, 1950), col. 1269.

This is an example of India's interest in the Himalayas naturally spilling over into Nepal. The statement regarding Nepal, cited above, is sufficiently general and showed the absoluteness of India's interests in Nepal.[25]

In this connection, it must be borne in mind what India did in regard to the other two Himalayan states, Bhutan and Sikkim. India forged special relationships with the two ; the treaty with Bhutan, signed August 8, 1949, earned for India the right of consultation on matters involving Bhutan's external relations, while allowing Bhutan its internal autonomy ; the treaty with Sikkim's Chogyal, signed December 5, gave India the right to protect Sikkim (thereby making Sikkim a protectorate of India).[26]

India's interest in the Himalayas in general and in the various sectors of the Himalayan borders (that included Nepal, Bhutan and Sikkim also) revealed as nothing else did what India thought about China. In September 1950, the Indian delegate to the United Nations, while trying to explain why India recognized China, said :

> ...For a variety of reasons, the main reason being that according to the best of our knowledge and information, it is sound and stable government. . . Obviously only a government exercising effective control over the territory and the People of the Republic of China can fulfil the obligations laid upon the Republic of China.... But how can we require the fulfilment of these obligations and yet deny that government its rights under the Charter, one of which is the right to be

---

25 In conformity with this interest India proposed that Delhi should continue to handle Nepalese foreign relations in the manner of the British before 1947 (August). Nepal having rejected it, Nehru promptly placed Nepal within the Indian defense orbit.

26 Lorne Kavic, *India's Quest for Security* (Berkeley : University of Calif., 1967), pp. 52-53. The Chinese did not like what the Indians did in reference to Bhutan and Sikkim. When Indit declared Bhutan to be her protectorate, *The People's Daily* (Jen Min Jih Pao) asked this rhetorical question : "Since the Nehru Government has announced its sovereignty over Bhutan and declared that Tibet had never recognized Chinese suzerainty, will it not declare suzerainty over Tibet ?" Cited by Bhabani Sengupta, *The Fulcrum of Asia* (New York : Pegasus, 1970), p. 105.

represented in the United Nations ? To deny rights, and in the same breath, to insist on obligations is clearly illogical and inconsistent.[27]

Behind this legalistic reason was the concern for friendship with China—friendship that was expected to buy defense for India.[28] This recognition was accorded to China at a time when the Korean War was about to begin, and when it did India wanted the United Nations to accord recognition to the People's Republic of China. For Nehru once declared that there would be "no settlement in the Far East [sic] or Southeast Asia till this major fact of the People's Government of China is recognized".[29]

Thus, India was interested in friendship with China for her own sake and for the sake of the salutary effect it may have upon the international situation in Asia. India's feeling in this matter was well put by B. N. Rau in this way :

India has historical and almost immemorial ties of culture and friendship with China. For us, situated as we are and where we are, the friendship of China is desirable and natural. We wish to do everything possible to promote the friendly relations that now prevail between us, because we feel that a free and independent China marching with India will be the most effective stabilizing factor in Asia.[30]

But after the Tibetan episode that ended in China's physical control of the area, making China a direct neighbor of India, India began to think more of that part of her

---

27 UNGAOR, Fifth Session, Plenary Mtgs., I, 9-10.

28 B. V. Keskar, Deputy Minister of External Affairs, said on March 28, 1951 : "We should keep in mind that a friendly China and a friendly Tibet are the best guarantee of the defense of our country." Cited by Kavic, *India's Quest for Security*, p. 44.

29 Cited by Vidya Prakash Dutt, "India and China : Betrayal, Humiliation and Reappraisal", in *Policies Toward China*, edited by A. M. Halpern (New York : McGraw-Hill for Council on Foreign Relations, 1965.), p. 205.

30 *Ibid.*, p. 206.

relations with China that was motivated by her security considerations,[31] until the Sino-Indian clashes over the Himalayas brought the relations between the two countries on the verge of total collapse.

There was perhaps another interest of India in China. This was inspired by her belief that in a bipolar world where the Soviet Union was in control of the whole bloc of communist nations, including China, the fate of world peace was in jeopardy. India by developing her relations with China and by helping China take her rightful place in the comity of nations, wanted to wean China away from the Moscow-dominated Communist bloc. Indeed, Peter Calvocoressi, an eminent British political commentator, said : •

> The Indian Prime Minister, Pandit Nehru, was eager to establish relations with Peking, because he believed that the Chinese Communists could be weaned from Moscow and that India and China could together constitute a third force, which might perhaps build a bridge between Washington and Moscow.[32]

Krishna Menon, who had great ability in articulating what Mr. Nehru felt to be the interests of India, summarizes India's interests in this way :

> To us it is not an academic question. We are not wedded to any compartmentalism. But neighbourhood, distance, geography, cultural affinity have impacts upon our relationship. Our security, our future, and our capacity to develop very largely depends upon the stability in the Far East and we would like representatives of Europe and of the American continent at least to carry away with them the impression that in taking the attitude they are taking they are isolat-

---

[31] In the Treaty which formalized India's acquiescence in China's occupation of Tibet (April 19, 1954), this concern for security was expressed in the preamble which contained the Five Principles.

[32] See Royal Institute of International Affairs, *Survey of International Affairs*, 1949-1950 (London : Oxford University Press, 1951), p. 335.

ing themselves from the large continents of Asia and Africa to a very considerable extent.[33]

Thus, India did not want "to put herself out of bounds" by putting China out of bounds, to paraphrase a statement by Krishna Menon.[34]

But the dominant consideration behind everything, it has to be admitted, was security. As one American, Herbert Elliston, has observed :

> The dominantly realistic side of Mr. Nehru 's foreign policy is Himalayan. Tibet 's great plateau with a Southern border of no less than 2500 miles overshadows the Indian plain. India has taken care to put the intervening Himalayan countries of Sikkim, Bhutan and Nepal under its protection. Included in the category of prudent diplomacy of course is exchange of words about coexistence with Peking. But roads and airfield construction which has marked Red China's transformation of Tibet offsets all these assurances. Security rises superior to fine sounding phrases even in India.[35]

The above areas (geographical territories) seemed to loom large in the perception of India's policymakers so much so that they could be considered as strategic interests. There were a few other territorial interests, particularly in Suez, but they were part of bigger world problems where India was only technically involved. Those interests will be dealt with as and when the question of India's interests in specific cases are taken up.

B. *General*

It has been found in Chapter II (in the section dealing

---

[33] India, Ministry of External Affairs, *Foreign Affairs Record,* IV (Sept., 1958), 173.

[34] *Ibid.,* p. 169.

[35] *Washington Post,* June 10, 1956, as cited by Kavic, *India's Quest for Security,* 60-61.

with general national interests of India) that security as abstractly conceived did not command a great deal of attention in India. Indeed this could be confirmed by reference to some of the statements made by topranking leaders of India. No less a person than Sardar Vallabhbhai Patel, the other man in the duumvirate that ruled India between 1947 and 1950, said in 1948 that no foreign country would dare attack India. Nehru is reported to have confided in 1951 to the then Secretary General Trygve Lie that "he was not concerned about the security of his country". And, N. R. Pillai, then Secretary General of India's External Affairs Ministry, wrote in 1954 in reference to the Communist threat to India that "we may be stupid or completely blind but where we do not see the menace we cannot pretend to do so, merely because we are so advised by no doubt wiser people".[36]

From the above it appears that India did *not* at least *openly* express great concern for her security. But her stances in regard to Nepal and the Himalayas to which references have been made already showed that her leaders were not unaware of what might come from that side. As for security concerning Kashmir and Pakistan, their statements are quite eloquent. Indeed, the verbalizations regarding Kashmir in particular, which have been discussed above, bear ample testimony to the threat to security that they felt came from Pakistan. Many times, Nehru made such a statement as this :

> Our relations with Pakistan and more especially those involving Kashmir issue and Goa—these two are the questions which affect us directly and immediately. They affect the integrity and they affect the *security* of India.[37]

Anti-Colonialism

India's interest in Goa has been discussed. One of the

---

[36] The statements referred to in this paragraph are all cited by *ibid.*, p. 2.

[37] India, Ministry of External Affairs, *Foreign Affairs Record,* III (Sept., 1957), pp. 177-178.

interests symbolized by Goa as has been pointed out already
was anti-colonialism. As a general interest also, anti-
colonialism commanded a great deal of attention in India,
as exemplified by one of the early pronouncements of
Nehru on the subject :

> ...No European country, whatever it might be, has
> any business to keep its army in Asia. The fact that
> foreign armies are functioning on Asian soil is itself
> an outrage against Asian sentiment. The fact that
> they are bombing defenseless people is a scandalous
> thing. If other members of the UN tolerate this or
> remain inactive then the UN organization ceases to be.
> So far as India is concerned we will give every help.[38]

The above statement reveals clearly that India was
interested in the elimination of the *physical* and *military
presence* of the colonialist as a first step toward the elimination of colonialism. This elimination would mean, according to Indians, the ushering in of freedom of the opp-
ressed peoples of Asia and Africa, and the elimination of
racial discrimination, illiteracy, disease and poverty which
affect the greater part of the world's population.

In a resolution adopted shortly after India's independence, the Congress Party, after reaffirming its age-old
principles, such as promotion of peace, freedom of all
nations, racial equality and end to imperialism and colonialism, added this statement : "In *particular*, the Congress
is interested in the freedom of the peoples of *Asia* and
Africa who have suffered under various forms of colonialism for many generations" [emphasis added].[39] The
above statement does reveal another facet of India's anti-
colonialist concern, which is that India's anti-colonialism
is Asia-and Africa-oriented, and that even though there
could be manifestations of colonialism elsewhere they may

---

[38] See N. V. Rajkumar (ed.), *Diplomacy of India*, 159.
[39] *Idem., India's Policy*, p. 41

not meet with India's wrath, notwithstanding occasional statements to the contrary.[40]

Indian leaders thought of racialism in the same breath with colonialism,[41] because every case of colonialism in Asia and Africa was an instance of White (European and American) colonialism affecting non-White people adversely. So, to India, elimination of colonialism meant an end to racialism.

All these interests were underscored when India called the Asian Relations Conference in Delhi in support of Indonesia's independence from Dutch rule, condemned the Anglo-French intervention in Suez, and strongly supported moves for withdrawal of Belgian troops in Katanga (in the Congo). Antiracialism was quite crystal clear in India's attempts in the UN for putting an end to discrimination in South Africa against people of Indian (and Pakistani) origin.

It must be pointed out here though that the interests of security and anti-colonialism, when divorced from such territorial interests as the Himalayas, Kashmir, and Goa, were only tactical in nature.

It remains now to discuss those strategic interests which were, and still are, internal in nature about which there could not be made any claim *at all* that others were affected. Mr. Nehru is quoted to have said : "We have to look after ourselves" and that he, in spite of his being the Minister of External Affairs, was "not interested in external affairs so much as *internal affairs* at the present

---

40 *Cf* : "We in Asia, who have ourselves suffered all the evils of colonialism and of imperial domination have committed ourselves inevitably to the freedom of *every other colonial territory.*" UNGAOR, Third Session, (1948), p. 376.

41 *Cf* : "In West Asia, in East Asia, in W. Africa and in S. and E. Africa there are social, economic and political problems creating a great ferment. And then there is the admixture of colonial domination and racialism and the other issues connected with them . . . India is interested in the removal of *colonialism and racialism everywhere.*"—Nehru before AICC, July 6, 1953. Cited by Doris L. Mack and Robert T. Mack, "Indian Foreign Policy since Independence", *Australian Outlook,* XI (March, 1957), pp. 25-26.

moment because external affairs will follow internal affairs. . . ."[42] Now what these internal interests were, have been fairly comprehensively discussed in Chapter I.[43] Maintenance of political stability, quarantining the country against the cold war epidemic, organization of the economy geared to removing mass poverty in the country without however doing away with parliamentary democracy—all these seemed to figure prominently in the calculations of Indian policymakers. The last two purposes engaged their attention from the earliest days of independence. Nehru said in the constitutent Assembly :

> The first task of this Assembly is to free India through a new Constitution to feed the starving people and to clothe the naked masses and to give every Indian the fullest opportunity to develop himself according to his capacity.[44]

And they were aware that this economic revolution must be achieved quickly or else India may not survive. But in achieving this, India must remain independent and non-Communist. One member of the Constituent Assembly put the matter succinctly : "The choice for India... is between rapid evolution and violent revolution... because the Indian masses cannot and will not wait for a long time to obtain the satisfaction of their minimum needs".[45] So the Constituent Assembly finally chose—and unanimously too—the parliamentary way, fortified by adult suffrage, to bring about this rapid evolution towards economic transformation of India.[46] The Indian leaders also felt that "democratic constitutions are inseparably associated with the drive towards economic equality" and therefore they decided during the debate

---

[42] See Section 2 of this chapter for fuller quotations.
[43] See Section 3.
[44] Cited by Granville Austin, *The Indian Constitution : The Cornerstone of a Nation* (Oxford : Clarendon Press, OUP, 1966), p. 26.
[45] Santhanam, who said it, was an important member of the Constituent Assembly. Cited by *ibid.*, p.27.
[46] *Ibid.*, Ch. 2.

on the Objectives Resolution that the Constitution must be dedicated to some form of socialism and to the social regeneration of India.[47]

Indian leaders, it has been pointed out already, wanted internal wellbeing which, in its turn, was construed largely in terms of economic wellbeing. And Nehru did indeed intend to use his foreign policy in such a way as to serve the purposes of economic wellbeing. In a foreign policy speech on December 4, 1947, he even said :

> Ultimately foreign policy is the *outcome of eocnomic policy* and until India has properly evolved her economic policy, her foreign policy will be rather vague, rather inchoate, and will be groping...I regret that we have not produced any constructive economic scheme or economic policy so far...Nevertheless, we shall have to do so and when we do so, that will govern our foreign policy more than all the speeches in this House. [emphasis added][48]

And the evolution of the economic policy was to take the shape of the Five Year Plans. The First Five Year Plan reiterated that economic wellbeing is to be brought about by democratic planning, and it defined democratic planning and the role of the state in this way :

> It is clear that in the transformation of the economy that is called for the state will have to play the crucial role. Whether one thinks of the problem of capital formation or of the introduction of new techniques or of the extension of social services or of the overall re-alignment of the productive forces and class relationships within one society one comes inevitably to the conclusion that a rapid expansion of the economic and

---

47 *Ibid.*, p. 41. Austin says : "Being, in general, imbued with the goals, the humanitarian bases, and some of the techniques of social democratic thought, such was the type of Constitution that the Constituent Assembly members created".—*ibid.*, p. 43.

48 *Indian Foreign Policy* (Selected Speeches, September, 1946 to April, 1961) (New Delhi : Ministry of Information and Broadcasting, Govern-

social responsiblities of the state will alone be capable of satisfying the legitimate expectations of the people. This need not involve complete nationalization of the means of production or the elimination of private agencies in agriculture or business and industry. *It does mean however a progressive widening of the public sector and a reorientation of the private sector to the needs of a planned economy.* [emphasis added][49]

After spelling out the main ways of bringing about economic regeneration of the country, the First Five Year

TABLE I

THE FIRST FIVE YEAR PLAN

Heading	Adjusted Plan Financial Estimates (in Crores of Rupees)	Percentage
Agriculture	354.32	14.0
Irrigation and Power	647.47	27.2
Transport and Communications	570.04	24.0
Industry and Mining	188.24	7.9
Social Services	395.86	16.1
Rehabilitation	135.70	5.7
Miscellaneous	86.02	3.6
Total	2,377.67	100.0

ment of India, 1961), pp. 24-25.
    49 India, Planning Commission, *The First Five Year Plan* (New Delhi : India Government Press, 1952), pp. 31-32. The ideas expressed in these were later developed in India's Industrial Policy Resolution, the Socialistic Pattern of Society Resolution and *The Second Five Year Plan.* As we will see later on, these last were not simple developments but are themselves the fallout effects of India's nonalignment-cum-neutralism (see next chapter),

Plan and the plans that followed it (the Second and the Third Five Year Plans during the period of our study) spelled the broad objectives of the plan. The First Five Year Plan aimed at laying "the foundations on which a more progressive and diversified economy could be built up". The first plan was nothing but a body of specific programs with a major emphasis on agriculture, as the table[50] at page 141 would reveal.

A close look at the Table reveals that more than 2/3 of the total expenditure were devoted to agriculture and community development, irrigation and power projects and transport and communications ; less than 10 per cent went for industrial development. By all accounts, it was a very ambitious plan which could be implemented only with a liberal dose of external assistance. In the Draft Outline of the First Five Year Plan, a resource gap of Rs. 655 crores was shown of which Rs. 290 crores was expected to be filled by deficit financing. The remaining Rs. 365 crores, it was estimated by the plan fathers, could be "met only from external resources".[51] It could be said without equivocation that the plan's fulfilment depended to a great extent on the availability of external assistance.

The Second Five Year Plan if anything was more ambitious as the objectives outlined below show : (1) a "sizable increase in National Income" ; (2) "rapid industrialization with particular emphasis on the development of basic and heavy industries" ; (3) "a large expansion of employment opportunities" ; and (4) "reduction of inequalities in income and wealth and a more even distribution of

---

50 Adapted from Arthur H. Hanson, *The Process of Planning : A Survey of India's Five Year Plans* (London : Oxford University Press for Royal Institute of International Affairs, 1966), Table no. 2, p. 110.

51 *The First Five Year Plan,* Chapter 3, "Assessment of Resources". Cited also by Hanson, *Planning,* p. 100. Although only Rs. 188 Crores or 10% of the funds for public outlays came from external sources. See Leo Tansky, *U.S. and USSR Aid to Developing Countries : A Comparative Study of India, Turkey and the UAR* (New York : Praeger, 1965), p. 93.

economic power".[52] The following table[53] shows the outlay for various heads :

TABLE II

THE SECOND FIVE YEAR PLAN

Heading	Adjusted Plan Financial Estimates (in Crores of Rupees)	Percentage
Agriculture and Community	510.00	11.3
Irrigation and Power	820.00	18.2
Industries and Minerals	950.00	21.1
Trade and Communications	1,340.00	29.8
Social Services, etc.	810.00	18.0
Miscellaneous	70.00	1.6
Total	4,500.00	100.0

But the most important point to remember from the perspective of our study is that the plan outlay as shown above depended on external assistance to the tune of about Rs. 1100 crores (of which it was estimated Rs. 982 crores actually came).[54]

The Third Plan was obviously more ambitious than the previous two as the following Table[55] reveals :

52 India, Planning Commission, *The Second Five Year Plan : Draft Outline* (New Delhi : India Government Press, 1956), pp. 6-8.

53 Adapted from Hanson, *Planning,* p. 134.

54 *Ibid.,* pp. 150 and 193. Tansky shows Rs. 1099 crores (2.4% of the resources for public sector outlays. See *US and USSR Aid,* p. 93.

55 Hanson, *Planning,* p. 204.

TABLE III

THE THIRD FIVE YEAR PLAN

Heading	Adjusted Plan Financial Estimates (in Crores of Rupees)	Percentage
Agriculture and Community Development	1,068.00	14.0
Irrigation	650.00	9.0
Power	1,012.00	13.0
Village and Smallscale Industry	264.00	4.0
Organized Industry and Minerals	1,520.00	20.0
Transport and Communications	1,486.00	20.0
Social Services and Miscellaneous	1,300.00	17.0
Inventories	200.00	3.0
Total	7,500.00	100.0%

The most important point here again is not what the actual physical targets were or what the expenditures for each of these heads would be. The most important point related to the question of financial resources. The plan fathers estimated that if the targets in the public sector were to be realized, they had to find external assistance to the tune of Rs. 2200 crores (or 30 per cent of the total outlay).[56]

The brief discussion of the objectives, social, political and economic, as enshrined in the Constitution and the Five Year Plans, will lead us to say that the leaders of India were intent on building a solid base for India's development. And, by a base is meant, in the words of Nehru :

First of all, the establishment of a democratic apparatus

---

56 *Ibid.*, p. 212.

with adult franchise—that is parliamentary democracy.... Then a sound base for economic development with the Five Year Plans, and heavy industries, particularly machinemaking plants, a strong
public sector commanding the strategic heights of our
economy, and the foundation for an independent self-
developing economy. You may also say socialistic
pattern of society based on the principles of gradual
economic organization and social justice.[57]

But this ambitious solid base could be built, as has been
seen before, on a sizable amount of external assistance.[58]
And, Indian policymakers were keenly aware that only by
following a particular type of foreign policy not only the sizable foreign exchange gap in the Five Year plans be met but
some of the other aspects of what he called the solid base for
India's development could be strengthened. India's policymakers realized that upon the successful building of this
base depended the future of Indian democracy. N. R.
Pillai, one of Nehru's principal foreign policy advisers in
the period immediately following independence, well articulated this as follows :

India is as definite as the United States in her view
that Communism is a danger, but she feels that the
danger will become serious only if the free nations in
Asia are unable to organize their economic and political life on a sound and stable basis. The competition
between democracy and Communism has to be fought
and settled in the internal structure of each state. If
India and the new nations of South Asia can improve
their standard of living, modernize their societies, utilize their resources to the best advantage, bring education and health to the people, then they will be able
to defeat Communism. This is the struggle in which

---

[57] K. Satchidananda Murty (ed.), *Readings in Indian History, Politics and Philosophy* (London : Allen and Unwin, 1967), pp. 204-205.

[58] W. W. Rostow, one of the top American economists who also
happened to be one of his country's top policymakers, sized up this need
correctly as "being whether expanded supplies of foreign exchange would
be available to India from abroad". Cited by Sarbadhikari, *India and Great
Powers*, p. 49.

India is engaged and in which she is determined not to fail.[59]

Section III :   Tactical and Instrumental Interests

India's emphasis on peace throughout the world generally has been well known. It has been found in Chapter II that of all the general interests, it is peace that was accorded the greatest emphasis (its score being 81).[60] It led many people to conclude that India is wedded to pacifism, and the Gandhian tradition of nonviolent noncooperation that largely succeeded in bringing India's freedom from foreign rule did little to remove this impression. Everybody considered it as a strategic interest of India. Although it is difficult to entirely disprove the appropriateness of such an interpretation, it could yet be averred in addition that it is one of the tactical interests of India. For, according to India's policymakers, war should be avoided and peace promoted not for the sake of the world only but because of herself, because India is part of it. Nehru once said : "The interest of peace is more important because if war comes everyone suffers, so that in the long distance view self-interest may itself demand a policy of cooperation with other nations, goodwill for other nations, as indeed it does demand."[61]   In other words, India wanted to further her national interests in the context of world cooperation and world peace, in so far as peace can be preserved.[62]   Peace, according to her spokesmen, was not merely desirable or preferable, "it is a vital necessity and a daily prayer", and she needed peace, not in order to become more powerful or more prosperous, but in order to exist—(wanted it) in order for her people "to eat, to be

---

59 "Middle Ground Between Russia and America : An Indian View", by "P" *Foreign Affairs*, XXXII (January 1954), 269.

60 See Table IV (Section 3) of Chapter II.

61 India, Constitutent Assembly, *Legislative Debates*, II (Dec. 4, 1947), p. 1263.

62 *Ibid.*

clothed, and housed and made literate".[63] Peace was thus
related intimately to economic wellbeing of the country,
and it is because of this relationship that it was so eagerly
sought. Maintenance of peace, it was calculated, would
ensure savings, "effected by the reduction of armaments
which could be used for developing underdeveloped areas",
as the then chief Indian delegate of the UN B. N. Rau
explained.[64] On another occasion, while advocating establishment of UN Peace Fund, the same Indian delegate
suggested how the money could be raised—by savings
through disarmament.[65] Time and again, Nehru did think
of giving "a better life to all our innumerable people" and
thought that "that can only be done if there is peace."[66]
On the other hand, he feared that the absence of peace
and war may endanger democracy and freedom. Indeed
he said, "If war is there, there is no democracy left, there
is no freedom, there is nothing worthwhile left."[67] That
peace was not an ultimate interest, a strategic interest,
to be emphasized in world problems but not in matters of
more immediate interest, is under-scored by India's refusal
to shrink from the use of force in Goa and in defence of
Kashmir.

And, finally, no discussion of tactical interests of
India would be complete without bringing into consideration
the interest that India had in nonalignment-cum-neutralism itself. So many things have been said already about
it.[68] One thing that has not been said clearly enough is
this : India's policy of neutralism in the global cold war
reflects her interest, a persistent one, in the balance between India's alignment with the two Super Powers, at
least during the period of time this study deals with. The

---

63 V. L. Pandit, "India's Foreign Policy", *Foreign Affairs*, XXXIV
(April, 1956), 435.
64 UNGAOR, Fifth Session, Committee I, Vol. I, p. 204.
65 *Ibid.*
66 *Times of India*, Nov. 8, 1961, 1 : 3.
67 India, Parliament, *Lok Sabha Debates*, IX : Part 2 (Nov. 20,
1956), col. 572.
68 See Chapter I (Section 6 included where it has been pointed out
that nonalignment-cum-neutralism is an aspect and technique of India's
foreign policy).

outline of such a balance was formulated by Nehru himself in the 1950's and the reasoning for it was, as put so
admirably by Ashok Kapur, as follows :

> USSR is India's strongest neighbour which has the
> capacity and the political will to harm India's interests
> if the latter was preceived as an adversary power.
> Rather than alienate Moscow, it is better for India
> to develop a sound working relationship—that is, if
> we can't beat them, join them. While Washington
> was too far away for effective action in defending
> India, it was nevertheless a source of valuable economic
> and technogical assistance to India. In this respect
> the USSR was also a source of valuable economic, tech-
> nological and military assistance. To promote
> India's material interests and political influence in
> the global community it is necessary to promote
> India's bargaining position vis-a-vis the two great
> powers. But to promote viable bargaining relations
> with Moscow and Washington it is necessary to have
> diversified sources of foreign assistance. Eventually,
> as India's dependence on foreign technology and capi-
> tal declines India could, in the spirit of Chanakya's
> "detached king", insulate the subcontinent from the
> "foreign interference" of the systematic environment in
> which the great powers presently predominate. But
> until such an ideal solution occurs, India must seek the
> optimum path of taking advantage of US-Soviet hos-
> tility and to induce the two powers to prevent the
> growth of a preponderant power in Asia.[69]

Section IV :   India's Interests in World
Crisis Situations

A. Korea

The Indian concern in the Korean War of 1950 was

---

[69] Ashok Kapur, "Indo-Soviet Treaty and the Emerging Asian
Balance", *Asian Survey*, XII (June, 1972), 470.

mainly because it brought the world on the verge of war and she wanted to prevent widespread war which she felt would be absolutely disastrous. In preventing the war from spreading, she did not attempt to gloss over the question of North Korean aggression. Indeed, Nehru's speech in the Parliament indicated little difference between the position of India and that of the USA : "Our policy is, first of course, that aggression has taken place by North Korea over South Korea. That is a wrong act that had to be condemned".[70] He also added, however, two other interests : "Secondly, that so far as possible the war should not spread beyond Korea. And thirdly, that we should explore the means of ending this war".[71]

Later on, however, with the United States Seventh Fleet ordered by President Truman to neutralize the Formosa Strait, India's interests underwent a change. She began to see the Korean war, as Berkes and Bedi point out so acutely, "less and less as vital demonstration of collective security and more and more as an American-KMT threat to reopen the Chinese Civil War, and to resettle one of the greater stakes in the Great Power rivalry" and this change in attitude developed into a "driving urge to terminate the war".[72] This was coupled with the realization that without China's admission this could not be done. As Nehru put it :

It was clear to us that no negotiations would have any value unless China was associated with it. China, apart from being a great power, is most intimately concerned with the events happening next door to her.[73]

India wanted a permanent solution of the Korean crisis. But a permanent solution could only depend upon the taking of smaller steps—the first of which was "the loca-

---

70 Cited by Berkes and Bedi, *The Diplomacy of India*, p. 107.
71 *Ibid.*
72 *Ibid.*, 108-109.
73 *Speeches* (1949-1953), II, 251-52.

lization of conflict". Nehru disclaimed any desire for honour, glory, prestige behind India's active part in the solution of conflict, and offered the following explanation "We went to Korea because, if we had not gone, there would have been no truce and no ceasefire and the war would have gone on, with a danger of its expansion".[74]

There was another question involved in India's participation in the solution of the Korean problem. Nehru's comment in the Indian Parliament on September 17, 1953 seems to clarify this :

> The question that we have been considering is an Asian question, a question of Asia, and is the will of Asia to be flouted because some people who really are not concerned with this question so intimately feel that way ? This is an extraordinary position,

and, continuing, he warned : "The countries of Asia however weak they may be, do not propose to be bypassed and certainly do not propose to be sat upon".[75]

India also liked to fulfil her responsibility to the poor people of Korea, and as Nehru put it : "We strongly felt that the utter ruin and destruction in Korea should be stopped at any cost".

B. *Suez and West Asia (Middle East)*

India was interested in this area for several reasons. As Nehru himself put in answer to Tibor Mende :

> Naturally we are interested because we have a large Moslem population. But also because, historically speaking, for a very long period of time we had close contacts with the Middle East [sic] Countries.

> For hundreds of years our official language was Persian. History is full with our contacts with Iran and with the other Middle Eastern [sic] countries,

---

74 *Ibid.* (1953-57), III (1958), 244.

75 India, Parliament, *Lok Sabha Debates,* VIII (No. 33), Part II, Sept, 17, 1953, cols. 3986-87.

cultural contacts.... Now that we are free again, naturally we are developing those contacts, we are picking up the old threads which were cut off by British rule in India. We are brought nearer also by the development of communications. That is only natural. But apart from all that, we are brought nearer to each other by the developments in international politics.

. . . We are interested also because of the dangers in the Middle Eastern [sic] situation which might lead to trouble.[76]

When in the aftermath of Suez nationalization, there was the Anglo-French-Israeli intervention in the area, India's main interest was in the quick peaceful settlement of the matter and in the establishment of "at least as much of *non-conflict* on the border (referring to Egypt-Israel border) which may lead gradually step by step towards a wider settlement of the question that involves the two countries and the other Arab states".[77]

On a more mundane level, however, India's involvement in the Suez dispute was necessitated by the fact of the realization that the Suez Canal :

> to a large extent, is much more our lifeline than that it may be the lifeline of the Western countries. In the Autumn last year, 70 per cent of our exports and 69 per cent of our imports passed through the Canal. This country carried somewhere about 650,00 tonnage through the Canal in that twelve-month period. Therefore, its opening which is vital to the progress of our Five Year Plans, is a matter of great concern to us.[78]

And, of course, colonialism was inherent in the situ-

---

[76] Tibor Mende, *Nehru* (New York : Braziller, Inc., 1956), 1935-36.
[77] Menon in Lok Sabha Debates, March 26, 1957. *Foreign Affairs Record*, III (March, 1957), 67.
[78] *Ibid.*, 68.

ation. India, by working against it, (while Pakistan, being a part of Western alliances, SEATO and CENTO, was aiding and abetting it) tried to make the greatest impact on the Arab countries so that the latter countries, all inhabited by predominantly Moslem populations, could be weaned away from Pakistan. This possibility could be, as the policymakers figured, of tremendous value to India in her struggle to retain Kashmir to which Pakistan had laid claim on grounds of the Islamic faith of the majority of her population.

C. *Hungary*

European problems have generally been quite remote from the consciousness of Indian policymakers. After an early interest in the Berlin crisis, India's general apathy gave way, willynilly, to a sort of forced interest because of the crisis in Hungary (1956), which emerged, by the way, simultaneously with the Suez crisis. The way India looked at the problem—and this is revealed from Nehru's speech of July 23, 1957—revealed the interests she had in the problem :

First, ... undoubtedly it was or it developed into a national uprising. Two, it is also true that this national uprising was forcibly crushed by the military, chiefly the Soviet forces that came in...in a certain context of events ; and three, all this coincided with what happened in Egypt at the time and Suez Canal. ...It is quite conceivable that the same thing (as happened in Poland) would have happened in Hungary but for what took place immediately in Egypt, the invasion of Egypt and the Suez Canal. That is, a situation arose when every country began to think in terms of war coming, in terms of security, in terms of seeing that it does not lose its strategic point...in terms of seeing that the hostile frontier did not come nearer to them...[79]

---

[79] Nehru's reply to the debate in the Lok Sabha, July 23, 1957. See *Foreign Affairs Record,* III (July, 1957), 148-49.

India thus wanted several things in regard to Hungary. One, Hungary should be allowed to decide its own future in her own way. But, whether or not Soviet troops should be asked to withdraw from Hungary, a question that fell within cold war politics, she was not clear about—if anything she was willing to give some benefit of doubt to the Soviets. She evidently did not consider Soviet presence in Hungary as another instance of colonialism. Second, since Hungary was sovereign—its membership of the UN attesting to it—she cannot be compelled to accept UN supervision of her own elections to determine the form of government her people wanted. By taking such a position India was in essence trying to oppose the setting up of a precedent that could be invoked in Kashmir.[80]

D. *Congo*

Even before the civil war in Congo and the consequences following from it, Nehru had looked upon Africa as a continent where the most naked form of colonialism and racialism prevailed, and in those parts where it formally ended, he felt an attempt was being made by the ousted colonialists and their colloborators to stage a comeback and he was afraid of it. He said :

We are afraid of a new type of colonialism in Africa, one based on powerful military resources and calling itself self-government there. Not colonialism of the metropolitan countries, but the colonialism of small, dominant group controlling the country and calling it self-government.[81]

From the very beginning of the crisis in the Congo, India looked upon the Congo as a single entity not to be split up. He said: "Our approach to the question is that the integrity and the sovereignty of the Congo should be maintained."[82]

---

[80] See Section 2 (D) of Chapter III.
[81] Mende, *Nehru,* 133-134.
[82] Nehru, *Indian Foreign Policy* (Selected Speeches, 1946 to 1961), (Delhi : Government of India Press, 1961), 512.

In a speech to the Members of the Rajya Sabha in
1961, Nehru outlined all the interests of India in regard
to the crisis in the Congo. He said :

> The question is today of trying to prevent a world
> catastrophe, trying to help the Congo to preserve its
> integrity and independence, trying to prevent foreign
> forces whoever they might be from going and dominat-
> ing over the Congo, trying to prevent the cold war com-
> ing—it has come but to prevent it coming more fully,
> trying to prevent civil war and all that....We have
> no selfish interest in the Congo, no selfish interest at
> all. We have interest of course in the countries of
> Africa becoming prosperous and independent....[83]

And the Indian Government supported the UN intervention in the Congo with the same objectives in mind. Mr.
Menon defined the objectives thus : "They are to obtain
the withdrawal or the evacuation of the Belgian forces, to
prevent the dismemberment of the territory and also to
assist in the nonemergence of factional disorder".[84] And,
India after seeing that the UN intervened in the Congo
saw to it also that it succeeded in its tasks. For, her
representative felt that :

> ...if the UN fail in the Congo, it will be a disaster,
> not only in the Congo, but for the world. If the UN
> cannot effectively deal with the situation, it would fade
> away in the Congo and its reputation will continue to
> suffer...it would really mean the collapse of the UN.
> It would mean most inevitably leaving the Congolese
> to fight it out amongst themselves, and it would also
> mean the intrusion of foreign nations with their troops.
> and therefore war.[85]

India did as has been seen already try everything not to
weaken the authority of the United Nations in the Congo.

---

83 *Foreign Affairs Record,* VII (February, 1961), 25.
84 *Ibid.,* VII (April, 1961), 88.
85 Nehru, *Indian Foreign Policy* (Selected Speeches, 1946 to 1961).
519.

India showed ample determination after the reentry of the Belgians in Katanga to get them out. Menon himself reflected such interest and determination thus :

> We are opposing a situation where the empire which happily went out of the front door has tried to get in by the rear door.... There is one thing an empire can decently do, and that is to end itself.... Suicide is not justifiable under our human system for individuals but suicide is justifiable for empires.[86]

So, the greatest reason that impelled India to involve herself in the Congo was because she put so much store in anti-colonialism.

It can be pointed out here that in the cases cited above, it is the tactical interests of India that were involved, such as war and peace, localization of conflict, abolition of colonialism in parts of the world outside of India, prevention of the establishment of certain precedents which might affect her strategic interests adversely, keeping the Muslim nations at bay so that they would not openly side with Pakistan, and of course mitigating the rigors of the cold war and not to unduly offend the Super Powers.

Section V : A Summary

It can therefore be stated in summary form that within the framework of such verbalizations as have been referred to above, the following were the actual, quintessential interests[87] that Indian policymakers would defend, pursue and further:

(1) incorporation of Kashmir

(2) protecting the northern boundaries vis-a-vis China

---

[86] *Foreign Affairs Record,* VII (April, 1961), 95.

[87] In a very perceptive article written in 1958, Adda Bozeman listed a number of interests that India would defend. Curiously enough, they seem to run almost parallel. See Adda Bozeman, "India's Foreign Policy : Reflections Upon Its Source", *World Politics,* X (January, 1958), 262.

(3) completing the liberation of India by driving the Portuguese out of Goa

(4) anti-colonialism, anti-imperialism, anti-racialism

(5) establishment of friendly relations with both major powers—so that India's "eggs would not be in one basket"

(6) internal wellbeing, broadly conceived, but more narrowly in the sense of political stability and betterment of the proverbially fragile Indian economy so that poverty of the masses could be removed or at least mitigated.

The first three, it must be noted, are territorial questions not unrelated to India's security. These were also among the most difficult interests, because they seemed to counter the vital interests of two neighbours, Pakistan and China (Goa was relatively unimportant, because colonialism in general was retreating from all over the world). All the above, not excluding the first three, were the irreducible minimum of India's interests as seen by her policymakers. All these interests India wanted to pursue wholeheartedly, through diplomacy if possible ; some through the arbitrament of sword when necessary. It has been indicated that nonalignment-cum-neutralism is the most precious part of India's diplomatic posture in the global arena. And this became an interest itself, and for the maintenance of this interest, India would get emotionally worked up. As late as in 1962, with China invading India, Mr. Nehru was still saying that abandonment of neutralism would mean a "terrible moral faliure."[88] Just as nonviolent noncooperation had played a major role in India's struggle against the British, in bringing India's freedom, similarly, after independence, confronted with a new reality in international relations—cold war—India's leaders

---

[88] *Hindustan Times*, January 28, 1962 as cited by M. S. Rajan, "India's Nonalignment Policy", *International Studies*, V. (July-October, 1963) 128.

fashioned neutralism as an instrument for the protection of national interests.

CHAPTER V

CONSEQUENCES OF INDIA'S POLICY OF NEUTRALISM IN TERMS OF INDIA'S NATIONAL INTERESTS

In the previous chapter an attempt was made to spell out the contents of those interests which India's policymakers thought to be the most important. The analysis hopefully has revealed that India has or rather had as her aim, during the period of our study, two different kinds of objectives—strategic (general and territorial) and tactical-instrumental. In this chapter an attempt will be made to find out as best one can the consequences in terms of these interests. While dealing with the question of consequences, however, the order of our discussion is proposed to be changed a little. Instead of dealing with the question of vital strategic interests first (a prior discussion of which would superficially appear to be more important or appropriate), the tactical-instrumental interests will be tackled first. Such a reversal of the order of our discussion seems to be necessitated by the realization at once simple, potent and important that considerations such as those that lay behind neutralism, India's main foreign policy instrument in a world racked by cold war, were mainly tactical in nature, geared to producing, rather inducing, certain conditions in world affairs most propitious for the protection or furtherance of the more vital and ultimate strategic interests of India. It appears therefore proper to start our discussion of the consequences with an outline of the general state of India's relations with the two Super Powers, the USA and the USSR, in particular, in the period of their contact or interaction with India's policies. The outline will be impressionistic, barely touching upon those points in their mutual relations which signified identity of views and understanding, therefore friendly relations, or misunderstandings, therefore tension leading to disharmonious relations. This would be accompanied by a brief summary of the results of India's intervention in the four cases, Korea, Hungary, Suez, and the Congo in terms of the specific interests inherent in them which tended to modify the international, particularly regional, milieu in which the pursuit of national interests, from the point of view of India, could take place. Such an analysis of their mutual relations and the international milieu will it is hoped provide the general framework or context of disposition of the two Super Powers in which their particular acts of omission or commission did seem, at least to this writer, to help, make, or mar India's own interests.

Section I : India's Neutralism and the State of Relations between India and the Super Powers

In Chapter III India's neutralist stances have been discussed, especially as they concerned the several global questions affecting East-West relations. Apart from the cases that have been discussed that reveal the nature of neutralism,[1] there were others that seem to polish up the nature of India's neutralism. It is impossible in this present study to cover those "other cases", because they are too numerous to be tackled in one study ; besides, there have been some studies of them too.[2] What can be done however is to give a look at the records of voting (roll call) of India on East-West issues during the period. There have not been too many studies on this aspect of India's foreign policy ; even of those that exist not a single one, to the knowledge of the present writer, covers the entire period of our study. There are three studies however, that, taken together, seem to reveal India's general leftward orientation—a greater readiness to agree with the Soviet Union. One dealing with the period from 1950 to 1958[3] reveals that, in the thirty-seven roll call votes in plenary sessions on East-West issues in Asia during this

---

1 See Chapter III, especially pp. 113-118.

2 Such as Berkes and Bedi, *The Diplomacy of India.*

3 John Rose Faust, "Foreign Policy Positions of Selected States Expressed in the General Assembly of the UN" (Unpublished Dissertation, North Carolina University : Chapel Hill, 1960).

period, India voted 12 times with the West, abstained 14 times, and voted with the Soviet Union 11 times, and as the study itself points out, if the three votes on Korean unification prior to the outbreak of hostilities are excluded, India actually voted more often with the East than with the West. This may be interpreted to mean that India did not adhere to strict non-partiality at least on East-West issues in Asia. If this is contrasted with India's voting alignments on East-West issues in Europe then the conclusion seems to be inevitable that India's strategic interests were affected qui*e differently by East-West issues in Europe.[4]

Another study on roll call votes in plenary sessions of the General Assembly from 1946 to 1957 shows that the correspondence of India's votes with the USSR was 49.3 per cent and with the United States 37.3 per cent.[5] Yet another study of 80 important roll call votes at the fifteenth and sixteenth sessions (plenary and committee session) of the General Assembly in 1960-61 reveals that India's votes coincided with those of the USSR 33 times (41.2 per cent) and with those of the USA 8 times (10 per cent) on issues where there was disagreement between the two Super Powers.[6]

The resultant picture that one gets then about India's nonalignment-cum-neutralism is that it tended to tilt toward the Soviet bloc, especially in matters affecting Asia of which India herself was a part. What did this mean in terms of overall perceptions of the two Super Powers and also China ? In other words, how did they look at India ? Did they share her preceptions *after* encountering India's neutralism ? What priority did they accord

---

[4] *Ibid.,* pp 166-67.

[5] See Gertrude Boland, "India and the United Nations : India's Role in the General Assembly, 1946-57" (Unpublished Ph.D. Dissertation, Claremont College, 1961), p. 21.

[6] Francis Wilcox, "UN and the Nonaligned States", *Headline Series,* No. 155 (Sept.-Oct., 1962), pp. 28-29 ; also, Idem., "The Nonaligned States and the United Nations" in *Neutralism and Nonalignment : The New States in World Affairs,* edited by Laurence W. Martin (New York : Praeger, 1926), pp. 121-51.

India in their overall scheme of things ? The ensuing discussion of the state of relations, US-Indian, USSR-Indian
and also Sino-Indian, is aimed at answering some of these
questions.

A. State of US-Indian Relations[7]

The relations overall between the United States and
India during the period (1949-1964) remained on a level
below that of full cordiality. There remained a number
of irritants arising out of their relative appreciation of the
world scene. The United States continued to believe that
there are two worlds that are inimical to each other, and
the one led by Washington must try to contain the other
led by Moscow, entirely untrustworthy, by military means
if necessary. To the extent Washington wanted to experiment with its ideas in Europe, India did not mind that much.
But with the emergence of China under a Communist
regime after the collapse of the US-backed Kuo-Min-Tang,
the United States "reacted almost instinctively to put the
new regime in China in the same perspective as had put
the Soviet Union in the other continent" and this caused
India to demur. For example, in Korea India attempted
to convince the United States of the inapplicability of the
formula in Asia.[8] America was chagrined : Dulles expressed the American mood on April 23, 1951, thus : that
neutrality in practice meant "conniving at aggression" ;[9]
and, when in the midst of Korean imbroglio, India's name
was suggested as a participant in the proposed political conference on Korea, Dulles, on behalf of the US Government,
opposed it by saying this: "exclusion from such a conference was the price India should pay for its policy of neu-

---

[7] For a masterly survey of US-Indian relations see Norman D.
Palmer, *South Asia and US Policy* (Boston :   Houghton Mifflin Co., 1966),
Chapters 1 and 2 were of help in preparing this section.

[8] See Chapter III, Section 2 (B) dealing with India's Korean policy.

[9] Dulles continued to distrust and dislike neutralism ; in 1956 for
example he said of neutralism :   "This has increasingly become an obsolete conception, and except under very exceptional circumstances, it is an
immoral and short-sighted conception",   "The cost of Peace", United
States, Department of State, *Bulletin,* XXXIV (June 18, 1956), 999-1000).

trality [sic]".[10] Additionally, the United States answered
negatively to Indian suggestions for a peace zone at least
in Asia even to the extent of vigorously pursuing the same
formula of containment-establishment of more alliance
systems. In fact, three political developments, all engi-
neered by the United States in Asia, brought the cold war
right up to the borders of India, and these were : one, the
US military aid to Pakistan (February, 1954) ; two, the
Baghdad Pact (the foundation of which was laid April,
1954 when Pakistan signed an agreement with Turkey) ;
and, three, the Southeast Asia Treaty Organization (September 8, 1954). The last development was of particular
concern to India, because Pakistan, a signatory to the
treaty, insisted at the Manila Conference that produced
the treaty—and the Conference agreed—that the word
"communist" before aggression be deleted in a vital SEATO
clause (Art. IV) ;[11] the United States, while not agreeing
with the Pakistani concept of aggression still affirmed that
"in the event of other aggression or armed attack it will
consult under the provisions of Art. IV(2).[12] The Indian
leaders were given the impression that the "USA sponsored and secured the...treaty as *pis aller* and a means
of exerting diplomatic coercion" on India and other sister
nonaligned countries.[13] Whatever be the case, it shows
clearly that India's neutralism and the perceptions that lay
behind it hardly succeeded in persuading the Americans to
change their perceptions regarding Asia or the world.
The Eisenhower administration, whose main foreign policy
spokesman was John Foster Dulles, remained distrustful
of neutralism as espoused by India. But this is not to
say that America became hostile to India. It was more a

---

10 Sarbadhikari, *India and Great Powers,* p. 49.

11 See Oliver E. Clubb, Jr., *The United States and the Sino-Soviet
Bloc in Southeast Asia* (Washington,, D.C. : The Brookings Institution,
1962), pp. 80-81, and Appendix 2, esp. p. 152.

12 *Ibid.,* p. 154.

13 A Study Group of the Indian Council of World Affairs, *Defence
and Security in the Indian Ocean Area* (New Delhi : ICWA ,1957),
p. 157.

case of America's overweening devotion to her global
strategic interests where India figured rather unimpor-
tantly than one of her overt hositility to India. The
United States of America was eager to have Pakistan in
SEATO in the aftermath of the Western debacle at Dien
Bien Phu ; and Pakistan's inclusion in CENTO was motivated by the American consideration that among Moslem
nations with anti-Western nationalism Pakistan's advocacy
of the Western cause would have a moderating effect.[14]
These factors notwithstanding, the United States stance
vis-a-vis India still contained some cordial elements. One
such element was the product of the US perception, howsoever superficial and imperfect, of the domestic character
of India as a democratic state, "committed to a struggle
against communism within its borders" and the fact that
India as one of the largest population centres of the world
could not be entirely ignored by her as cold war participant,
interested in keeping as many people as possible from
joining the other side overtly.

However, with the accession of Kennedy to the pre-
sidency of the United States in 1961, there appeared to be
a marked change in the mood of the US toward the nonaligned and the neutralist India in particular.   John
Kenneth Galbraith, Kennedy's ambassador to India, notes
in his memoirs how Kennedy mused once that "with so
many nations opting for neutralist policy, may be the
United States should be neutralist too".[15]   The new administration also took into account the increasing might
of the Soviets in scientific, military, economic and cultural
matters, and began to think of the non-aligned nations
(including neutralist India) in terms of their value as
buffer or cushion in world politics. Kennedy was also

---

[14] U.S. Congress, House, Committee on Foreign Relations, *Mutual
Security Act of* 1958, *Hearings,* House of Representatives, 85th Congress,
and   Session   (Ap. 15-16, 1958), p. 1753 as cited by Khalid B. Sayeed,
"Pakistan and China :   The Scope and Limits of Convergent Policies" in
Policies Towards China, edited by A. M. Halpern, p. 232.

[15] John Kenneth Galbraith, *Ambassador's Journal : A Personal Account
of the Kennedy Years,* Signet Book (New York : the New American
Library, 1970), p. 54.

interested in India, which he had long regarded as the "key area" in Asia. The new administration of John F. Kennedy, at once more understanding and professionally more competent, recognized the economic needs of the developing world, particularly India, at this time in border conflict with the People's Republic of China, from which she also faced a stiff economic competition. The possibility that India might fail to meet the challenge of China in economic development of the people spurred the new administration to get more involved in India's future. The new President, who, as Senator, had said earlier : "We want India to win that race with China.... If China succeeds and India fails, the economic development balance of power will shift against us",[16] now got the chance to revise American Policy toward India. As regards the new US administration's attitude toward the twin powers of the subcontinent, India and Pakistan, that also showed a certain change and now seemed to favor India. Of the straws in the wind, the appointment as US Ambassador to India of such a liberal Harvard economist and braintruster of the Kennedy campaign as John Kenneth Galbraith was the most obvious. But the initial promise of the new administration's support for India, especially in terms of economic aid, was never redeemed ; in fact economic assistance to the other country of the subcontinent, Pakistan, increased proportionately more than the aid to India under Kennedy.[17] But there was an unmistakable improvement in the psychological component of India-United States relations. India contributed a little to this improvement—the record of cooperation that she set in her dealings with the USA particularly in the Congo was a bit reassuring to the Americans. However, Mr. Kennedy's

---

16 Cited by Arthur Schlesinger, Jr., *A Thousand Days : John F. Kennedy in the White House* (Boston : Houghton Mifflin Co., 1965), p. 522.

17 In fact the annual average of Pakistan's total economic assistance for the three fiscal years of the Kennedy administration, 1962-1964, was 47 per cent higher than the annual average for the four years preceding, 1958-61. The equivalent figure for India was 42 per cent. Cited by Paul Y. Hammond, *The Cold War Years : American Foreign Policy since 1945* (New York : Harcourt, Brace and World, Inc., 1969), pp. 178-179.

interests in and sympathy for India were to a certain
extent dampened by the unhappy encounter that he had in
1961 with Mr. Nehru—Kennedy having described the meeting as "a disaster...the worst head of state visit I have
had".[18]

At the same time, however, it must be remembered that
for the entire period of our study, despite India's successful attempts in mediating cold war disputes, she did not
at all seem to loom large in the scheme of the US State
Department in particular and the American policymakers
in general. Chester Bowles, who was US Ambassador to
India twice, has regretfully discussed in a recent article
how India was consistently ignored thus :

> ... (This nation) most of our harassed top policy-
> makers in the State Department, White House, Penta-
> gon, and Congress have visited only briefly or in many
> cases have never seen, and of which consequently they
> have had only a limited knowledge and a hazy under-
> standing. The Bureau of Near East and South
> Asian Affairs, which has jurisdiction over our
> relations with India, stretches all the way from
> the India-Burma border to Libya. Understandably,
> the time of its key officials has largely been absorbed
> by the explosive Middle East. The average number
> of Representatives and Senators visiting India each
> year during my eight years there as Ambassador was
> nine—most of them for relatively short visits in and
> around the large cities.[19]

B. *State of USSR-Indian Relations*[20]

It can be immediately said at the outset that just as

---

[18] Schlesinger, *A Thousand Days, p.* 526.

[19] Chester Bowles, "America and Russia in India", *Foreign Affairs,*
XXXXIX (July, 1971), 638-639. In this connection, see Palmer, *South
Asia,* pp. 2-11.

[20] For a reliable survey of the USSR-Indian relations of the period
see Arthus Stein, *India and the Soviet Union* : *The Nehru Era* (Chicago :
University of Chicago Press, 1969).

India could not agree with the United States in viewing Communism directed from Moscow as the villain of the piece and to her policy of its containment by military means, similarly she could not view with equanimity the Soviet attempt, especially in the domestic field, at ruthless suppression of all unorthodox opinion and wholesale regimentation of thought.   Nor she could connive at Soviet Russia's attempts to communize the areas surrounding her home territories by violent means.   It is no wonder then that in early years India was angrily denounced by the Soviet leaders as a "lackey of Anglo-American war-mongers". So this period of Soviet-Indian relations almost verged on hostility ; to be sure, it was not a period of warm relations. Yet, after an initial period of coolness, things began to move for the better.   India's nonalignment-cum-neutralism that forced the United States to be on the defensive in regard to certain world issues, Korea, in particular, later led the Soviet Union to reconsider the whole situation, and to improve relations with India.   Since refusal by India to join the United States bloc was by itself regarded by the Soviet leaders as defeat for the United States if not a straight gain for the Soviet Union, they began to encourage India's neutralist role and her commitment to the idea of the "peace area", particularly in Asia.   Every American move in reaction to India's neutralism that exacerbated Indian sensibilities was taken advantage of by them. When the USA scorned India's antipathy to alliances, especially in the latter's backyard, by forming SEATO that included Pakistan, India's arch-enemy, the Soviet Union accepted such antipathy to alliance systems with as much grace as possible ; and the Soviets' good faith in accepting it appeared more plausible to Indians simply because the Soviets, apart from their bilateral military relations with the People's Republic of China, did not try, during the period of our study, to sponsor any security pact in Asia.   What is more, they proposed to practice a policy of peaceful coexistence vis-a-vis the Indian Union in spite of the latter's quite different political and social system.   And, when the regime in India began to experience difficulties with the People's

Republic of China in the late Fifties[21] which curiously enough conicided with her own difficulties with the same country, the Soviet Union saw in India a possible balance against China. As one observer puts it :

> While the USSR certainly hoped for some additional dividends—India's support for Soviet foreign policy generally, the expansion of the "socialist camp" etc. —the motivation of the USSR in assisting India has since the mid-1950s been primarily based upon the Soviet estimation of India's geopolitical importance as a partial balance to the political influence and potential military weight of China.[22]

So, the USSR which initially had no more interest in South Asia, beyond ideology—and that too in a negative way in the area, her Marxist-Leninist interpretation having been predicated on the assumption that post-war nationalism in the countries of the area was only a phase of bourgeois reaction and were not therefore truly independent, now developed the view, in reaction to political developments such as nonalignment-cum-neutralism the evolving Chinese strategy attributed to Mao Tse-Tung himself,[23] and the Bandung Conference of 1955—and the death of Stalin might have facilitated the view—that India (other newly independent countries of Asia and Africa not excluded) and the policies she espoused could not only be not ignored but be positively encouraged. The new view of the Soviet Union found its most representative articulation in the speech Khrushchev gave to the Twentieth Congress of the Communist Party of the Soviet Union in February, 1956 : "An extensive zone of peace comprising both Socialist and nonaligned [sic] states in Europe and Asia, with a population of nearly 1500 million had entered upon the world

---

21 For details, see the   discussion on Sino-Indian border dispute in the following section of this chapter.

22 Chester Bowles, "America and Russia in India", pp. 637-638.

23 For this point see the following subsection dealing with Sino-Indian relations.

stage." Accordingly, the Soviet leader saw the task ahead of his nation in terms of "re-informing indefatigably the bond of friendship and cooperation with India... and other states that stand for peace".[24] Thus, as the years rolled by the Soviet assessment of India's role and significance in international affairs changed quite perceptibly as could be gleaned from the following statement from a Soviet scholar in 1957 :

> Free India quickly achieved full independence for itself in the sphere of foreign policy. In contradiction to Pakistan which entered the Baghdad Pact... India conducts an independent, peaceful policy differing sharply from the policy of the USA and England, maintains friendly relations with the USSR and the Chinese People's Republic, and supports the peoples of the colonies and semi-colonial territories in their struggle against imperialism... The peaceloving foreign policy of India is a great defeat for the Western Power (bloc) who hoped to use India against the other nations of Asia.[25]

It must be concluded then that the Soviet assessment was much more helpful, and their attitude much more cordial, to India than those of the United States.

That India fared much better in the Soviet scheme of things is apparent from the frequency of visits by their high ranking officials to India. Indeed, practically every high ranking official of the USSR visited India during

---

24 Cited by Study Group of ICWA, *Defense and Security,* pp. 145-147 passim.

25 See E. Varga, "A Post-Stalinist View of India" in *The Foreign Policy of the Soviet Union,* edited by Alvin Z. Rubinstein (New York : Random House, Inc., 1960), pp. 397-399. It should be remembered however that toward the latter half of this period, the Soviet assessment of India's internal situation did not coincide with, or correspond to, their assessment of India's foreign policy stances. Indeed the Soviet ideological sight into the internal situation of India continued to be lowered until 1960 when the questions relating to the ideological sight were expressed in published form in *Fundamentals of Marxism-Leninism* (Moscow : Foreign Languages Publishing House, 1960), pp. 506-12 ; Cited by B. Sengupta, *Fulcrum of Asia,* p. 251.

Nehru's lifetime—Khrushchev, Brezhnev, Kozlov, Voroshilov, Suslov, Kosygin, Gromyko, Mikoyan and others. The visit of Khrushchev and Bulganin to India in 1955 was their first outside their fatherland. Nor was it an accident that Tereshkova and Nikolaev, two of their most famous cosmonauts, came to India for their honeymoon.[26]   And, it must be added that some of them visited India not just once but a number of times.

A further corroboration of the importance given to India by the Soviet policymakers is gained from the organization of the Soviet Foreign Ministry *(Minindel)*.   The South Asia Division, which is one of the fifteen political geographic divisions into which the *Minindel* is organized, is charged with foreign policy questions affecting only four countries, the most important amongst which is India.[27] Thus there was no attempt, as in the organization of the United States State Department, to dilute the importance of India by including countries from beyond the region of South Asia.

C.   State of Sino-Indian Relations[28]

It has been pointed out before[29] how India tried to befriend the People's Republic of China from the very beginning. Indeed she worked for the new regime's recognition ; she wanted the world community to sympathetically consider the needs of the proud people the regime represented ; she recognized the rights of China in the region of Tibet and relinquished her own rights there.   Also, she did many

---

[26] Stein, *India and the Soviet Union,* p. 240.

[27] See   Vernon C. Aspaturian, "Soviet   Foreign   Policy" in *Foreign Policy in World Politics,* edited by Roy C. Macridis (Englewood Cliffs, New   Jersey : Prentice-Hall   Inc.,   1967),   p. 210 ; Kurt London, *The Making of Foreign Policy : East and West* (Philadelphia and New York : J. B. Lippincott Co., 1965), p. 191.

[28] For an able survey of relations between India and China, see John Rowland, *A History of Sino-Indian Relations : Hostile Coexistence* (Princeton, New Jersey : Van Nostrand, 1957).

[29] See Chapter III, Section 1.

other things too numerous to recall here to get China's participation in international affairs. However, her efforts on behalf of the regime and China in the counsels of the world were only perfunctorily reciprocated by China in spite of the much-publicized honeymoon, *bhai-bhai* ("the Chinese and Indians are brothers") period from 1954 to 1957. However, in the early period, immediately following China's emergence as a Communist state, Maoist ideology, as brought up to date, contained three points that led most to conclude that China would, at least, be not inimical to nonaligned nations in general, and to the neutralist India in particular. These points were : (1) The People's Republic embodies only a "bourgeois revolution" against a foreign imperialism and local feudal reaction ; (2) People's Democracy is a Dictatorship, *not* clearly by a single class, the proletariat over all others as under Marxist procedure, but of several classes considered revolutionary by it ; and (3) in its progress from these two to the Socialist Revolution and the Dictatorship of the proletariat it is the intention of Chinese Communism to conform intellectually to the Marxist-Stalinist thesis.[30] And, indeed, in regard specifically to India, a neighbour of China, China's new rulers seemed to try to take a posture based upon the realization that India, an ex-colonial country herself, would not, in league with the Anglo-American imperialist bloc, be against China, as evidenced from this statement in the *People's China* in November, 1950 :

> We cherish the friendship that has been developing with the Indian people who are also struggling for complete emancipation from imperialist intrigues. If China hopes and believes that India will not become …a cat's paw of the Anglo-American imperialist bloc against China, it is because the Chinese people have faith in the value of the costly lessons that both peoples have learnt from the oppression of the imperialists.[31]

---

30 Study Group of ICWA, *Defense and Security*, pp. 149-150.
31 Cited by Sengupta, *Fulcrum of Asia*, p. 110.

The meaning of these points was actually clarified through specific stances of China or political developments with which China's rulers chose to associate themselves : (1) signing of the Chou-Nehru Declaration of Peaceful Coexistence based on the Five Principles or Panch Shila in May, 1954, and (2) holding of the Bandung Conference (in which China participated) in April, 1955.[32]

Ironically enough, China's Bandung participation, which India's Nehru laboured so hard to bring about, marked also the beginning of rivalry between China and India. Bandung, bringing China out of her quarantined existence (imposed upon her by the United States in East Asia) into the arena of world diplomacy, provided China with an opportunity to woo the Afro-Asians away from India's leadership. From this point on, India's being a parliamentary democracy, wedded to the goal of economic improvement of her masses through democratic planning,[33] (therefore a rival to Communist totalitarianism of China) coupled with the fact that she was, by 1954 legally, China's immediate neighbour to the south, who, according to China's policymakers, had been in occupation of some Chinese territory, added to the intensification of rivalry, nay tension ; and, after 1959, their relations became distinctly cool, if not openly hostile, posing for India a definite security threat.[34] Under such conditions of rivalry, China began to see Soviet help for India, especially in economic matters, as betraying the interests of the Communist bloc, since she felt that resources diverted as aid to India could have been utilized for developing the more orthodox Communist nations of the world.

---

[32] Study Group of ICWA, *Defense and Security*, p. 150.

[33] Cf. "A stable India, friendly with both blocs, and receiving economic assistance from both, making slow but steady progress under a system of mixed economy and a democratic framework—this being the essence of Nehruism—became a thorn in Peking's side..." V. P. Dutt, *China and the World : An Analysis of Communist China's Foreign Policy* (New York : Praeger, 1964), p. 209.

[34] This threat became an actuality with the outbreak of war in 1961. For a discussion of the war and other related interests, see the section 1(C) of chapter VI dealing with the consequences relating to Sino-Indian boundaries.

It is said that this difference between the Soviet Union
and China contributed in no small measure to the development of schism in the Communist bloc starting a period
of polycentrism in the Communist world.[35]

D. *Further Modification of International Milieu— Consequences in Terms of India's own Interests in Korea,
Suez, Hungary, and the Congo*

In the cases that have been discussed before,[36] it can
be said that India's actions did help localize the conflict in
Korea, Suez, and the Congo. In Korea India tried her best
to settle the conflict through negotiations, and it must be
conceded that without India's mediatory role, particularly in
the matter of prisoner of war repatriation, whatever chances
of cessation of hostilities existed could have been nipped
in the bud, in which case peace would have remained a hope
or chimera. In the Suez Crisis, India's actions together
with those of others—the United States and the Soviet
Union for various reasons of their own, not all of them
compatible, decided to team up[37]—led to the calling off
of the neocolonialist adventure of the Anglo-French-Israeli
bloc. The invasion that they launched came to nought ;
peace came back to the troubled Middle East, a vital area
in the world by keeping which free of turmoil and tension
and war India could help solve her domestic problems. The
Suez Canal as a vital supply line, the logistical 'must' of a
reasonably healthy economy of India, became operational
again. Also, by effectively mobilizing international support
on behalf of Egypt, a sister neutralist nation, vis-a-vis
Israel, Britain and France (this should be contrasted with
the Pakistani stand in the crisis), India not only succeeded in embarrassing the Pakistani but also brought about

---

35 For an elaborate discussion of the causes of Sino-Soviet rift, see
Edward Crankshaw, *The New Cold War : Moscow vs. Pekin* (Baltimore :
Penguin Books, Inc., 1963).

36 See Chapter III.

37 Stoessinger, *UN and Super Powers,* ch. 4.

a perceptible change in the Egyptian attitude, a factor in the immediate external milieu where she could pursue her national interests with greater freedom and less anxiety. Hungary, where colonialism of the Soviets was involved, was not matter of great worry for India. And, India's efforts, when they were made finally, assisted by those of others, did achieve precious little, if any, in putting an immediate end to the Soviet military occupation of Hungary. But India's interest in seeing that Hungary, whose sovereign independence had already been recognized by the United Nations (Hungary was already a member of the UN General Assembly), was not allowed to be compelled to hold elections under UN auspices, was upheld or vindicated ; this vindication meant, in effect, that there would not be any precedent for a UN initiated and operated plebiscite in Kashmir also. In the Congo, India wanted an end to colonialism or rather neocolonialism (return of the Belgians for example) and end to civil war and restoration of peace. All these interests were more or less satisfied. She could also get the United Nations strengthened by her very eager cooperation in the matter of establishing the UN peacekeeping forces and their operation in the Congo. This accretion of strength of the United Nations principally benefited the small powers (derided as mini-powers) which could, especially in the General Assembly , still sway the decisions of the Big Powers on questions of peace and war and their economic development. And, so far as India's relations with the United States were concerned, her close record of cooperation with the latter in the Congo, as contrasted with the rather unhappy record of cooperation with the Soviet Union in the same case, brought about some improvement in the mental climate of the United States policymakers vis-a-vis India and her nonalignment-cum-neutralism.

Section II : **Summary**

The above impressionistic survey of the relations US-Indian, USSR-Indian and Sino-Indian brings into relief certain interesting points. The mood of US policy toward India as can be seen from our study is one of cool tolerance not untouched by misunderstandings. So far as the mis-understandings were concerned, they were caused by the contradictory perceptions by the two nations' ruling elites of the world scene. Whatever understanding the USA showed was because of India's commitment to democracy with accompanying beliefs in the dignity and freedom of the individual and the fact that India was too large a coun-try to be ignored without detriment to US interests. There was a decrease of misunderstanding when India's percep-tion of China, consequent upon the latter's belligerent moves vis-a-vis India, almost tallied with that of the USA. How-ever that happened rather late in the period.

The Soviet mood, in contrast, as is perceptible from the survey, in the entire period with the possible exception of the Stalin years, was one of friendliness. This friendliness, reversing the old attitude of hostility or indignant indiffe-rence, was caused to a large extent by India's world percep-tions which led her to embrace nonalignment-cum-neutra-lism. The USSR trying her best to encourage Indian leaders to persevere with their chosen policy of neutralism went to the extent of accepting without demur India's domestic social and economic policies which, to any Communist, local or international, were simply perverse.

But so far as the mood of China as discernible from the survey is concerned, and which could be described as distinctly unfriendly, it was partly a product of India's international perceptions (some of them corresponding to hers), but motivated by factors born primarily of her close proximity to India. It could be observed that the enmity of China for both India and the USSR made of China's enemies mutual friends, willing to present a joint front against China. It could also be pointed out that, consequent upon China's menacing posture vis-a-vis India in the late fifties, the United States appeared to develop a greater interest in the survival of India as a viable democracy, able to relieve the economic distress of her teeming masses. Thus India became an area in regard to which the Americans and the Russians came to have a stake in India that was essentially alike.

This change in the psychological climate or complex of the Super Powers which India's neutralism succeeded or failed to bring about was accompanied by certain other changes in the political climate in the world as a whole. India, it has been seen in the section just preceding, could satisfy certain interests through her intervention in such cases as Korea, Suez, Hungary, and the Congo. Prevention of largescale war, acceleration of the process of liquidation of colonialism, in one case leading to neutralization of Arab opinion vis-a-vis Pakistan and in the other to the consolidation of African-Asian solidarity and strengthening of the United Nations peacekeeping machinery through which this solidarity could be expressed to the betterment of their interests—were indeed satisfied. These were the changes that provided the framework under which the specific strategic interests could be satisfied.

CHAPTER VI

CONSEQUENCES IN TERMS OF NATIONAL INTERESTS OF INDIA (CONTINUED)

Now that the problem of changes in the psychological climate of the Super Powers in particular and the international milieu in general has been disposed of, it is possible to turn to the question of consequences in terms of India's national interests that such changes might have directly or indirectly led to. Consequences would be discussed in terms of three broad categories of interests : (1) Strategic Interests (Geographic-Territorial) that involved other countries directly, (2) Strategic Interests (economic) as determined by India's domestic requirements, and (3) other interests that are mostly political. The following sections will deal with the consequences in the order just mentioned.

Section I : Strategic Interests (Geographic-Territorial) that Involved Other Countries Directly

A. Kashmir (or Indo-Pakistan Conflict in Regard to Kashmir)

Since the battle for Kashmir (for its retention by India and annexation by Pakistan) has been fought mainly in the Security Council, it is the stances of the Super Powers, the USA and the USSR, that would be taken into account. These stances were taken during three clearcut periods : (1) 1948-1950, (2) 1957, and (3) 1962. First the US policy toward Kashmir and the elements of that policy can be gleaned from the following facts :

First, in the late forties and the early fifties, when the Security Council was virtually under the control of the US bloc, the Council quite unfailingly evaded a decision on the Indian charge of Pakistani aggression in Kashmir. This, in spite of the reports of the UN Commission on India and Pakistan that the Pakistani troops were indeed there,

Second, the original resolution of the UNCIP (August 13, 1948)[1] envisaged that Pakistani forces should first be withdrawn from Kashmir, that the Pakistani-occupied areas should be administered by the local authorities under the control of the UNCIP, and *then* a plebiscite would be conducted.[2] The US did not only not lend her support to this resolution, but also sought to make out that India had not fulfilled the UN resolutions on Kashmir. Also, the United States blocked the fulfilment of the first two portions of the United Nations resolution which were the necessary prerequisites for the plebiscite. By a number of moves, the resolution of 1948 was allowed to be emasculated, with India, a victim of aggression, being finally equated with Pakistan, the aggressor. Third, Sir Owen Dixon's verdict in 1950 that Pakistan had violated international law when her forces crossed into Kashmir[3] was allowed by the United States dominated Security Council to be entirely[4] dropped.

In the second period, when in January, 1957 Pakistan complained to the Security Council that India was trying to incorporate Kashmir into India through a Kashmir Constituent Assembly resolution, the Security Council passed a draft resolution by Pakistan's partners in military alliances (by the five powers, viz., US, UK, Australia, Columbia, and Cuba—only the last two not being direct military allies of Pakistan) which finally reaffirmed the position of the Security Council that any action that the Constituent Assembly of Kashmir might take would not constitute a disposition of Jammu and Kashmir.[5] Fifth, on

---

[1] UN Doc. S/995, August 13, 1948.

[2] The formalization of these obligations on Pakistan took place by a resolution of January 5, 1949.

[3] UNSCOR, Fifth Year, *Supplement for September through December*, 1950, p. 29, para. 21. UN Doc. S/1791 (September, 1950).

[4] For an excellent study of US stances in Kashmir, see Gupta, *Kashmir*, especially pp. 179-180, 186-189, and Ch. 9.

[5] UN Doc. S/3779, January 24, 1957. Also, see Karunakar Gupta, *India in World Politics : A Period of Transition* (Calcutta : Scientific Book Agency, 1969), p. 35.

February 19 of the same year, the Security Council tried to pass a resolution which proposed that the President of the Security Council (Mr. Gunnar Jarring of Sweden) be sent to the subcontinent to examine proposals for demilitarization or for the establishment of other conditions for progress toward the settlement of the dispute, bearing in mind the Pakistani proposal for the temporary UN force in Kashmir.[6] The draft resolution in question was sponsored by the USA, together with UK, Australia, and Cuba in spite of their knowledge that India would never accept such provisions.[7] Although this resolution could not be adopted, another resolution tabled by the same Western powers proposing a mission to India by Jarring to examine proposals for demilitarization *with no operative clause* was finally passed.[8]

Sixth, when Mr. Jarring, after completing his mission, submitted his report to the Security Council on April 29, wherein he expressed his view that the US military aid to Pakistan had brought about a substantial change in the strategic, political, and economic factors thereby obstructing the implementation of international agreements of an *ad hoc* character and therefore without this major obstacle there could only be grave troubles surrounding any holding of plebiscite,[9] the response of the Western powers (US, UK, Australia, Colombia, and Philippines) came rather late in the shape of a new draft resolution on November 16, 1957.[10] This resolution, without thinking of tackling the main problem raised in the Jarring Report, referred to the need for demilitarization as a first step towards a plebiscite to determine the future of the state and proposed that another mediator (this time an American, Dr. Frank

---

6 UN Doc. S/3787.

7 The two aspects in the draft resolution—(1) the reintroduction of a UN mediator and (2) the expression of a preference for a UN force were considered "undesirable" and "totally unacceptable" respectively by India. See Gupta, *Kashmir*, p. 317.

8 UN Doc. S/3793, February 21, 1957.

9 UN Doc. S/3821, April 29, 1957.

10 UN Doc. S/3911, November 16, 1957.

Graham) should be sent to the subcontinent to devise a scheme of demilitarization. Thus twice in 1957 the Western powers led by the US came very close to imposing a plebiscite on India.

In the third period (beginning 1962), after the failure of a series of direct negotiations between India and Pakistan in 1962 (early), the Security Council attempted once again to resolve the dispute. This time a resolution, introduced by Ireland, and supported by the United States and her allies in the Security Council, proposed unsuccessfully for direct negotiations between India and Pakistan for the implementation of the UN resolutions of August, 1948 and January, 1949.[11] The main purpose of this could only have been to pressurize India into settling the dispute on terms that could only help Pakistan.

Another attempt was made by the Security Council in 1964. This time short of a formal resolution, to force the hands of India at least in regard to the principle of mediation to which India was opposed, the idea was to use the Secretary General, U Thant, as the mediator. It is interesting to note that Pakistan proposed it with the approval of the whole Security Council (barring the Soviet Union and Czechoslovakia).[12]

It must be pointed out also that it is not by taking a political stance within the United Nations Security Council that the United States opposed India's interests in Kashmir. She also took at least two rather overtly cold war measures that affected India rather adversely ; one, in 1945 (February) she announced her bilateral military agreement with Pakistan ; and two, some months later, she formed the SEATO and CENTO, with Pakistan as a member. These measures tended to encourage Pakistan to think of a military solution to the dispute.

Indeed, the record of the United States and other Western Powers in regard to the Kashmir dispute has been so consistently against Indian interests that Nehru reflec-

---

[11] UN Doc. S/1534, June 22, 1962.
[12] Palmer, *South Asia*, p. 236.

ted on June 23, 1962, in the Rajya Sabha thus :

It is a matter for deep regret to me that when subjects which concern us greatly and about which we
feel rather passionately almost, like Goa and Kashmir,...the United States (and UK) should almost
invariably be against us.[13]

The Soviet Union's stances, on the other hand, looked
much more helpful from the Indian point of view. In the
early days and years of the Security Council debate, the
Soviet Union was mostly silent, taking no substantive
policy stand in regard to the dispute. However, this silence
was broken in 1952, in the course of a Council hearing on
Kashmir whose main purpose was to hear the views of
Dr. Frank Graham on Kashmir. The then Soviet Ambassador to the United Nations Security Council made a rather
comprehensive statement of the Soviet view of the
problem :

The USA and the UK are continuing as before to interfere in the settlement of the Kashmir question,
putting forward one plan after another...These plans
in connection with Kashmir are of an annexationist
imperialist nature, because they are not based on the
effort to achieve a real settlement. The purpose of
these plans is interference ... in the internal affairs
of Kashmir, the prolongation of the dispute between
India and Pakistan on the question of Kashmir, and
the conversion of Kashmir into a protectorate of the

---

[13] *Jawaharlal Nehru's Speeches : Sept.* 1957-*April* 1963, IV (New
Delhi : Ministry of Information and Broadcasting, 1964), p. 300.   The
United States opposition to India seems not to have diminished since. Two
new facts show that the United States is not   yet reconciled to India's
position. In 1965 when Pak forces crossed the ceasefire line, the
Security Council did not act ; but when   India retaliated by moving across
the ceasefire line in the Punjab, it demanded   immediate ceasefire.
More recently, in 1972, the Nixon-Chou communique from Shanghai
demanded withdrawal of occupying forces behind the ceasefire line in
Kashmir, which meant   simply that Indian forces should be withdrawn,
because Pakistan could not get far into Indian territory. See *New York
Times,* February 28, 1972.

USA and the UK under the pretext of rendering assistance through the United Nations. Finally, the purpose of these plans in connection with Kashmir is to secure the introduction of Anglo-American troops into the territory of Kashmir and convert Kashmir into an Anglo-American colony and a military and strategic base....

The USSR Government considers that the Kashmir question can be resolved successfully only by giving the people of Kashmir an opportunity to decide the question of Kashmir's constitutional status by themselves without outside interference. This can be achieved if that status is determined by a Constituent Assembly democratically elected by the Kashmir people.[14]

The above statement reveals for the first time that the Soviet Union was in agreement with India. However this was still in the nature of an *indirect* support to the Indian position.

In the second period, in 1957, in answer to the first Western resolutions in Kashmir (known as the Five Power resolution), the Soviet Union accepted the idea that there cannot be any final disposition of the Kashmir question through the action of the Constituent Assembly of Kashmir. But the other resolution of February 19 (UN Doc. S/3787) proposing to send Jarring to India with a view to using a temporary UN force in Kashmir (and it was dubbed by Nehru as "collective aggression or collective approval of aggression"), was vetoed by the Soviet representative in apparent agreement with the Indian contention. In fact, even before the voting, the Soviet representative Mr. Sabolev had said on February 18, 1957, that there was no question of a plebiscite on Kashmir and that the Soviet Government considered that territory as an integral part of India, and therefore the attempt to send a UN force to Kashmir "was flagrant contradiction of the purpose of

---

14 Cited by Gupta, *Kashmir*, pp. 244-45.

the Charter and an offence to the Kashmir people".[15]   But when the Jarring mission was proposed without any operative clause, the Soviet Union neither supported it nor opposed it (she merely abstained).   When, late in the same year, on November 16, another resolution spoke in terms of demilitarization as a first step towards a plebiscite, the Soviet Union's representative by threatening to veto it scotched it.   The Soviet representative, Mr. Sabolev, referred to his objection to the proposed Graham visit ; he also extended the definition of demilitarization to include the withdrawal of military aid to Pakistan by the United States.   Mr. Sabolev, after pointing out that the resolution took into account only the position of Pakistan, asked this rhetorical question :

> What purpose can be served by adopting another resolution that merely repeats the proposals which experience has proved to be fruitless and not in the interest of a peaceful settlement of the Kashmir dispute ?[16]

In the third period, in regard to the June resolution (UN Doc. 1534) of 1962, the Soviet Union exercised her veto.   This time, Mr. Morozov, on behalf of his country, said :

> The USSR delegation considers that the Council should reject all attempts, at this stage of the discussion and after such significant delays and protraction of the debate under various pretexts, to impose on it at all costs a draft resolution which reflects a onesided and hence incorrect view of the question of Kashmir.[17]

From the above discussion, it seems obvious that the United States was from the very beginning in favour of

---

[15] UNSCOR, Twelfth Year, 770th Mtg., 1957. In fact, the Soviet Union also proposed during this time an amendment to the four power draft resolution that seemed to reflect the points made by Sabolev as referred to.   See UN Doc. S/3789.

[16] Cited by Karunakar Gupta, *India in World Politics,* pp. 36-37.

[17] Cited by Gupta, *Kashmir,* p. 352.

some solution that would mean loosening of the Indian grip over Kashmir, and give greater leverage to Pakistan to finally annex it. The United States did not even shrink from an imposed solution to the detriment of the interests of India. This policy, however, was more than balanced by the policy or stances of the Soviet Union. Thus, the Soviet Union over a period of years beginning with 1952 thwarted the US-led pro-Pakistani moves of the Security Council. In 1957 alone she saved the Indian cause twice. In 1962 also, with the Chinese invasion of India impending and her own difficulties with China worsening, she stood by India and her threat of a veto and its actual use was enough to silence the Pakistani and Western guns. That India continued to hold on to Kashmir throughout Mr. Nehru's years of power was largely because of Soviet help, and this help came largely because of India's global stances, and partly because of the Western stances that such stances induced.

B. *Goa (India-Portugal Dispute in Regard to Goa)*

Although the United States policymakers from the very beginning accepted the desirability of accelerating the process of elimination of colonialism from the world (e.g., their decision to grant independence to the Philippines, their erstwhile colony in Southeast Asia), in regard however to the abolition of Portuguese colonialism in India in general, the United States seemed to have reversed her position. As early as on December 2, 1955, the then Secretary of State Mr. John Foster Dulles in a joint statement with then Foreign Minister of Portugal Mr. Cunha described Goa and other Portuguese colonies in India as Portuguese Far Eastern Provinces. Confronted with angry reactions from India and other anti-colonialists, Mr. Dulles tried to justify this description by citing rather legalistically that according to Portuguese law Goa was indeed part of Portugal.[18] This justification seemed a

---

[18] Cited by Study Group of Indian Council of World Affairs, *Aspects of Indian Foreign Policy*, Paper No. 1 (New Delhi : Indian Council of World Affairs, 1958), pp. 33-34. (The justification by Dulles came a few days later on Dec. 6 to be precise.

little bit lame too since he and other US decisionmakers had previously been unable to accept the legality of India's occupation of Kashmir. The only saving grace in this US stand was the denial that Goa or for that matter any other Portuguese territories in Asia were covered by the North Atlantic Treaty.[19]

In contrast, the Soviet Union's stand in regard to Goa was clear and absolutely pro-India from the very beginning. Only a few days back, on November 27, 1955, Mr. Bulganin, then Soviet Premier, had said : "There is no justification for the Portuguese Colony of Goa to exist still on the sacred soil of India. It is a shame on civilized people." This point was underscored by N. Khrushchev when he described the Portuguese reluctance to quit India as "the reluctance of a leech to part from the body whose blood it is sucking".[20]

But the solidity of the US opposition and the firmness of the Soviet position for the Indian cause in India could be ascertained only after the Indian Government, after being repeatedly baffled by the Portuguese intransigence and by the failure of the international organization to correct the direction of the Portuguese policy, decided to satisfy the growing Indian public opinion in favour of some action against the Portuguese in Goa. On the 17th day of December, 1961, the Indian army moved into Goa in an apparent attempt to compel the Portuguese to get out of the colony. Within twenty-four hours Goa was rid of the Portuguese and incorporated into India.[21]

---

[19] *Ibid.* Later, after Kennedy's accession to power and before India's invasion of Goa in Dec. 1961, there was some change in US opposition to India in Goa. In 1961, the United States' revealed Ambassador Galbraith in course of Senate hearings on Foreign Assistance on April 25, 1966, did try to persuade Portugal to accommodate India regarding the colony. See Richard Siegel, *Evaluating the Results of Foreign Policy : Soviet and American Efforts in India,* Social Science Foundation Monograph Series on World Affairs, VI, No. 4 (Denver : University of Denver, 1969), p. 12.

[20] Cited by Stein, *India and the Soviet Union,* p. 73.

[21] The actual decision to take the police action might have been made on Dec. 7, 1961. See India, Parliament, *Lok Sabha Debates,* XL ; 15 (December, 1961), col. 3864.

The Soviet Union's support for the action in Goa as expressed before and after the incident was complete. Mr. Leonid Brezhnev had announced on Dec. 17, while on a goodwill tour of India, the Soviet people's "full understanding and sympathy for the Indian desire to achieve the liberation of Goa, Daman and Diu". A day after the liberation of Goa he again assured the Indian people of Russia's firm support for the action. Some suspect that the Soviets were informed beforehand of the Indian plan to annex Goa.[22]

The Western world, the United States in particular, however, was entirely dismayed. The Indian action in Goa aroused strong emotions—the response in the USA was "one of shock, variously tinged with distress, perplexity, or resentment, not always free from malice".[23] Thus immediately after the start of the police action, the United States in league with others (Britain, France, Turkey) sponsored a resolution calling for the cessation of hostilities. In course of the debate in the Security Council on December 18, the US delegate the same Adlai Stevenson, who, in 1955 had criticised Dulles' policy in regard to Goa, now said :

> ...We are meeting to decide what attitude should be taken when a UN Member casts aside the principles of the Charter and seeks to resolve a dispute by force.... What is at stake today is not colonialism. It is a bold violation of one of the most basic principles of the UN charter....If the UN is not to die an ignoble death as the League of Nations, we cannot condone the use of force on this instance and thus pave the way for forceful solutions of other disputes. ...This body cannot apply a double standard with regard to force....[24]

---

[22] Stein, for example, says : "It remains a moot point whether or not the Soviets were informed beforehand of the Indian plan to annex Goa." Stein, *India and the Soviet Union,* p. 137.

[23] Margaret W. Fisher, "Goa in Wider Perspective", *Asian Survey,* II (April, 1962), p. 3.

[24] UNSCOR, Sixteenth Year, 987th Mtg. (Dec., 18, 1961), pp. 21-26.

Mr. Zorin (USSR), on the other hand, objecting to the draft resolution, declared first that the "situation in the territories which are part of a sovereign state cannot in keeping with the UN Charter be the subject of consideration by any" UN body, and that the Portuguese enclaves "are connected" with India for "geographic reasons, as well as by history, culture, language, and tradition", and finally upheld the Indian action thus : "Today saw...the expression of the will to defend colonial countries and peoples and their right to life, freedom, and independence".[25] Thus defending the Indian action, the Soviet Union cast her ninety-ninth veto. And Stevenson, seeing Western efforts thus thwarted, simply lamented : "We are witnessing the first act in a drama which could end in its death".[26]

It can be seen therefore that India got support from one and opposition and condemnation from the other. But in the contest between the opposition as expressed in the Security Council in terms of voting for cessation of hostilities and support in terms of vetoing it, it is the support and veto that prevailed. This meant in effect that India could secure her national interests—territorial and security —as symbolized by Goa's full integration with the rest of India. It was a victory for India as total as could be conceived under the circumstances.

C. *Sino-Indian Dispute Regarding the Northern Boundary Areas*

In a previous chapter[27] India's interests, as seen by her policymakers, have been shown to be at variance with those of the People's Republic of China. It has also been seen how China's occupation of Tibet and India's recognition of her occupation brought China face to face with India. China looked upon the British negotiated, nay

---

[25] *Ibid.*
[26] *Facts on File,* 1961, XXI, 462.
[27] Chapter IV.

imposed, MacMahon Line as particularly galling and un-acceptable, and began to sound out Indian feelings about it from the early fifties. It is not in regard to the North-eastern boundary areas (MacMahon Line) that there were clashes of interests. In the Northwest also, Indian interests clashed with those of the Chinese ; the Chinese had already built a road through Aksai Chin (that ran through Ladakh in Kashmir). The Chinese apparently considered this of greater strategic value, and were willing to negotiate with the Indians regarding the MacMahon Line provided the latter accepted that the MacMahon Line was a symbol of a colonial era and that the Chinese would not be dislodged from Aksai Chin (they in fact wanted a lease there). The Indian Government would not some-how budge from its legalistic stand that the MacMahon Line, as an international line, is entirely sacred and cannot be the subject of any negotiation with the Chinese. This territorial dispute was not the only matter that exercised the minds of the leaders of these two giant states of Asia. They were competing in two other fields : ideological-political, and economic. The Indians, wedded to democracy and neutralism in foreign affairs, had apparently succeeded so far in both ; their democratic economic planning, geared to bringing about a total transformation of a colo-nial economy, was on the threshold of a big leap forward. China, a totalitarian Communist state experimenting with Communist techniques of economic planning, saw India's progress with some misgiving, rather dismay. And thus Chinese leaders apparently decided in 1962, after some provocations from the Indian Government ("Forward Policy"),[28] to use the territorial dispute as an excuse to bring India down, to destroy her image as a relatively successful democracy with a neutralist clout in inter-

---

[28] Neville Maxwell in his book *India's China War* (New York : Pantheon Books, 1970) considers these provocations as mainly respon-sible for the outbreak of war.

national affairs.[29] So began the invasion of India.[30] What were the stances of the two Super Powers in regard to the Sino-Indian boundary dispute ?

Although American sentiment had always been against the People's Republic of China, strangely enough the United States Government did not express its full sympathy for India in the dispute with China until August, 1962, and it did not officially state that it regarded the MacMahon Line as the sacred boundary between India and the Tibet region of China in the NEFA area until October 27, 1962, shortly after China had moved her forces there. This American reticence was the result of endeavour by two friends of India who had also been ambassadors, Chester Bowles and John Sherman Cooper, who had reasoned that closer American interest and espousal of India's cause would be misconstrued by the Chinese, as also by the world as a whole, as intrusion of the cold war into the India-China dispute, which would have made the problem all the more intractable and insoluble.[31] The Government of India had apparently agreed with this line. This period of US reticence was however marred by one statement by the then Secretary of State, Christian Herter, made in the fall of 1959, which indicated that the United States was rather uncertain about the relative merits of the border claims of India and China, and this caused considerable resentment in India.[32]

However this period ended when in August 1962, the United States signified her approval of the Indian position on the border dispute. The official American endorsement of the Indian position in sticking to the MacMahon Line was expressed by Ambassador John Galbraith on October

---

29 For an elaborate discussion of the point, see Dutt, *China and the World,* especially pages 208-222. Also, Sengupta, *The Fulcrum of Asia,* pp. 113-140.

30 It must be remembered that the invasion of India, although massive, was not sudden. It followed a period of clashes between the armed forces of the two countries. For a chronology of the events preceding the invasion, see *ibid.,* pp. 157-162.

31 Palmer, *South Asia, p.* 266 *passim.*

32 *Ibid.,* p. 266.

27 in this way : "The MacMahon Line is an accepted international border and is sanctioned by modern usage. Accordingly, we regard it as the Northern border of the NEFA area".[33]

Although border skirmishes had been going on for some time between the two Asian giants, the first clashes that could truly be called massive took place in both NEFA and Ladakh on October 20, 1962, and the clashes continued up until November 20, 1962, when the Chinese unilaterally initiated a ceasefire and began withdrawing their troops from the occupied territories on December 21.

In this crisis India received almost immediate aid from the United States and her allies. Nehru's request for Western aid, sent on October 29 was acceded to by the Western allies within three days when "the first American C-135 jet transports took off from American bases, in Frankfurt, Germany, loaded with light infantry weapons, artillery, communications and transportation equipment. Very shortly, C-135s were flying arms to India on a round the clock airlift from Germany".[34] Although total military aid received from the United States and her allies did not amount to much,[35] it must be conceded that its psychological and symbolic value, which was considerable, more than offset its meagre material value. There is reason to believe that the ceasefire that the Chinese initiated was as much due to American (and Western) endorsement for the Indian position and military intervention on behalf of beleaguered India as to other factors.

And, among the other factors was the Soviet position in regard to the dispute. It must first of all be mentioned that before the outbreak of the massive clashes of October, the Soviet Union already had taken a very significant stance in regard to the dispute. The Soviet Government through a Tass statement of September 9, rallied to India's support in a sense by first coming out with neutrality

---

[33] Cited by *Ibid.*, p. 267.

[34] *Ibid.* About the details of the military aid given after the invasion by the United States, see K. Subrahmanyam, "US Policy Towards India", *China Report,* VIII (January-April, 1972), 44-46.

[35] *Ibid.* This point is taken care of in the following section.

between "Chinese brothers and Indian friends".[36] After the outbreak of the war however, the Soviet Union called for ceasefire. When, on October 24, the Chinese proposed that the line of actual control on that date should serve as a ceasefire line, and that both sides should then with-draw their troops twelve and a half miles, the Soviets seemed to accept the Chinese proposal for the demarcation of the northern borders on the following day.[37] This was indeed unexpected from the Indian point of view, since this appeared to India that perhaps the Soviet Union was trying to get out of a pro-India neutrality to a position more favourable to the Chinese. But this change, if that was a change, was purely tactical necessitated by the events surrounding Soviet missiles in Cuba.[38] On October 31, however, the Russians seemed to correct their position ; Mr. Khrushchev on that day speaking at the Supreme Soviet regretted the Ladakh incident and urged friendly negotiations to find a solution "to the mutual satisfaction of both sides". In a volunteered comment to the *New Age* correspondent, the Soviet leader suggested that "China should be generous in settling the border dispute with India, as the USSR had been with Iran".[39] And, by the first week of November, the Soviet Government came to completely support the Indian stand. The Soviets indicated that they would not only not curtail their assistance to India but would even speed up supplies in certain respects ; and the Indian Ministry of Defence announced that arms "have been coming according to schedule" from the USSR.[40] What is more, the Soviets seemed to endorse Mr. Nehru's request to the Western Powers for military help. And, finally, on Noverber 6, Alexei Kosygin, at that time Soviet Deputy Premier, called for a ceasefire on "a reasonable

---

[36] Cited by Sengupta, *Communism in Indian Politics* (New York : Columbia University Press, 1972), p. 55.

[37] Stein, *India and the Soviet Union,* p. 152.

[38] *Ibid.*

[39] Cited by Sengupta, *Communism,* p. 55.

[40] And, on Nov. 9, 1962, Nehru expressed confidence that the Soviet Union would fulfil its pledges of assistance, including MIGs.

basis" which seemed to the Indian Government to reveal the stand of the Soviet Government to be basically sympathetic to India's. It might also be added that the USSR encouraged mediation by the six non-aligned Afro-Asian states which finally met in Colombo in December, 1962 and put forth the socalled Colombo Proposals.[41] Incidentally, it might be mentioned that some observers think that "the Colombo proposals were the best that India could hope for, given the realities of the de facto situation".[42] Subsequently India made diplomatic use of China's refusal to accept the proposals without qualification.[43]

It must be said then that, in spite of the military setbacks and relatively large square miles of northern boundary areas lost (this loss also did not mean much since Nehru himself had said some years ago that these areas were barren, "where not a blade of grass grows") India did indeed sort of become an "area of agreement" in the relations between the big powers. One serious student of Indian affairs observes :

> ...India received largescale military assistance from the United States and Great Britain. This aid was given immediately and virtually without conditions (it was valued at an estimated $ 100 million). And the Russians—after the Cuban crisis had passed its peak—tried in their own way to bolster India's posi-

---

[41] Stein, *India and the Soviet Union*, pp. 155-156, *passim*.

[42] *Ibid.*, p. 157.

[43] *Ibid.*, pp. 155-156. It must be mentioned that the main proposals put forward by the nonaligned powers that met at Colombo were : "In the Western sectors (Ladakh) : (a) Chinese forces were to withdraw 20 kms. from the actual line of control on Nov. 7, 1959 (both India and China accepted), and (b) pending final solution of the border dispute, the area of Chinese withdrawal was to be a demilitarized zone, to be administered by civilian posts of both sides, without prejudice to claims (India accepted but China insists on Chinese posts only in the demilitarized zone) ; in the Eastern Sector (NEFA) the line of actual control in areas recognized by both Governments was to serve as a ceasefire line to their respective posts, the remaining areas to be settled in the future discussions (India accepted, the Chinese insist that Indian troops do not return to the MacMahon Line)". See Brecher, *The New States of Asia*, p. 172 ; also cited by Stein, *India and the Soviet Union*, pp. 156-157.

tion. And, at least momentarily the Indian nation was united—in the common cause of opposing China.[44]

Mr. Currimbhoy Chagla, then Indian High Commissioner in London, attributed this to nonalignment-cum-neutralism, to its ability to prevent the two Communist giants from coming together and bringing about the ever widening gulf between them. He added : "Therefore in a strange twist of history, we may succeed by our nonaligned [sic] policy in bringing the West and Russia closer together and isolating China".[45] For the moment at least it appeared that Mr. Chagla's assessment was more or less correct. Set against this Indian success however was the failure brought into relief by the loss of about 40,000 square miles of northern strategic territory, to which reference has already been made.

Section II : Strategic Interests as Determined by Domestic Requirements

A. *Foreign Aid (Economic)*

India has been the recipient of foreign economic aid from many quarters,[46] including the United States and the USSR, the arch rivals in the cold war. By the end of September, 1965, as reported by one authority, Rs. 5,455 Crores ($ 11·4 billion at the official rate of exchange) had been extended to India in the form of loans, credits, and grants.[47] Of this total, the United States accounted for 54 per cent.[48] It can be said that in absolute terms the aid

---

44 Stein, *India and the Soviet Union,* p. 157.

45 Cited by *ibid.,* p. 162.

46 Over 21 countries as well as international agencies and private foundations have given economic assistance to India—says Warren Ilchman, "Political Economy of Foreign Aid", *Asian Survey,* VII (October, 1967), 680.

47 Tansky, *US and USSR Aid to Developing Countries,* p. 97.

48 *Ibid.* A year and a half earlier, by the end of March, 1964, the total of US aid was 5,743 billion dollars, thus comprising 50 per cent of all aid received from all the countries combined. Sadhan Mukherjee, *Who Really Aids India : The USA or the USSR ?* (New Delhi : People's Publishing House, 1972), p. 14.

received by India from the US was one of the largest that
any developing countries received ; however, per capita-
wise, India's share was among the lowest (during the
period of our study). The following table[49] gives a comparative estimate of US assistance to four countries and
how it works out per capita (in the period from January
7, 1950 to March 6, 1964) :

TABLE I

Country	Total Value of US Assistance $	Per Capita $
India	5,743 m.	10
Pakistan	2,742 m.	20
S. Vietnam	2,150 m.	134
Philippines	822 m.	25

On the other hand, the USSR's economic aid to India
in the first decade ending February, 1965 comprised an
estimated Rs. 4·84 billion or $ 1·017 billion for Indian
development projects,[50] which comprised about 9 per cent
of the total aid received by India during the period end·ng
September, 1965.[51] It is also said that as a result of
this comparatively large a·d, India ranks among the
largest recipients of Soviet aid among the thirty-nine
developing countries.[52]

---

[49] *Ibid.* However Burton cited a report by the *Far Eastern Economic Survey,* Oct. 18, 1962 which gives a slightly different picture, based
undoubtedly upon an earlier survey : $ 6.20 per capita—see J. Burton,
International Relations : A General Theory (Cambridge : Cambridge
University Press, 1965), p. 193. But then in 1965, according to another
report, the per capita aid to India was only $ 2.7 compared with $ 3.3
for Asia, and $ 4.2 for all world recipients. See Indian Council of
Current Affairs, *Foreign Aid : A Symposium, A Survey, An Appraisal*
(Calcutta : Oxford Book and Stationery, 1968), p. 461.
[50] Arthur Stein, "India and the USSR : The Post-Nehru Period",
Asian Survey, VII : No. 3 (March, 1967), p. 172.
[51] Tansky, *US and USSR Aid to Developing Countries,* p. 97
[52] Mukherjee, *Who Really Aids India ?,* p. 39.

13

Yet looking at the whole picture of foreign economic aid (aid coming from all countries), it can be said that India's share per capita remained among the world's lowest.[53] This meant in effect that India had to depend mostly upon her own domestic resources ; the ratio of domestic resources to total investment was almost 70 per cent at the end of the Second and Third Plans.[54] It could be said therefore by some students that "India was unable to get anywhere near the extent of assistance required for the transformation of her economy, nor even anywhere near the assistance that many other poor societies... received."[55] And this nonavailability of adequate foreign aid was one of the principal reasons for the condit.on of virtual stagnation obtaining at the end of the Nehru period.[56]

Yet the significance of whatever aid India received from the countries of the world, including the United States and the USSR, could not be minimized—because "it covered almost every sector of the economy and most forms of social organization."[57] Indeed, the American aided projects, as listed by an Indian authority on US aid in India, included 38 projects in the field of agriculture, 33 projects in industry, 18 in health, 6 in transportation, 18 in education and a further 18 that could be called miscellaneous.[58] The Soviet aid projects although less numerous

[53] See the Table in India, Ministry of Finance, *Pocket Book of Economic Information* (New Delhi : Government of India Press, 1963) as reproduced in S. L. N. Sinha, *Development With Stability* : *The Indian Experiment* (Bombay : Vora and Co., 1963), p. 111.

[54] *Ibid.*, p. 110.

[55] Ronald Segal, *The Anguish of India* (New York : Stein and Day, 1965), p. 191.

[56] Jayantanuja Bandyopadhyay, *The Making of India's Foreign Policy*, p. 45. Compare also the statement : "In short, a higher proportion of per capita foreign aid with the same rate of domestic savings helps a country to accumulate a much greater amount of capital assets and this cannot but accelerate the rate of economic growth." See ICCA, Foreign Aid, p 461.

[57] Warren Ilchman, "Political Economy of Foreign Aid", 680.

[58] Sripati Chandrasekhar, *American Aid and India's Economic Development* (New York : Praeger, 1965), Appendix I, pp. 207-210.

and concentrating mostly on heavy industry and related fields included such projects as Bhilai Steel Plant, Heavy Machinery Plant, Coal Mining Machinery Plant, Drugs Projects, Power Projects and Oil projects, etc.[59] Be that as it may, the significance of the aid by the two countries (and others) should be measured not in terms of 'gross figures of aid' but in its ability to bridge or narrow the 'foreign exchange gap'. As Ilchman observes :

> More important than gross figures of aid or number of countries granting it, however, is that the foreign assistance provides a resource worth many times its official rate or statistical proportion in that the most sensitive area of planned change is the 'foreign exchange gap'. The ability of India to import raw materials and capital equipment works a multiplier effect throughout the economy.[60]

This indeed is a kind of advantage that no one can easily ignore. And if it is remembered that most of the foreign exchange came primarily from the USA and the USSR (US supply of foreign exchange was four times larger than the Soviet), then it could be considered a *"politically happy situation* wherein India could rely on receiving resources from all sides and thus avoid depending on any single country" ; and this could be further exemplified by the fact that when "the United States backed down on the Bokaro Steel Plant, the Soviet Union agreed to finance it".[61]

This is indeed a kind of competition between the United States and the USSR, and is a by-product, at least indirectly, of India's nonalignment-cum-neutralist policies. But the dynamics of this competition is such that it was transformed, in due course, "into a contest between two programs for economic development, the Soviet one stressing public ownership and heavy industry and the American

---

[59] For a fuller account of the various projects aided by the Soviet Union, see Stein, *India and the Soviet Union,* Appendix A, pp. 285-296.
[60] Ilchman, "Political Economy of Foreign Aid", 680-681.
[61] *Ibid.,* 683.

stressing acceptance of private foreign capital and development of private agriculture".[62] This point is corroborated by Stein who says, "the Indo-Soviet economic collaboration which began with a credit of Rs. 647·4 million for the Bhilai Steel Plant in 1955 has been extended through the years to a variety of development projects in the public sector".[63] With the establishment of the Bhilai Steel Plant with its better performance in comparison with similar plants with Western help as Durgapur and Rourkela Steel Plants, the Government of India felt encouraged to insist on public control for many other projects including the Bokaro Steel Plant.[64] The Socialist transformation of the society, the will to which as it would be seen[65] was to some extent supplied by better relations with the Soviet Union and its bloc which included at one time People's Republic of China, was thus made easier ; the concept of public sector no longer remained an abstract concept, it became a living reality ; and the Government of India gradually took control of the "commanding heights of the economy"—a very important aspect in the socialist transformation of society that India's leadership was bent on bringing about. In this matter, breaking up of the monopoly control is another important aspect. At least in one sphere, in the matter of petroleum industry, the Soviet help proved to be invaluable in breaking the iron grip of "a closely coordinated cartel of three Western firms". The then Petroleum Minister in the Government of India, Mr. K. D. Malaviya, moved successfully to secure Soviet help in oil exploration, the purchase of cheap crude

---

62 Siegel, *Evaluating the Results of Foreign Policy,* p. 22. Siegel also says that only about 5 to 6 per cent (about 290 million dollars) in government credits were provided directly for any industrial plants in India. *Ibid.,* p. 5.

63 Stein, *India and the Soviet Union,* p. 285. Stein also gives a detailed picture of the various public sector projects that the Soviet Union has been assisting—see *ibid.,* pp. 286-292.

64 Siegel, *Evaluating the Results of Foreign Policy* p. 22.

65 In our discussion of the political consequences this point will be touched upon. See the following section.

oil, and project aid for several refineries.[66]   Michael Kidron has observed in this regard : "Oil is the paradigm for the use of nonalignment [sic] in underpinning Indian economic independence".[67]   Indeed, Moscow's actions in this regard have thus bolstered "the Indian Government in an area in which New Delhi was anxious to alter an indefensible status quo".[68]

But it must be noted that American help, although not forthcoming substantially in the public sector, has indeed led to increased food supply. Senator McGovern, while Director of American Food for Peace Program, had said in 1962 :

> Of the $ 4000 million in US aid that has come to India since independence, over one half has been in the form of P.L. 480 Food for Peace commodities.... The total tonnage of food grains in the P.L. 480 program and earlier agreements such as the Wheat Loan of 1951 provide for the supply to India of over 31 million tons.[69]

In the remaining two years of Nehru's term, the supply could only have further increased. The enormity of this aid could only be imagined. But, S. Chandrasekhar makes our work a little easier by the following statistical evaluation :

> The total amount of these American supplied agricultural commodities is the equivalent of 160 pounds of food grains for every man, woman, and child in India. The total value exceeds Rs. 12,000 crores or about 30 rupees for every inhabitant of India.[70]

This apart, American assistance was of more cons-

---

[66] For detailed discussion of this point, see Mukherjee, *Who Really Aids India ?*, pp. 48-49.

[67] Michael Kidron, Foreign Investments in India (London : Oxford University Press, 1965), as cited by Siegel, *Evaluating the Results of Foreign Policy*, p. 23.

[68] *Ibid.*, p. 23.

[69] Cited by Chandrasekhar, *American Aid and India's Economic Development*, p. 103.

[70] *Ibid.*

tructive value in the field of agricultural production and education, and in the matter of power generation. In this last area the United States supplied more than 60 per cent of capital ; and, the help she gave in the construction and staffing of eight agricultural universities and in the modernization of railway transportation in India[71] could be cited as of greatest significance but for which India's problems of economic development would have appeared even grimmer. Indeed all the above help in the various fields has helped trigger the socalled 'green revolution', more power for the industries, holding promise of selfsufficiency in food production and assuring more credibly that the wheels of industry will keep running. More importantly, America's help has kept alive the prospects of a mixed economy in India under democratic planning. While the United States always felt a sort of "dilemma of assisting in the development of a 'socialist pattern of society', the American aid expenditures, even when not helping the public sector, at least acted as supplement to domestic savings in India, and thus helped the overall goals of the Indian Government in the direction of 'socialist pattern of society'. Leo Tansky argued :

> Assuming that the agricultural commodities imported under the aid program enabled India to import an equivalent amount of investment goods, then US outlays comprised 16 per cent of total investment in India during the first two plans. Furthermore, such aid equalled 30 per cent of total investment in the public sector.[72]

On the other hand, says Leo Tansky, Soviet econom'c aid,

---

71 For some details, see K. Subrahmanyan, "US Policy Toward India", 40 ; also, Siegel, *Evaluating the Results of Foreign Policy,* p. 5. Statistics recently compiled by United States, Aid for International Development, in *India : Briefing Book* (Washington D.C. : Government Printing Press, Dec., 1966) as cited by Siegel reveals that of the total aid $ 6.4 billion by the end of June 30, 1966, 11.8% was allocated directly to transportation and power infra-structure and slightly more than 80% directly for agricultural or industrial commodities, almost 70% of the latter offered under the special provisions of US PL 480. See *Ibid.,* p. 5.

72 Tansky, *US and USSR Aid to Developing Countries,* p. 111.

while almost completely concentrated in the public sector, provides India with needed capital, "facilitates India's plans to achieve her development goals within the framework of a free and democratic society."[73]

B. *Foreign Aid (Defense)*

In regard to foreign aid in the field of defense of India, it must be said that it played a comparatively minor role. The United States aid in this field was minimal over the entire period. Only after the Chinese invasion, the US policy showed a noticeable change, when President Kennedy responded to Nehru's request for arms help more or less positively. The United States, after President Kennedy's meeting with Prime Minister MacMillan of Great Britain in December, 1962, agreed to pay half of $120 million (the balance to be paid by the Commonwealth countries).[74] Another agreement between Kennedy and MacMillan in 1962 at Birchgrove (England) led to a program of joint military assistance to India under which the United States and the Commonwealth would contribute $ 50 million each. While these two were in the nature of grants, there was a credit for $ 10 million in 1964. But as three experts point out, only $ 82 million of supplies were actually delivered ;[75] the same experts estimated that these aid supplies would have been adequate to cover six mountain divisions (then nine in number) only and were to be used not against Pakistan but only against China.[76] The insignificance of this aid becomes quite apparent when one remembers that Pakistan, a military ally whose defense needs were less than those of India, received much more military aid, somewhere above $ 1 billion, between $ 1.2 to $ 1.5 billion during the comparable

---

[73] *Ibid.,* p. 101
[74] Subrahmanyan, "US Policy Toward India", p. 44.
[75] Paul Streeten, Michael Lipton, and General P. S. Bhagat as cited by *ibid.,* p. 46. Mr. M. C. Chagla, Minister of External Affairs, stated that military aid valued at $ 75.6 m. was received—see Siegel, *Evaluating the Results of Foreign Policy,* p. 10 (fn 1). .
[76] Subrahmanyan, "US Policy Toward India", p. 46.

period.[77]

In contrast, the Soviet Union's defense aid has been quite substantial. India started getting military aid from the Soviet Union in 1960. Since then she has supplied India not only transport aircraft and helicopters but MIG-21s as well. India has now been given the licence to manufacture MIGs in India. In addition India has received other aircraft and surface to air missiles and tanks and rocket launchers. One estimate made in 1964 revealed that Soviet aid up to that time totalled the equivalent of $ 130 million.[78]

The above discussion, although brief, reveals that both the US and the USSR have to a certain extent helped India meet the threats to her security. Warren Ilchman has said in this regard :

> The recent drain on India's political resources (referring to China's invasion and the expenditures on its account) has seen this happy collaboration by cold war combatants continue in the offering of arms aid. Nonalignment [sic] has, for defense purposes, become coalignment.[79]

What are the implications of the total foreign aid situation ? To the extent the Government of India did receive economic aid, it could take care of India's defense needs on the basis of resources internally available without being accountable to any nation. Also, to the extent that India also received some military aid, either in the form of credits or grants, this also must have saved some worry in regard to development projects, for without money coming for defense from abroad, she would have

---

[77] Richard Weekes, *Pakistan : Birth and Growth of a Muslim Nation* (New York : The Asia Library, 1964), p. 258 ; also, Khalid B. Sayeed, *The Political System of Pakistan* (Boston : Houghton Mifflin Co., 1967), p. 279.

[78] Cited by P. J. Eldridge, "India's Nonalignment Policy Reviewed" in *International Politics of Asia,* edited by George P. Jan (Belmont, Calif. : Wadsworth Publishing Co., 1969), p. 140. But another estimate by the US State Department made in 1968 of the Soviet military aid (arms committed) to India between 1960 to 1967 put at $ 610 million—see Siegel, *Evaluating the Results of Foreign Policy,* p. 11.

[79] Ilchman, "Political Economy of Foreign Aid", p. 683.

been constrained to find money from domestic resources, which would have meant curtailment of development projects. So both forms of aid are related, and it seems rather unfair, at least in a sense, to separate the two.

It has been seen that both the US and USSR have given foreign aid (economic and defense) to India. It behooves now to see how aid from one country or the other affected the stability, popularity or solvency of the Government of India (dominated for most of the time by the Indian Congress Party) ?

One way of answering the question is by way of asking, as Ilchman does, whether the externally assisted projects contribute to the political resource position of the Indian Government and then answering it.[80] Ilchman answers the question by referring to a study by B. R. Nayar[81] where the latter, using a sample of 67 legislative assembly constituencies in West Bengal, of which 39 had received assistance under the Community Development and National Extension Programs, concludes, after comparing the voting pattern of the aided and nonaided constituencies in the 1952 elections thus : First, Congress improved its percentage of votes in both categories, but did so more substantially in areas which had not received aid. Second, the votes for the CPI and the Marxist Left increased in both categories, but especially in those that had participated in development programs. Non-Marxist Left declined in aided areas. Thus Ilchman makes this rather sedate observation which the present writer thinks all can accept without much reservation :

> While the time period is too short and the constituencies' complexity too great for the following conclusion, it might be argued that development programs *do not* cost the regime the resource of political support. [emphasis added][82]

---

80 *Ibid.*

81 "Community Development Program : Its Political Impact", *Economic Weekly*, XII (Sept. 17, 1960), 1401-12, which is said to be the only study so far linking development expenditures with political support.

82 Ilchman, "Political Economy of Foreign Aid", p. 684.

Nor political support increases in those constituencies where there are foreign assisted development projects. Ilchman's quite rational conclusion is :

> Development projects do not dramatically increase support for the regime. Nor do Soviet projects spawn anti-democratic parties.... What the results are of the political investments made with resources freed by those projects is not known. Even if they too did not enhance Congress support, the Indian regime has considerable political capital to live on and can continue to invest in future political coalitions and political infrastructure.[83]

A final point may now be discussed—whether or not the relatively large economic aid (combined with the aid on defense account) led to the recipient country's loss of independence. So far as the question of US success in pressurizing India through economic aid is concerned, there are some instances during the period when India's Government had to give way. For example, in lieu of the food aid of 1961, India was asked and she agreed, that the repayment should be "by export of materials in short supply in the United States" (which meant supply of uranium) and a noted foreign economist referring to this had said : "...a principle had been attached to an aid bill which constituted a challenge to India's concept of sovereignty, foreshadowing subsequent conflicts".[84] And there have been other instances, including those where the United States attempted to change the direction of India's economic policies from socialism to a system which required a greater reliance on the private sector as the instrument of progress. But the Government of India could largely succeed in meeting such pressure, because of certain factors. John P. Lewis, a former US AID administrator in India, gave the following reasons why the US pressure could not

---

[83] *Ibid.,* p. 687.

[84] Eldridge, *The Politics of Foreign Aid,* pp. 30-31, as cited by Mukherjee, *Who Really Aids India ?,* pp. 3-4.

be driven home. First, India was not one of those 'defense support' countries as South Korea and South Vietnam. Second, the official US posture in regard to India had been one of 'diffidence' ; in the words of Lewis : "The US Government sometimes has acted as though it were treading on eggs in its aid transactions with India. A very high estimate has been placed on the Government of India's sensitivity to its sovereign prerogative". Third, the US managers of aid in India differentiated India from other developing countries—(i) India was a rare example of a new nation with a politically accountable government, (ii) India's economy was massive, making outside assistance a lesser ingredient in the development formula, (iii) US was not the only aid-giving country, (iv) US authorities confronted an 'underdeveloped economy' government whose "top political, professional and administrative cadres were highly sophisticated in a Western sense". This last point was emphasized by Lewis in these words :

> It was a government that as the leader of the Afro-Asian 'neutralist' bloc not only represented an outlook on international affairs distinctly different from that of the West, but confronted the US more nearly as a de facto equal in the realm of power politics than any other government it had assisted economically, at least since the Marshall Plan.[85]

The USSR, on the other hand, which was sort of satisfied with India and her nonalignment-cum-neutralism, did certain things which tended to strengthen the Indian government domestically, giving the latter a greater flexibility. Her support for India's public sector projects and especially in ridding the petroleum industry of the vicious grip of monopolistic cartels helped India pursue domestic socialistic policies with greater success. It is certain that in some matters the Soviet Union also wanted to influence

---

[85] John P. Lewis, *Quiet Crisis in India : Economic Development and American Policy,* Anchor Book (Garden City, New York : Doubleday and Co., 1964), pp. 272-273, *passim.*

or even pressurize India, but the same factors that inhibited the US in driving the pressure home as well as she
might have must have deterred the Soviets also.

Section III : **Other Interests (Primarily Political)**

Although India started her independent career with
a faith in democracy and parliamentarianism, Nehru and
his government rightly felt that this faith was not widely
shared by all the parties outside the Congress system. The
Communist Party of India in particular was deeply distrustful of the bourgeois-led Congress Party and its motives
in adhering to the democratic system. The then leadership of the CPI even were thinking in terms of toppling it
through armed uprisings under their banner. The Telengana uprising of 1948, although eventually aborted, was a
serious enough challenge not only to the Nehru regime but
also to the fledgling democratic order in general, dedicated
as it was to the improvement of people's condition through
parliamentary means. The strategy of the new regime,
in meeting this challenge, consisted in, *inter alia,* not
adding to the number of tensions that already were there
between one segment of Indian people, followers of Communist Party who seemed to reject the democratic parliamentary system, and the rest, led mostly by the Congress,
who were bent upon preserving this order. Foreign policy
matters had, and still have now, a great deal of relevance
in this regard. And the Nehru regime's first attempts in
controlling tensions included the development of a foreign
policy—that of nonalignment-cum-neutralism which was a
way of balancing not only the West against the East and
cutting an independent path in international politics but
was also a way of assuring stability in internal politics,
where democracy and parliamentary means of governance
could be carried on relatively unhampered. By deftly
taking an independent stance in foreign affairs, especially
in matters affecting the Super Powers, by appearing to be
at least nonaligned Nehru helped change the Communist

Party of India and its avowedly anti-parliamentary character.

Indeed one of the first fallout effects of India's foreign policy of nonalignment-cum-neutralism was the retraction by the CPI of the Telengana solution of India's manifold ills. The CPI apparently decided in 1951 that, given the objective conditions of India, it had to go through a long period of legal struggle, making use of parliamentary methods. Whether it was due to the failure of the Telengana uprising or due to changes in Soviet perceptions of the world, born of, *inter alia,* Soviet contact with nonaligned India, is very difficult to say. But that this occurred in the period of India's nonalignment-cum-neutralism is perhaps to a certain extent significant. With the intensification of the cold war, the Soviets came to put greater value in nonalignment-cum-neutralism, considered Nehru in the 'peace camp', and wanted the CPI to lend the former increasing support. One Indian authority on Communism in India, Bhabani Sengupta, points out that between the Third Congress of the Party at Madurai and the Fifth Congress at Amritsar, the CPI rapidly embraced 'the international line' that is to say of the Soviet Party and Government, amounting to acceptance of the strategy of the parliamentary way.[86]

This change in line of the CPI meant in effect the emergence of those leaders who were centrist, who were skilled in parliamentary ways : and indeed the CPI leadership in Lok Sabha (House of the People) after 1952 General Elections, included such men as Hiren Mukherjee, Dange, Renu Chakrabarti, A. K. Gopalan, and their contributions to India's parliamentary system, to the uphold-

---

[86] Sengupta, *Communism,* pp. 37-40, *passim.* It must be pointed out in this connection that there still remained in the party a group of leaders, "by no means contrite", who continued to challenge the official leadership. In fact, because of the continued schism within the party, there had to be a compromise. The political resolution adopted at Madurai represented an uneasy compromise. The party chose to oppose the government, but to support its specific acts. Gene Overstreet and Marshall Windmiller, *Communism in India* (Berkeley and Los Angeles : University of California, 1959), Chapter XIV, and p. 312 in particular.

ing of parliamentary traditions, were second to none.[87]

Thus, in the period 1954-57, many of the reservations the Communists had in regard to the new order in India largely disappeared. India had signed an agreement with China in Tibet in April, 1954, the Chinese and Soviet leaders, including Chou En-Lai, Khrushchev, and Bulganin had visited India and the Soviets had offered economic aid to India not long after. These developments, particularly the last, convinced the CPI leaders that Nehru's domestic policies were not that anti-people. The Congress Party also tried to accommodate them by moving toward the left— the Avadi session of the Congress Party having adopted the 'socialistic pattern of society' in 1957. After the Fourth Congress of the Party at Palghat in April, 1956 (held interestingly after the Twentieth Congress of the CPSU which heard Khrushchev's denunciation of Stalin). the CPI accepted the possibility that India may accomplish a peaceful transition to socialism. And this meant in effect that the CPI offered the olive branch to the Congress Party under Nehru to accomplish things the parliamentary way.[88] The role the Communists decided to play in the Indian political system was defined by themselves :

> In order that the Communist Party may pursue such a revolutionary and flexible policy and play its rightful role as the builder and spearhead of the democratic movement, it must come forward as an *independent national force*. It must act as a Party of Opposition in relation to the present government.[89]

This stand of the Communist Party redounded to the credit of the Nehru Government. The latter indeed succeeded first in domesticating the Communists of India, and in making them, at least temporarily, upholders of the Parliamentary system. Secondly, by keeping the Soviets humoured in particular Nehru and his government could

---

[87] Sengupta, *Communism,* pp. 39-40
[88] *Ibid.,* pp. 41-43, *passim*
[89] *Cited by ibid.,* p. 44.

still keep the Communists out of real decisionmaking process of the nation. By invoking Russian help, in addition, the Congress Party led by Nehru could beat the Communists in national elections, as was proved in Andhra, and, after seeing them in power as in Kerala, it could, without inviting any visible Russian retaliation, dislodge them from power.[90]

It can be said that the increasingly nationalist stances of the CPI might have afforded them an opportunity to woo the Indian masses more persuasively, as perhaps the election statistics showed ;[91] at the same time by working within the perimeters of parliamentary traditions they gained not so much strength for themselves or won victory for their cause of socialist transformation of society as they helped the cause of political stability under the Congress Party banner, and thus helped parliamentary traditions to grow.

The above discussion has stressed that the CPI, thanks to nonalignment-cum-neutralism, was transformed into a parliamentary party, trying to influence things in the domestic arena through parliamentary ways. It can be pointed out in this connection that to the extent CPI became more interested in parliamentarianism, it also tried to restrain its adherents from taking to politics of streets. Although it would be hard to prove that it is *only* the Communists that take to politics of streets to agitate violently for or against some thing, it could be mentioned that during the period immediately following the change, at least tactical in nature, in the CPI, the number of riots, as studied by two major newspapers of India, was not actually on the increase : in 1955, there were seventy riots, and in 1957,

---

90 *Ibid.*, pp. 51-54, *passim.*

91 For example the Communists continued to get a greater percentage of votes in successive elections. In 1952 they had only 3,484,401 votes (that is 3.3% of the total votes cast) ; in 1957 their support jumped to 10,754,075 (8.92%), and in 1962 to 11,450,037 (9.94%). Only in 1967 this pattern changed, due largely to the split of the party consequent upon the Sino-Indian clash of 1962 and other related events. For election statistics, see W. H. Morris-Jones, *The Government and Politics* of India (London : Hutchinson University Library, 1971), pp. 184-185.

only sixty riots.[92]   Another study shows figures for 1958 and 1960 as 7 (per month) and 9.8 (per month) respectively.[93] These figures, if taken against large population increases in the country appear to be quite a formidable index of change for the better in so far as the recrudescence of riots as a way of political expression quite opposed to parliamentary politics is concerned. That there was no increase of violence or riotous demonstrations in India during the period under discussion can be further stressed by pointing out that it is only before the period (i.e., in 1950) and in 1967 that the Government of India felt it necessary to abridge personal freedom and judicial review in India through the Preventive Detention Act of 1950 and the Unlawful Activities Prevention Act, 1967.[94] That the Government of India showed greater confidence in meeting the threats of violence without resorting to such means was undoubtedly because they felt the other parties especially the CPI would be more restrained, and they were indeed so, particularly from 1952 to 1962, the years of domestication and parliamentarianization of the Communist Party of India.

It could be pointed out that the resultant domestic consensus, consequent upon the domestication of CPI that followed India's nonaligned-cum-neutralist stances, was to a large extent helped by the Indian regime's own tilt toward leftism or socialism in internal politics. This will to socialism was reflected in the form of a number of socialist ideological objectives, which comprised a number of key policy choices particularly in the field of Indian agriculture, such as : (1) recommendations (in the First Five Year Plan) to establish ceilings on the size of individual holdings as part of a comprehensive program of land reform ; (2) the decision in 1953 to achieve all-India

---

92 The two papers were *The Times of India* and ,*The Statesman.* The figures are cited by David H. Bailey, "Public Protest and the Political Process in India", *Pacific Affairs*, XLII (Spring, 1969), 8.

93 Alan Wells, "Mass Violence in India Since 1960", *The Indian Political Science Review,* VII (April-September, 1973), p. 126.

94 Bailey, "Public Protest", pp. 10-11.

coverage under the Community Development program as rapidly as possible, and (3) a set of decisions in 1956 to establish cooperatives as the basic unit of economic organization in the rural sector.[95] There is reason to believe that this will to socialism was partly traceable to this period of India's peaceful coexistence with the Communist bloc, especially China. Indeed it is widely inferred that the third component of the will to socialism was the result of Mr. Nehru's travel to China in 1955 which seems to have impressed him deeply, he came back with a rejuvenated desire "to move India decisively to the left internally";[96] he came determined to challenge the bureaucratic and conservative forces of his Congress Party to achieve socialism. Thus the 'socialistic pattern of society' resolution was adopted by his Congress Party in its Avadi session in January, 1955 at his behest. The more concrete evidence of the impact of Nehru's China visit was the following : for the first time Indian economic planning, as evidenced from the Second Five Year Plan, not only emphasized primary industries and the public sector,[97] but also adopted largescale cooperative societies, previously rejected by Nehru himself on grounds of their economic inefficiency, on the newly acquired belief from China that they would help preserve the essential characteristics of cooperation, close contact, social cohesion and mutual obligations.[98] The National Development Council followed this up with a series of steps that seemed to underscore this tilt to socialism : Strict regulation of private traders,

---

[95] Francine R. Frankel, "Ideology and Politics in Economic Planning : The Problem of Indian Agricultural Development Strategy", *World Politics*, XIX (July, 1967), p. 624. Francine also argues in her article that these objectives indicate that the Indian leaders "were genuinely committed" to their ideological objectives, to the extent that they were "prepared to sacrifice gains in output and resource mobilization in order to advance their image of a socialist society". *Ibid.*, pp. 629 et seq.

[96] Eric Hansen, "The Impact of the Border War on Indian Perceptions of China", *Pacific Affairs*, XL (Fall and Winter, 1967-68), 236.

[97] *Ibid*, Interestingly those (Professor B. N. Ganguly included) who had a hand in the preparation of the second plan also had been to China.

[98] Frankel, "Ideology and Politics in Economic Planning", p. 629.

14

announcement of maximum controlled prices for wholesale transactions in foodgrains, government purchases of
rice and wheat, compulsory levies on the stock of private
millers and traders, rapid expansion of the network of
government supplied fair price (retail) shops in major urban
centers, and programs for state trading in foodgrains.[99]

By the same token, India's difficulties with China as
evidenced from the border clashes with that country
particularly in 1959 and later led to certain developments
which showed a weakening of this will. The seeming
treachery of the leaders of China produced a revulsion in
the Indian mind against ideas associated with China, including those aspects of socialism that seemed to have
been inspired by the Chinese example. The Ministry of
Food and Agriculture, now under a new steward S. K.
Patil who did not have faith in the socialist transformation of India,[100] seemed ready to turn away from the socialist policies. It proposed some measures that at least
diluted the socialist commitment of the Government of
India ; they included the following : (1) an intensive
agricultural development program in approximately one-
tenth (as opposed to *all*) of the cultivated area ; (2) satu-
ration of this area with a 'package' of units, especially
high-yielding seeds, chemical fertilizers, etc. ; and (3)
price incentives to farmers as a stimulus for increased
private investment in improved practices.[101] By 1965,
the Ministry, no longer inhibited, openly called for "a reorientation of agricultural programs, if necessary, even to
the extent of clearly departing from some old principles
having a bearing on production".[102] The emergence of a

---

99 Frankel, "Ideology and Politics in Economic Planning", p. 632.

100 S. K. Patil's stewardship of the Ministry of Food and Agriculture
itself represented a weakening of the socialist will. Hansen, "The Impact
of the Border War", pp. 243-244.

101 Frankel, "Ideology and Politics in Economic Planning", p. 632.

102 Hansen, "The Impact of the Border War", pp. 243-244. Frankel
also argues that the Ministry's proposals represented in broad outline "a
return to the abortive pre-1953 approach of concentrating scarce inputs
and facilities in areas and among farmers best able to utilize them".
"Ideology and Politics in Economic Planning", p. 643.

significant political party, the Swatantra (or the Independent) Party that openly rejected socialism as a panacea for India's ills seemed to further emphasize this weakening of the will to socialism.[103]   However, socialism was spared the total annihilation partly because of the positive image of socialism that the other Marxist nation the USSR (that remained friendly) still seemed to project in India in general and in the circle of India's planners in particular.

The consensus in regard to India's foreign policy might also have suffered after 1959. A study of foreign policy views of the Indian Right (which included Swatantra and Jan Sangh) revealed the inclination of the rightist parties in the latter half of the period to depart from the main pillars of Nehru's foreign policy even while they made genuflexions in the direction of nonalignment-cum-neutralism.[104]   These departures[105] could be taken to indicate that the nonacceptance of the major assumptions of the foreign policy by a major party or parties, particularly the Swatantra, having access to much of the wealth of the country, although lacking popular support, indicated in no uncertain way a poignant erosion of the consensus regarding foreign policy that previously existed.

Yet this erosion of consensus as reflected by the Swatantra policy program on foreign affairs did not essentially weaken its edifice built as it was on the support from the center of the Congress Party and left-of-center (PSP

---

[103] Before this almost all the political parties, be they of the right or left, used to affirm socialism in some form or another. Even the Jan Sangh, the rightist communalist party, had somehow supported socialism. See Craig Baxter,   *The Jan Sangh :   A Biography of an Indian Political Party* (Philadelphia : University of Pennsylvania Press 1969). pp. 60-62.

[104] For a fuller discussion of the foreign policies of the Swatantra and the Jan Sangh, see Howard Erdman,   "The Foreign Policy Views of the Indian Right", *Pacific Affairs,*   XXXIX (Spring and Summer, 1966), 13-15.

[105] For departures from Nehru pillars of foreign policy, see *ibid.,* 15. They led to these considerations :   Western colonialism is no threat, racialism is of little concern ; nonalignment is suicidal ; notions of third force and of mediation in cold war are bunkum, etc. *Ibid.*

and CPI) political parties. Indeed a content-analysis by Warren Ilchman of the position of these parties after 1954 reveals little difference among these parties on foreign policy questions ; the Congress, PSP and CPI emphasized the more general international aspects of nonalignment-cum-neutralism 60.73 per cent, 76.34 per cent and 68.08 per cent of the time respectively, although these parties "may have played variations on a general theme ot non-alignment [sic] and modes of conducting that policy".[106]

It appears then that except for a brief period at the end of the Nehru era, India continued to bask at the achievements that were largely brought about by her neu-tralist foreign policy. She continued to consolidate demo-cratic (parliamentary) government (untouched by milita-rism) on the basis of a widely shared consensus and re-mained determined to bring about social and economic wel-fare of the people through socialistic planning. Pakistan's very different situation seems to bring these achievements into a sharper focus. Indeed Pakistan, with a policy of military alliance with the United States which was diame-trically opposed to neutralism, found herself continuously strengthening her military establishment, all based in West Pakistan, until such time that the military leaders usurped the entire state authority to bring the civilian and democratic elements in the country under their subjuga-tion. They, in their arrogance, began to suppress even the most widely shared popular demands and grievances, there-by almost compelling the eventual secession of the eastern province from the Pakistani federation in 1971. India's policy of neutralism, on the other hand, because of its being more or less dependent upon the people's consensus, could reflect and even promote in many instances the repre-sentative character of India's political system even in the teeth of pressures inherent in India's enormously plura-listic society. Indeed, the truth of the statement that "a

---

106 Warren Ilchman, "Political Development and Foreign Policy : The Case of India". *Journal of Commonwealth Political Studies,* IV (November, 1966), 226.

government which denies the national aspirations of its people in the international field is bound to deny them in the domestic sphere"[107] was made manifest by India's leaders by their better representation of national aspirations in the international arena through nonalignment-cum-neutralism. A perceptive Indian commentator has observed : "It may seem ironic but it is true that India's refusal to join the Western camp is also a refusal to repudiate parliamentary democracy at home".[108]

Beyond this particular point, nonalignment-cum-neutralism for India did mean a particular type of defense capability. This point could be understood in the context of India-Pakistan quarrels that degenerated into a general war in 1965. Pakistan, an ally of the USA, fought neutralist India over Kashmir in 1965. Pakistan was almost completely dependent on the US for military supplies. So when the United States Government, on the outbreak of general hostilities, stopped arms shipments to both the belligerents, it was Pakistan, the US ally, who was hurt more than India whose supplies that were purchased came from varied sources, including the Soviet Union. This relative advantage of India could be traced to nonalignment-cum-neutralism. In the case of the Sino-Indian conflict of 1962, too, the actual developments after the brief clash showed that India, which had no prior understanding with the USA or the USSR, could continue to procure arms, through grants, loans or purchases, from various countries, including the arch rivals of the cold war. This indeed facilitated the build-up of India's defenses against China. The above two examples do indeed demonstrate the military significance of neutralism, which one student has put in this way :

It avoids a complete military alliance with any one power in order to permit limited military agreements

---

[107] K. P. Karunakaran, "Domestic and Afro-Asian Requirements", in *India's Nonalignment Policy,* edited by Paul F. Power (Boston : D. C. Heath, 1967), pp. 58-59.

[108] Commentator in question is K. P. Karunakaran. *Ibid.*

with all powers.   Facilitating our armament in this way was not the most original intention of the policy, but it has now become its most cherished advantage.[109] Another related contribution of neutralism centers round the question of defense expenditure. During the period before the Chinese invasion, India's external policy was quite successful in keeping expenditures on defense or military preparedness down, allowing the Government of India to spend a greater share of her budget on nation-building projects.   Only threat to security in the earlier half of the period of our study, as seen by policymakers, came from Pakistan, especially in regard to Kashmir, and this did not require major military expenditures.   The following table[110] reveals the total outlay on defense by the Government of India from 1951 through 1963-64. These figures not only are comparatively low,[111] but also over the first ten years seemed to be remarkably stable. These points could be taken to mean, as they have appeared to mean to George Rosen, that "India was able to carry out its development plans with relatively minor diversion of resources to military purposes and without involving the military in economic planning for development".[112]

All these consequences combined to give India a certain prestige.   Ever since India's successful mediatory role in the Korean imbroglio, many nations, big and small, have at least grudgingly acknowledged India's pre-eminent position as a voice for peace.   This recognition has taken various forms.   In the Korean case itself, all the parties finally agreed to give India the Chairmanship of the Neu-

---

[109] Raj Krishna, "A Need for Nuclear Arms" in *India's Nonalignment Policy*, 49.

[110] The Table is from Eldridge, "India's Nonalignment Policy Reviewed" in *International Politics of Asia*, 138.

[111] In the first years the defense expenditure was as low as 2.4 per cent of the gross domestic output. Even when it reached its peak in 1963-64 it did not exceed 6 per cent when most of the underdeveloped countries spent a greater percentage. See M. S. Rajan, "Nonalignment without Myth" in *India's Nonalignment Policy*, 90.

[112] George Rosen, *Democracy and Economic Change in India* (Berkeley and Los Angeles : University of California Press, 1967), p. 237.

TABLE II

TOTAL INDIAN OUTLAY ON DEFENSE,
1951-52 TO 1963-64

Year	Total Outlay in Crores of Rupees (1 Crore of Rs.=Approx. $2.1.m.)
1951-52	196·45
1955-56	190·00
1956-57	212·00
1957-58	279·00
1959-60	266·00
1960-61	282·00
1961-62	317.00
1962-63	478·00
1963-64 (estimate)	873·00

tral Nations Repatriation Commission ; and the success of India there further contributed to her image. At the end of the Vietnam War in 1954 (signified by the collapse of the French in Dienbienphu), the powers that participated in the Geneva Conference and finally signed the Geneva Agreements felt that peace could not be implemented without the services of India,[113] among others ; thus India was once again chosen the Chairman of the International Control Commissions in Indo-China. India was similarly requested at the end of the Suez Crisis to provide a contingent to keep peace there (this honour became all the

---

113 Although India was not invited to participate in the Conference India's six-point proposal as made by Nehru and the good offices of Krishna Menon, who remained behind the scenes in Geneva throughout the length of the Conference, proved to be of great value in so far as the successful completion of the Conference was concerned. M. Pierre Mendes-France, Premier of France, later acknowledged this Indian help. See Study Group of ICWA, *Aspects of Indian Foreign Policy,* Paper I, pp., 18, 26.

more significant in the face of Arab nations' refusal to accept any contingent from Pakistan, a sister Islamic nation). Finally, in the matter of peacekeeping in the Congo and Cyprus, particularly the first, Indian initiated moves really made the final resolution of the conflict possible. Of the Super Powers, the Soviet Union came to openly advocate, on July 19, that India be given a seat in the proposed five-power summit to deal with the Middle Eastern crisis.[114] Later she came to propose a permanent seat for India in the Security Council of the UN as well. Although nothing came of these proposals, it is reasonable to conclude that India came to occupy a position of considerable prominence in the United Nations. As an influential spokesman of Asia-Africa bloc in the UN, her movements were watched with a great deal of interest, and she was given seats in many of the most important Councils and Committees of the UN (including the Security Council, Trusteeship Council, and the newly constituted, after 1958, UN Disarmament Conference). Many of her representatives came to occupy some of the most prestigious offices in the UN ; Mrs. V. L. Pandit became the President of the General Assembly, Dr. Sarvepalli Radhakrishnan became the UNESCO Chairman, Mr. B. N. Rau became an early Justice of the International Court of Justice at The Hague. Also, a good many UN administrative positions went to prominent Indians, including that of the UN Undersecretary-General (and Chef du Cabinet of U Thant) to C. V. Narasimhan, Director Generalship of the FAO to Dr. B. R. Sen. These do indeed attest to the tremendous prestige that India gained in the world. In the world outside the UN, her sponsorship of the Asian-African Conference in Bandung held in April, 1955 (where 29 nations met) made it possible for the governments of these two continents to move toward some kind of solidarity, boosting at the same time the cause of nonalign-

---

[114] The beginning of the Sino-Soviet rivalry, according to some, could be traced to this date. See V. P. Dutt, "India and China : Betrayal, Humiliation and Reappraisal", 213.

ment-cum-neutralism and the concept of the peace zone. As a result of this her voice as the spokesman for the anti-colonialists acquired greater resonance. This high prestige of India among the Afro-Asians and in the councils of the world continued right up until 1960. India's Goa action might have contributed to her losing a bit of it especially in the Western capitals. But in Africa and Asia, where some of the Western colonies still remained, her stand against Portuguese colonialism boosted her image as the arch anti-colonialist and the friend of all peoples suffering from imperialism-colonialism. But after the disaster striking India in the form of Chinese invasion in 1962, India's prestige as a power to reckon with in military-political, social and economic matters suffered badly, and this was quite evident from the lukewarm support that the fellow neutralist countries gave to India in her cause against the Chinese Communists. And it must be added that India has not yet fully recovered from the blow.

CHAPTER VII

CONCLUDING OBSERVATIONS

In the previous three chapters an attempt was made to outline the contents of India's national interests—strategic (geographic-territorial and general) and tactical, and to find out whether or not those interests were realized during the Nehru era of India's foreign policy, which moved round the pivotal principle (at once an interest by itself) of neutralism in global policies. It could be said, without fear of contradiction, on the basis of our discussion in Chapters V and VI, that India did achieve some notable successes in terms of those national interests. First of all, the main strategic interests, as reflected in such territorial questions as Goa and Kashmir, in the direction of which other foreign powers, e.g., Portugal and Pakistan cast their covetous glances, were indeed mostly satisfied. Goa became undeniably a part and parcel of India, thereby freeing India completely from the vestiges of colonialism for the first time ; in regard to Kashmir, India successfully thwarted the attempts by Pakistan and friends (military allies) to impose a solution (plebiscite for instance) that could only have been detrimental to the interests of India. The success in the latter case however could only be considered tentative and incomplete since Pakistan continued to dispute it as an Indian territory after the period of our study. India's ideology—which comprized nationalism, secularism, anti-colonialism—was thus saved in so far as her victory in Goa and Kashmir could indicate. As regards other aspects of her ideology—that had to do with internal requirements—they were also largely fulfilled. India, a poor country with little propensity to save, got as we have seen much needed capital in the shape of grants and loans and foreign private and public investment. Although the amount received never exceeded 30 per cent of the entire outlay in the first three Five Year Plans, it could be said firmly and unequivocally that without this India would have been in direr straits. It is now known that American economic aid did help in the matter of agriculture, transportation, and generally in keeping alive the prospects of private enterprise in the emerging mixed economy of India. At the same time, the Soviet cooperation with India in economic matters, although comparatively modest in relation to the American aid (the Soviet aid amounting roughly to merely one-fourth the size of the American aid) during the period of our study, proved to be quite useful in supplementing the US and Western aid and in strengthening the Government of India in the matter of controlling the "commanding heights" of the economy. Thus, the concept of the public sector which the Government of India took pains in developing could become a reality ; monopoly of foreign economic interests, particularly in a strategic economic sector such as the petroleum industry in India could be broken only with the support of the Soviets. Other domestic requirements, no less important because they related to ideology[1] —democracy, socialism, nonalignment-cum-neutralism—also could be satisfied, at least up to a certain extent, not wholly but substantially. In this regard, the acceptance by the Communists (the Communist Party of India) of the Indian democratic system, their readiness to operate as a loyal opposition party, loyal not to the Congress Party but to the democratic parliamentary system, contributed to the domestic order, stability and tranquillity. Whatever will to socialism the leaders of the fledgling regime had was, at least, augmented and strengthened, contributing further to the growth of the domestic consensus—it has already been pointed out before how the cause of democratic socialism was helped by the nature of support (economic aid in particular) from both the power blocs.

If successes in strategic matters are quite considerable,

---

[1] For example, Richard Rosecrance says that "on some occasions nations look upon the maintenance of their ideology as important to the maintenance of basic security. Ideology then becomes linked to the more fundamental objective of security". *International Relations : Peace or War ?* (New York : McGraw-Hill, 1973), p. 213.

those were largely brought about by successes in tactical matters. Over the entire period of our study, both the United States and the Union of Soviet Socialist Republics, it has been seen already, retained at least their cool—and to a certain extent developed a bit of warmth too—in their relations with India ; the former by retaining her interest in not alienating the large population of a large country which happened at the same time to be democratic ; the latter (USSR) by positively welcoming the role of non-alignment-cum-neutralism, which was not incorrectly considered by the latter (Soviet Union), as an indication of loss for the Western bloc, since it meant refusal by the nonaligned, especially neutralist India, to join the bloc of their opposition (the US), even though it did not signify any eagerness to join their side (the Soviet). That the USA and the USSR did indeed seem to have some stake in the Indian freedom and security and overall viability was indicated by their support, concrete (military hardware) and political-diplomatic, of India during the latter's conflict with the People's Republic of China in the late 1950s and the early 1960s (and thereafter), particularly after the massive Chinese invasion of India in October-November of 1962. India's efforts in Korea, Suez, Hungary, and the Congo, proved to be of some value in localizing these international conflicts. In Korea her mediatory role led to the arrangement of the ceasefire. In Suez her efforts did help in sealing the fate of colonialism or neo-colonialism ; and, additionally, since these efforts were essentially pro-Arab they might also have helped her in keeping the Moslem Arab nations at least from going to the side of Pakistan[2] and also in getting a measure of political support from the Arabs, particularly the Egyptians, when China

---

[2] It is interesting to note how Pakistan's policymakers took this particular failure. Field Marshal Ayub Khan, former strong man of Pakistan, for one, tried to explain away this failure to establish close affinity with other Moslem countries by saying that "the upsurge in other Muslim countries is, by and large, racial, territorial, anti-imperialistic, and anti-colonial. It is not to any large extent religious". See Mohammed Ayub Khan, "Essentials of Pakistan's Foreign Policy", *Pakistan Horizon*, Fourth Quarter, 1961, p. 263. as cited by Palmer, *South Asia and US Policy*, p. 165.

attacked India in 1962.[3] In the Congo, her role strengthened the United Nations machinery as an instrument of peace and for the protection of independence of the smaller nations recently freed from colonial domination.

Does the above discussion (mostly of successes) mean then that all was well and there was no indication of any failure anywhere ? The answer seems to be : No, there were failures too. In one of the most strategic areas (territorial-geographic), in regard to her northern boundary areas contiguous to the Tibet region of China, India's failure was quite pronounced. Additionally, India lost in 1962, and has not recovered since, valuable territories— about 40,000 square miles—to the Chinese ; but the most precious part was not territory—but her policy of friendship toward China. The Chinese successes against the Indian army in 1962, which were, from the point of view of India, in the nature of military debacle of the first magnitude, led to serious loss of face for India in the Afro-Asian region in particular and the world in general ; and although the sister nonaligned-neutralist nations did give support, it was only a halfhearted effort. The entire episode degenerated into a period of domestic unrest that was unthought of before. Nehru, who until recently or this particular time was almost beyond or above criticism, came under heavy barrage of criticism—he had to bow to the opposition demand for Menon's dismissal from the Defense Ministry ; even more, he had to undergo the ordeal of the first "No Confidence" move against his government in the aftermath of the border crisis ;[4] India's socialism came to be diluted a little ; the split in the Communist Party of India into Nationalist wing (with affiliations with Moscow) and Maoist wing did not paradoxically

---

3 For the role of Egypt in the Sino-Indian dispute, see M. M. Rahman, *The Politics of Nonalignment* (New Delhi : Associated Publishing House, 1969), pp. 214-233.

4 This was in August, 1963 ; although the motion for 'No Confidence' was defeated 346-61, to many observers this marked the end of an era. See Margaret W. Fisher, "India in 1963 : A Year of Travail", *Asian Survey,* IV (March, 1964), p. 742.

enough strengthen the domestic consensus, but simply added
to the potentiality of domestic unrest through the very
split, making at least the Maoist wing irresponsible because
of its helplessness from shrinking support consequent upon
the nationalist upsurge. Defense services came to be given
a much larger share of the national cake, which meant
diversion of scarce resources from nationbuilding projects
that included anti-poverty programs and those for industrialization. India did indeed thus appear to be a flabby
giant, almost a "paper tiger", to China who defeated her,
but also to the other neighbouring countries of Asia and
Africa, to which it appeared that in a competition between
totalitarian way of life as symbolized by China and democracy as represented by India, it is the former that has
greater chance of success, of coming out on top. So, India
lost a great deal of prestige.

Another great failure of India's foreign policy had to
do with Pakistan. It has been noted previously how India
through the support of the Soviet Union came to prevail,
at least up until the end of the Nehru era, over Pakistani
intransigence in regard to Kashmir. But, India's efforts
in the direction of a peaceful resolution of the outstanding
conflicts with Pakistan have largely gone astray. Here
again the United States' disenchantment with India's nonalignment-cum-neutralism based as it was upon a wholly
different image of the post-World War II international
realities has to bear some responsibility. Of course, the
Pakistani and Indian perceptions coloured as they were by
their own conflicting ideologies, one theocratic and the other
secular, were poles apart from the very beginning. But
America's intervention—her bilateral military aid agreement with Pakistan and her inclusion of Pakistan in the
SEATO and other cognate alliance systems (even when
Pakistan made clear in the protocol of the SEATO treaty
that the aid she received from the United States could be
used against *any* adversary, meaning only India)—represented an Indian diplomatic defeat of the first magnitude, since it not only meant the coming of the cold war
to India's borders but also strengthening of the Pakistani
military machine and jingoism with the simultaneous

weakening of the roots of democracy in Pakistan with all that it meant for foreign policy. This meant in effect an effective neutralization, with all its implications, of India's natural dominance in subcontinental politics. It meant more, not less Pakistani hostility toward India, and of course it showed in 1965 in the form of Pakistani aggression over Kashmir. India in short found herself in the regional (South Asian) straitjacket of balance of power.

The question now is : Whether it was indeed non-alignment-cum-neutralism that lay at the root of all these developments. A look at the tactical side of the picture, viz., friendship or lack of it of the two Super Powers— the United States and the Union of Soviet Socialist Republics —with some discernment, will reveal that the United States coolness toward India is not exactly a case of the former *reacting* to Indian nonalignment-cum-neutralism in a certain negative way. For, as some writers have pointed out, even before the development of India's nonalignment-cum-neutralism, India was not seen with sympathetic eyes by some very influential American decision-makers. As early as in January, 1947, John Foster Dulles, who was later to become the Secretary of State under Eisenhower, had said in a speech published in the *New York Herald Tribune* of January 18, 1947, in apparent reference to India's UN complaint against South African Government's racial discrimination, that "in India Soviet Communism exercises a strong influence through the Interim Government". Dulles and other Americans in the decisionmaking processes of their country might have acquired the British prejudices and strategic ideas about India and her people. Americans seemed to imbibe wholesale the ideas of such British strategic thinkers as Sir Olaf Caroe (author of *Wells of Power*) that it was the Muslim world —the whole of the Middle East from Turkey to Pakistan —that was important for the security of the West. This might provide the clue to the American decision to establish the CENTO and to provide military supplies to Pakistan. The Americans seemed to imbibe other British prejudices too, such as, "Nehru a crypto-Communist", Congress a "subversive organization", and Hindus "non-beef-

eaters and (therefore) nonmartial...complex and therefore
unreliable partners".[5] So their assessment of India and
her people was coloured from the very beginning, and thus
the Indian policies were suspect in the US eyes. India's
nonalignment-cum-neutralism that became prominent after
the outbreak of the war in Korea might only have corroborated these suspicions and prejudices, but it did not produce them ; it was *not* the antecedent to the consequent
of US policies. On the other hand, however, the Soviets,
who had previously formed some ideas, on the basis of
their Communist ideology, mostly negative and disdainful
if not worse, regarding India before 1950, decided to respond affirmatively to India's nonalignment-cum-neutralism.
It could be that, without Stalin's death and Khrushchev's
accession to power, this Soviet *démarche* would have been
delayed or its form would have been different ; but that
this would have been taken seems certain. It is India's
nonalignment-cum-neutralism, embraced later on by other
nations of the Third World simply because it reflected so
very adequately their common concerns,[6] that brought
about this change in world affairs, and which proved, from
India's point of view, quite wholesome. But this policy
which also proposed friendship with China did not seem
to bring much dividend in that regard. It has been pointed out before that, in spite of a *bhai-bhai* period in Sino-
Indian relations from 1954 to 1957, India has had to endure
a number of pinpricks, even outright hostile reactions from
China. During and after the Korean imbroglio, in spite
of friendly gestures from India, China continued to be in
turns indifferent, disdainful, and hostile, and this sort of
relationship could only be occasionally assuaged by India's
signing of the Panch Shila Agreement of April, 1954 that
apparently developed the idea of peaceful coexistence as an

---

[5] Subrahmanyan, "US Policy Toward China", 36-43 *passim*.

[6] As Scalapino put it : "Nehru may be the father of neutralism, yet
Nehru for all of his unique qualities, is in a certain sense, a type. In
this sense, there are many Nehrus in Asia—Nehrus without India, Nehru
without Gandhi, Nehrus of right and left, with or without power. They
are a response to the broad forces...." Robert Scalapino, "Neutralism
in Asia", 51.

essential ingredient of nonalignment-cum-neutralism itself. But this very agreement, by normalizing, rather legalizing China's occupation of Tibet, brought China physically nearer India, to the point of making her a 'real' contiguous neighbour. But even then India, instead of thinking in terms of security through military means,[7] continued to stick to certain perceptions about China—of a socialist underdeveloped country that could not, and will not, because of her very socialism and underdevelopment, launch wars of aggression against countries similarly situated—the perceptions which the Chinese did not reciprocate about India.[8] India forgot her own Kautilya and his maxim that a neighbour is apt to be hostile and it is by taking adequate military precautions that such hostility could be met. Arthur Lall, a former leader of the Indian delegation to the United Nations makes this observation about lack of adequate military preparedness :

Even a neutral nation needs military preparedness. India, a nonaligned nation, failed to assemble the

---

[7] India did not exactly seem to be blind to the security threat from China ; but she continued to believe especially in relation to China that that security should or could be had through friendship or anything else that should be left to the politicians to evolve. As late as July, 1962, General K. S. Thimayya for one articulated this belief in this way : "Whereas in the case of Pakistan I have considered the possibility of a total war, I am afraid, I cannot do so in regard to China. I cannot even as a soldier envisage India taking on China in an open conflict on its own. China's present strength in manpower, equipment and aircraft exceeds our resources a hundredfold with the full support of the USSR, and we could never hope to match China in the foreseeable future. It must be left to the politicians and diplomats to ensure our security". Cited by Subrahmanyan, "1962 : The Causes and Lessons", *International Studies,* XI (October, 1969), 161.

[8] It is ironic that Nehru, whose sense of history was profound and who had himself come to the conclusion long before he became his country's Prime Minister that China had always been an expansionist power, reacted to China and conducted his diplomacy in relation to China against his own reading of Chinese history and his own interpretation of the nature of Chinese Communism. As one student views it : "The only explanation seems to be that his sense of history *temporarily* deserted" and added, "The romantic politician in Nehru got the better of Nehru the hardheaded historian". See H. Venkatasubbiah, "An Approach to Sino-Indian Relations", *Asian Affairs,* Vol. 60 (New Series Vol. IV), Part II, p. 148. Nehru himself confessed in the aftermath of Chinese invasion of 1962 : "We were living in an artificial atmosphere of our own creation", see his speech on October 25, 1962—*The Statesman* (Calcutta), October 26, 1962.

15

essential elements of a viable system of national security. The European neutrals base their posture on
what is for their size formidable military preparedness, as in the case of Sweden and Switzerland, or on
international treaty guarantees as in the case of Austria. India fell between two stools ; it neither built
adequate military strength nor sought guarantees.[9]

However, fortunately for India, her period of difficulties with China coincided with the latter's difficulties with
the Soviet Union. It could be pointed out that the Soviet
Union's subsequent friendship for India, itself largely
helped by nonalignment-cum-neutralism and her (Soviet
Union's) readiness to play the diplomatic game by the
Kautilyan maxim,[10] mitigated to a certain extent the failure of India's policy toward the People's Republic of China.
Even so, it must be conceded that India's starry-eyed perceptions—mostly   impractical—continued even when the
Indian leaders found that their Chinese counterparts were
not willing to reciprocate the same vis-a-vis India, and almost brought about the total collapse of the Indian foreign
policy.[11] But India was saved because of the joint response
of the United States and the Union of Soviet Socialist
Republics, which added another shade of meaning to the
concept of nonalignment-cum-neutralism, at least so far
as that of India was concerned, something that has been
variously described as 'bialignment', 'coalignment', and
'equal proximity'. And it must be added that such a development followed almost logically from India's friendship with all, which implied an effort to bring reconciliation
and better understanding between the two Super Powers

---

9 Arthur Lall, "Reinvigorated Nonalignment", *Seminar,* No. 77
(January, 1966), p. 16.

10 Kautilya defined an enemy as that state which is on the frontier
of one's state. Kautilya also defined a friend as that state which is
on the border of the state which is on the border of one's state. K. P.
S. Menon, "Relations with the Soviet Union", *International Studies,* V
(July-October, 1963), p. 155.

11 For a detailed discussion of India's perceptions about China, see
Krishna Prakash Gupta, "Indian Approaches to Modern China—I and
II", *China Report,* VIII (July-August, 1972), 36-51 ; also *ibid.,* VIII
(September-October, 1972), 38-57.

as indeed she wanted to be a bridge between the two. This brought dividends—the big powers developing their own channels of communication—and India became, instead of a mere bridge, an 'area of agreement'.[12]

As regards the Indo-Pakistani situation, although India's difficulties with Pakistan had undoubtedly been exacerbated by the US posture vis-a-vis the Indian subcontinent (bilateral military aid agreement with Pakistan, etc.), the roots of Indo-Pakistani hostility predated any US maneuvering. The whole history, culture, religion, ideology, etc. of the two young states as they seemed to be reflected in the constitutional make-up of them pointed to the inevitability of a clash between the two. So under these circumstances, the failure which was inherent or implicit was made only more obvious by the US intervention.

But the overall picture suggests a success of sorts—for neutralism. It has indeed contributed, with the aid of other international developments, to the loosening of the rigidity of the two Super Powers. This has meant, in effect, that the world has moved from bipolarity of rigid politics, involving no direct dealing between two Super Powers to a situation where they, more relaxed than ever, can deal with each other directly allowing little scope for any mediatory role that neutralism promises. That is to say, the success of this policy required, in a sense, the existence of violent differences between the Super Powers. This condition no longer obtains, thanks to the success of neutralism itself. Relaxation of this bipolar rigidity has to a certain extent facilitated entry of new actors, some

---

[12] Curiously enough here also India found herself in opposition to the PRC. As Sisir Gupta says : "Unlike the inverse relationship that exists between Russo-American and Russo-Chinese relations, Indo-Russian relations can continue to improve only as a part of a broad historical process : the replacement of the present conflict between the United States and the Soviet Union by a phase of cooperative existence. While China has believed in the inevitability of war between the two camps and her foreign policy is based on expediting this crisis, the foreign policy of India aims at the improvement of relations between the United States and the Soviet Union." Cited by Varma, *Struggle for the Himalayas,* p. 225.

of them powerful too, into the world scene. Could non-alignment-cum-neutralism be operative in this kind of new world ? The very success of nonalignment-cum-neutralism thus suggests a possible failure unless it is suitably amended to fit changing circumstances of world politics. The August, 1971 Indo-Soviet Treaty of Peace, Friendship and Cooperation perhaps is based upon this kind of awareness.[13]

Another factor might have contributed to the success of nonalignment-cum-neutralism : the modest nature of India's objectives. Both strategic and tactical interests that India's leaders outlined in order to realize through the chosen instrument of nonalignment-cum-neutralism were not too many, nor too ambitious—the fourth chapter of the present study hopefully adequately attesting to that. India's strategic considerations related to matters close to herself ; some of them were entirely domestic in their import. Tactical interests related only to those global matters that affected the Super Powers. Both these seemed to underscore a rather conservative orientation of India's policymakers. Indeed, it could be argued that India's policymakers were firstly quite realistic ; they cut their coat of national objectives according to the cloth of domestic requirements and military and economic strength. The only exception to their broad realism seems to relate to India's posture toward the Chinese, to which reference

---

[13] The treaty was signed August 9, 1971 in New Delhi by Mr. Swaran Singh, Foreign Minister of India, and Mr. Andrei Gromyko, Foreign Minister of the Soviet Union. The most interesting parts of the treaty are to be found in Art. IV, which reaffirms Soviet support for India's nonalignment. (sic), and in Art. IX, considered to be the operative part of the treaty, which averred that the two sides will "abstain from providing any assistance to any third party that engages in armed conflict with the other party. In the event of either party being subjected to attack or threat thereof, the High Contracting parties shall immediately enter into mutual consultations in order to remove such a threat and to take appropriate effective measures to ensure peace and security of their armies". For an elaborate discussion of the implications of the treaty, see Ashok Kapur, "Indo-Soviet Treaty and the Emerging Asian Balance", *Asian Survey*, XII (June, 1962), 464-465.

has already been made.[14] Secondly, since the Indian leaders intended to utilize (and also to a certain extent solve)
global differences between the Super Powers to achieve their
own national interests, they could not be considered to be
entirely selfish ; they were simply aware that India could
not be separated from the rest of the world, nor divorced
from every internationalist belief or ideal. They were
rather enlightened pursuers of national interest. And
it could be added, much of the success they achieved was
due to this careful, conservative, and modest definition of
national objectives. What would have happened if these
were defined by megalomaniac men harbouring grandilo-
quent ideas or ideals—with the main purpose of project-
ing themselves on to the world scene to reap maximum
publicity and possibly applause for themselves ? Nehru
and his associates who participated in the foreign policy-
making processes of their country were not megalomaniac
men ; they were men with visions of public good—large
yet manageable, based as they were on the reality of domestic and international circumstances. Only occasionally
they showed lapses—in regard for example to perceptions
of China. They might also have failed in the matter of
implementing their goals—there were a number of inexperienced diplomats who were suddenly called upon to
tackle the complexities of international problems.[15] The
limited nature of foreign policy decisionmaking might have

---

[14] Apart from the unrealistic misperceptions that have been referred
to before, there was one more. Ashok Kapur for one suggests that India's
posture toward China was based upon thinking of the British—to have
a balance of power in Central Asia—and this led to their idea of British
Indian 'forward policy'—a combination of preventive diplomacy and military deterrence.   But, Ashok Kapur suggests that "the destruction of
the strategic unity of India after 1947 made this type of thinking obsolete,
yet Nehru held on to this concept.   He underestimated the nature of
threat to India from China while overestimating   Indian potentialities".
Ashok Kapur, "Peace and Power in India's Nuclear Policy", *Asian
Survey*, X (September, 1970), 782.

[15] Bandyopadhyaya, a former member of the Indian Foreign Service,
gives some examples of inexperienced handling of diplomatic problems by
India's diplomats.   See Bandyopadhyaya, *The Making of India's Foreign
Policy*, ch. 4.

allowed such faulty foreign policy perceptions, etc., to continue to go unchecked until the final shock came. The corrective for such defects or deficiencies would certainly be a restructuring of foreign policy decisionmaking with inclusion of more knowledgeable people with expertise in international relations and contingency foreign policy planning far beyond the immediate future.

CONTENTS OF THE SPEECHES WITH THEIR DATES, PLACES, AND SOURCES

Date	Where Made	Source	Interests General and Abstract	Interests Geographical Priorities
1949 March 22	Indian Council of World Affairs, New Delhi	Dorothy Norman, *Nehru—The First Sixty Years* (New York : The John Day Co., 1965), II, 460-471	War and Peace—"indivisible" One World Economics—"basic matter"—Problems of Asia are essentially problems of supplying the primary human necessities. Preservation of Freedom. The whole world wants peace. United Nations. Racial Equality. Our policy should aim primarily at avoiding war or preventing war.	Priority 1: The nearby countries have a special interest in one another, and India must inevitably think in terms of its relations with the countries bordering her by land and sea. These countries : Pakistan, Afganistan, Tibet, China, Nepal, Burma, Malaya, Indonesia and Ceylon. It is inevitable for India and Pakistan to have close relations. We cannot be just indifferent neighbours. Priority 2 : The second place goes to the other countries of Asia with whom we are also fairly intimately connected : China, Middle East, Southeast Asia.

Date	Where Made	Source	Interests General and Abstract	Interests Geographical Priorities
			Nonalignment.	Problem of Indonesia is more important to us than many European problems.
			We want at least ten or fifteen years of peace in order to be able to develop our resources.	Indians in S. Africa.
			Asian problems — primary human necessities.	Freedom of Indonesia—a most vital problem affecting the whole of Australia, Asia, and perhaps America.
			Problem of preserving freedom.	Berlin, Indonesia.
			Economics—the basic matter.	There are two issues which may well lead to conflict on a big scale —Indonesia and Indians in S. Africa. It is a matter of vital significance to the world.
			Racial Equality.	
March 15	New Delhi, Constituent Assembly	Constituent Assembly, *Legislative Debates*, VIII	Promotion of Peace and the avoidance of war.	
			Maintenance of Peace a huge problem.	
			"It ought to be our.... positive policy to overcome the general trend towards war...."	

Date	Where Made	Source	Interests General and Abstract	Interests Geographical Priorities
			"The fundamental problem for an Indian patriot must be necessarily Indian freedom, India's progress, economic and the rest…"	
1950 Feb. 3	New Delhi, House of the People	Parliament, *Parliamentary Debates*, I : 5	War—it is so terrible to contemplate.	South Africa. Pakistan. Kashmir.
Dec. 6	*Ibid.*	*Ibid.,* VI : 17	Peace and War—a matter of greatest import and consequence. We should try our utmost to prevent it.	Relations with Pakistan—"important and subject of primary importance for us".
			Racialism—a vital matter.	Foreign possessions in India—"raise big questions on which we have strong feelings".
			Atomic Bomb—"a symbol of incarnate evil"	"South Africa raised vital issues of racialism."
				Formosa—"not an immediate issue that it must be settled immediately".

Date	Where Made	Source	Interests General and Abstract	Interests Geographical Priorities
				Tibet. Nepal—"With Nepal our relationship is intimate. Every country must realise this intimate, geographical, cultural and other relationship of India and Nepal. We can not risk our own security by anything going wrong in Nepal. Our chief need is peace and stability in Nepal at present.
1951 Feb. 12	*Ibid.*	*Ibid.*, (Pt. 2), VIII : 6	Maintenance of peace in the world...A widespread war is the most terrible disaster and we should strain every nerve to prevent it.	Far Eastern crisis. Europe—"the danger spot". Rearmament of Germany—"the most vital issue in Europe". Korea—another vital issue. The most immediate issue before the Prime Ministers' Conference was that of Korea and other connected issues in Far East. Taiwan—Formosa's reversion to China. China's recognition.

Date	Where Made	Source	Interests General and Abstract	Interests Geographical Priorities
				Tibet—"We did not allow that to affect our policy to maintain friendly relations with the People's Republic of China." "Kashmir is not just a piece of territory to be bartered. It is a struggle of progress against reaction, of a secular nationalism against communalism. If we succumb to the forces of reaction, then we would have failed indeed, for we would have given up everything that has made life worthwhile for us."
Mar. 28	*Ibid.*	*Ibid.*, IX	Nonalignment.	Foreign Possessions in India. Korea. (Far East) Europe. "In our dealings with foreign countries, perhaps the most important country is Pakistan." Kashmir.

Date	Where Made	Source	Interests General and Abstract	Interests Geographical Priorities
1952 June 12	*Ibid.*	*Ibid.*, (Pt. 2) II : 1	Peace. Imperialism danger to Peace. Prevention, avoidance of that disaster, and if comes to obtain a position in which we are able to stop even after it has started. World's Peace. Anti-colonialism — "To colonial rule, wherever it might exist, we are unalterably opposed."	Atlantic Pact (NATO)—"It is not my concern as to what certain other countries do for their defence. It is now a defence of the colonial possessions of those nations and that is a very serious matter, so far as we are concerned". Tunisia. Korea—"It is a matter of concern to us."
Aug. 17	*Ibid.*	*Ibid.*, VI	Peace—"indivisible" "so also is freedom". "No world peace can be built on the denial of freedom to countries…"	

Date	Where Made	Source	Interests General and Abstract	Interests Geographical Priorities
			Racial discrimination—"One of the outstanding problems of today. This overrides national boundaries—an affront to the men and women of Asia and Africa."	
1953 Mar 17	*Ibid.*	*Ibid.*	Colonialism.	Kashmir.
				Burma and Ceylon—"We are deeply interested in the fate of large numbers of people of Indian descent who have gone there in the past."
				Pakistan.
				S. Africa.
				NATO—"If it is a defence of colonialism, then we will react strongly against it."
				Foreign pockets in India—"unthinkable for us to continue".

Date	Where Made	Source	Interests General and Abstract	Interests Geographical Priorities
Dec. 23	Ibid.	Ibid., X:29	Peace—"We passionately seek it, from our point of view and the world's". It is essential.	Korea—"One of the subjects of high importance. It is important especially for us because we have got tied up to that in a variety of ways...". US military aid to Pakistan—"Of great interest and concern to us." Kenya, Africa. Sudanese Elections.
1954 Mar. 15	New Delhi, Lok Sabha	Parliament, Lok Sabha Debates (Pt. 2), II:10	Peace in Asia, in the world. Real importance of this ...is in re. nonaggression, recognition of each other's territorial integrity and sovereignty and non-interference with each other. Peace "for us—an emergent necessity".	French settlements in India. Agreement between India and China in re. Tibet—"a very important event. By this agreement, we ensure to a very large extent peace in a certain area of Asia". Korea. Indo-China-Geneva Conference. "In a sense the fate of Asia depends upon a good deal on what happens in Indo-China or Korea." Tunisia.

Date	Where Made	Source	Interests General and Abstract	Interests Geographical Priorities
			Disarmament.	Morocco.
			Economic problem — "Another matter in which we are deeply interested was the economic problem of S. Asia."	Afro-Asian Conference. Problem of Goa. People of Indian descent in Ceylon.
Sept. 29	*Ibid.*	*Ibid.*, VIII : 3	Rearmament. Peace. War—"a terrible disaster."	India in the Commonwealth. "One of the major issues before the world today is what happens to Germany and German Rearmament". Geneva Conference on Indo-China, Korea. NATO—"It was for defence, but today it covers Goa too in its scope. I do submit that when decisions are made of vital significance excluding the views of the vital part of the vital area, then there is something wrong in that very procedure".

Date	Where Made	Source	Interests General and Abstract	Interests Geographical Priorities
				SEATO, NATO—"Unless something is done to it, it will become more and more harmful to the interests of peace in S. E. Asia and the world at large".
				Quemoy—"If war occurs, it would be a terrible disaster for the whole world."
				Recognition of People's Republic of China—"One of the biggest factors towards ensuring security in SE Asia and in the Far East."
				Ceylon.
				Pondicherry, Goa.
1955 Mar. 31	*Ibid.*	Ministry of External Affairs, *Foreign Affairs Record,* I:3 (March, 1955)	"Asian and African countries obviously aim at two things—peace and opportunity to progress. We want peace in the world."	Indo-China—"a most extraordinary situation."
				Formosa and mainland China—"a very dangerous situation".
				Middle East.
				Rearmament of Germany.

Date	Where Made	Source	Interests General and Abstract	Interests Geographical Priorities
			"All I want is to be left in peace to work for the destinies of my country".	South Africa—"Racialism and racial separation may become more dangerous than any other problem that the world has to face."
			"Interested in the peace of the world—it is of high importance to my country."	Goa and Ceylon—"Our immediate problems."
			"War—if there is war all over the world, we cannot escape the consequences...."	Kashmir—"a very big question. It is not a thing to be bandied about ...it has a soul of its own."
			Comm/Anti-comm—	
			Important.	
			Rearmament.	
			Disarmament.	
			Panchshila.	
			Racialism.	

Date	Where Made	Source	Interests General and Abstract	Interests Geographical Priorities
Mar. 29	*Ibid.*	*Ibid.*, II : 3 (March, 1956)	War Disarmament. Disarmament. Question of economic growth—"good deal of importance to SUN-FED".	West Asia (Middle East)—"a very explosive region of the world—conflicts between Israel and the Arab countries and the region of the Bagdad Pact." Indo-China. Commonwealth. Baghdad and SEATO—"wrong, dangerous, and harmful." "They affect us intimately and in a sense tend to encircle us from two or three directions." Pakistan, Kashmir—"Even if Kashmir had not acceded to India, then too it would be our duty to defend it, India being a continuing entity."
1956 July 31	*Ibid.*	*Ibid.*, II : 7 (July, 1956)	Promotion of Peace. Disarmament.	"Significance of Asia ; of the situation in Middle East and Far East."

Date	Where Made	Source	Interests General and Abstract	Interests Geographical Priorities
			Improvement in the standards of life.	"The problem of German Unity"
			Recognition of Parliamentary Government as a hertiage.	China's cooperation "imperative for peace".
			Freedom and self-government.	"Just and peaceful solution of the problem of Algeria."
			Furtherance of economic devolopment.	
			The "basic aims" of preserving and strengthening peace.	
1957 Mar. 25	*Ibid.*	*Ibid.*, III : 3 (March, 1957)	Hydrogen Bombs and Nuclear Weapons.	Middle East—"a very serious situation in Egypt, because of a military invasion of Egypt".
			Disarmament — "Real reason for it is that without this there would	Also, in Central Europe a serious situation has been created in Hungary.

Date	Where Made	Source	Interests General and Abstract	Interests Geographical Priorities
			be utter disaster—economic development would be frustrated."	"Looking at the whole picture as it is today, ME might be said to be the most difficult and potentially explosive region."
				SEATO and Baghdad Pacts—"these two naturally affect us, India, much more intimately and directly than any other pact" "were directed against us in Kashmir". "The NATO alliance or Warsaw pact, we can view distantly."
				Indo-China-Vietnam Peace.
				Ghana's independence.
				Poland.
				Kashmir issue.
				Goa—"live and vital issue" "affects us deeply."

Date	Where Made	Source	Interests General and Abstract	Interests Geographical Priorities
Sept. 2	*Ibid.*	*Ibid.*, III : 9 (September, 1957)	World Peace. Colonialism.	Middle East—"At the present moment, probably, that is the most difficult and explosive part of the world surface." "In connection with the Suez Canal or intervention of other powers in which we were interested, if you like emotionally interested, but ultimately, politically interested..." "Dangerous and explosive situation" in Syria. Pakistan-military aid—"it has an immediate direct effect, and adverse effect on us." Goa "affects us—where India's interests are directly threatened, whether in Goa or in Pakistan, we must have our say, a loud say, a positive say. There we cannot remain quiet". Commonwealth.

Date	Where Made	Source	Interests General and Abstract	Interests Geographical Priorities
1958 **April 9**	*Ibid.*	*Ibid.*, IV : 4 (April, 1958)	Peace. Racial Discrimination	"the most important thing is Disarmament" "Questions of most immediate concern to us are, if I may say so, two or three—the matters re. Pakistan, Goa (and in a different category the question of racial discrimination in) S. Africa..." "At least as much import as any other matter is this question of racial conflict..."
Aug. 14	*Ibid.*	*Ibid.*, IV : 8 (August, 1958)	*Panchshila.*	Middle East—"Our sympathies are with Arab countries." "Element of danger in the relations between the Arab countries and Israel. Only when the other problems of W. Asia have advanced towards a solution and present day passions have cooled...can this difficulty be tackled."

Date	Where Made	Source	Interests General and Abstract	Interests Geographical Priorities
1959 Mar. 17	Ibid.	Ibid., V : 3 (March, 1959)	War Peace	"From the world point of view, the biggest problem, judged from the point of war or peace, is still the problem of Berlin in Germany..."
				Middle East—"recriminations between Iraq and the UAR—unfortunate and most deplorable."
				Africa—"Continued colonial domination. For us there is an emotional feeling too about it, because having gone through the same mill we react constantly to something happening elswhere."
				S. Africa—"Atavistic activities of emotion and feeling..can only lead to utmost disaster in Africa and elswhere. We might have to face a most terrible catastrophe."
				Tibet.

Date	Where Made	Source	Interests General and Abstract	Interests Geographical Priorities
				US Pact of mutual aid with Pakistan—"They bring insecurity."
				Baghdad Pact—"Symbol of disturbance."
				SEATO—"has not functioned very much though it has been on paper very much."
1960 Feb. 22	Ibid.	Ibid., VI : 2 (February, 1960)	Disarmament—"a matter of tremendous significance."	"This very important issue relating to our border, relating to the intrusion of Chinese forces on our territory and recent steps taken in regard to this matter."
			World Peace.	Revolutionary upheavals in Africa—"a most important thing in the world." "A big thing".
Aug. 31	Ibid.	Ibid., VI : 8 (August, 1960)	"The most vital question in the world today is that of disarmament."	"Leaving aside disarmament, the most significant features of the world today are these developments in Africa."

Date	Where Made	Source	Interests General and Abstract	Interests Geographical Priorities
			"Disarmament has become of the most urgent consequence, because of nuclear weapons.... it was important before, but now it has assumed an importance which is quite different from the previous we looked upon it."	"A measure of anxiety re. more especially the Congo."
				Algerian freedom.
				Potuguese Africa—"Apart from our direct interest in...Goa obviously—that has an indirect effect on that too."
				Pakistan.
				"Another international question that affects us in India is that of our border with China or Tibet."
1961 April 3	Ibid.	Ibid., VII : 4 (April, 1961)		Pakistan, Afganistan, Nepal, Ceylon, Malaya, Burma—"Our nearest neighbours." "We have always tried to send our leading and most distinguished ambassadors to the neighbouring countries, more especially to Pakistan, Burma, China...." Nepal—"a very import-

Date	Where Made	Source	Interests General and Abstract	Interests Geographical Priorities
				ant post in our foreign service, and that applies to some extent, to Burma also and to roundabout countries."
				Africa-Congo—"is a very big matter today in world affairs—in itself it is big because it affects the whole of Africa, and naturally all the newly independent countries of Africa."
Dec. 7	Ibid.	Ibid., VII : 12 (December, 1961)		China—its border aggression—"It is of the most profound importance to us."
				Goa—"this is a far more important subject, except one subject" (China presumably) "This is of the highest importance."
				China—"We are constantly thinking about it." Algeria.

Date	Where Made	Source	Interests General and Abstract	Interests Geographical Priorities
1962 Mar. 19	Ibid.	Ibid., VIII : 3 (March, 1962)	Disarmament — "The most important thing at present happening on the world stage. We feel strongly about Disarmament." War—"Looking at it even in the context of disarmament and all that is happening in the world, it would be utter absence of prudence to rush into some step, the end of which we can't see."	Algeria. Goa—"What I want to lay stress on is this, that Goa was part of our struggle for independence as much as any other part." "Chinese agression is serious : No country with any self-respect can ignore such a problem." China-India conflict—"It is not an easy matter for any responsible person the kind of long term hostility with a permanent neighbour."
May 14	Ibid.	Ibid., VIII : 5 (May, 1962)	Peaceful settlement. Disarmament.	European Common Market—"It is not good for us. . . it will do us some harm." Commonwealth.

Date	Where Made	Source	Interests General and Abstract	Interests Geographical Priorities
				Tibet. Algeria. Chinese Border. Pondicherry.
				Berlin—"another important question which lies behind Disarmament is the Berlin issue. If Berlin issue is solved, there is no doubt that a very big step will have been taken."
				India-China Border Question—"Any war between India and China is going to be tremendously disastrous affair."
1963 Sept. 2-3	New Delhi, Rajya Sabha	*Ibid.* IX : 9 (September 1963)	Nuclear Test Ban Treaty —"A most important thing."	Sino-Indian Conflict.
			Partial Test Ban Treaty —"Highly important."	Pakistan—"In regard to both, any understanding should be according to our honour, integrity, and all that."

Date	Where Made	Source	Interests General and Abstract	Interests Geographical Priorities
			Nonalignment—"a vital apporach."	Kashmir—"Handing over Kashmir to Pakistan, will be the death of India and the ruin of Kashmir."
			"We attach great importance to nonalignment... We arrived at a state when any other policy may lead to world disaster."	China and Pakistan—"It is obvious that International affairs, so far as we are concerned, we are largely affected by our conflict with China and to some extent our strained relations with Pakistan."
				Sino-Soviet Schism—"It is a matter of world importance. It has an effect on the Sino-Indian conflict."
				Vietnam—"is not so much of world importance as of local importance."
				Sino-Indian conflict—"A solution can only be in keeping with our honour, self-respect, and integrity."
				China—"We cannot take a risk and we must prepare ourselves with all our strength to meet such contingencies as might arise."

Date	Where Made	Source	Interests General and Abstract	Interests Geographical Priorities
Mar. 19	New Delhi, Lok Sabha	*Ibid.,* IX : 3 (March, 1963)	Peace—"Essential" "important to us".	Africa.
				China—"The mentality of peace must remain there all the same, not with China, but with the whole world."
			Elimination of colonial control.	"I still stand for peace, but I have to fight a war if China attacks."
			Disarmament.	
			Communism/Anti-Communism.	Nepal—"No change of attitude." Admission of PRC in UN.
				Sino-Soviet relations—"This is the biggest question in the world today."
				Chinese occupation of Tibet—"partially a threat to us."
1964 Feb. 19	*Ibid.,* Speaker : L. B. Shastri (Minister Without Portfolio)	*Ibid.,* X : 2 (February, 1964)	Disarmament.	Kashmir.
				Chinese Border Aggression.

Date	Where Made	Source	Interests General and Abstract	Interests Geographical Priorities
April 13	Ibid.	Ibid., X : 4 (April, 1964)	"Nonalignment is not a basic policy of ours". "It is a reaction to events."	"Our chief concern, for the present, is about our two neighbors, China and Pakistan."
			Disarmament—"This is of vital consequence to the world."	"But such settlements must be in keeping with the honour and integrity of India."
			Peaceful settlement.	Pakistan.
				Colombo proposals.
				Seventh Fleet in the Indian Ocean.

BIBLIOGRAPHY

Government Publications

India. Constituent Assembly. *Legislative Debates,* 1947-1949. Delhi : Government of India Press.

————. Ministry of External Affairs. *Foreign Affairs Record* (monthly). 1955-1964.

————. ————. *India, 1961 : Annual Review.* London : Information Service of India, no year.

————. Ministry of Information and Broadcasting. *Jawaharlal Nehru's Speeches 1949-1953,* II ; *1953-1957,* III ; *1957-1963,* IV. Delhi : Government of India Press, 1953, 1954, 1958, 1964.

————. ————. *India's Foreign Policy : Selected Speeches of Nehru, September, 1946 to April, 1961.* Delhi : Government of India Press, 1961.

————. Parliament (Lok Sabha Secretariat). *Lok Sabha Debates,* 1954-56. New Delhi : Government of India Press.

————. ———— (Secretariat). *Parliamentary Debates,* 1950-1954. New Delhi : Government of India Press.

————. Planning Commission. *The First Five Year Plan.* New Delhi : Government of India Press, 1951.

————. ————. *The Second Five Year Plan.* New Delhi : Government of India Press, 1956.

————. ————. *The Third Five Year Plan.* New Delhi : Government of India Press, 1961.

United States. Department of State. *Bulletin.* XXIV, January 29, 1951.

————. ————. ————. XXXIV, June 18, 1956.

United Nations Documents

Department of Public Information. *Yearbook of the United Nations, 1950, 1951 1952.* New York : Columbia University Press, 1951, 1952, 1953.

General Assembly. *Official Records.* Fifth Session, 1950.

————. ————. Sixth Session, 1951.

————. ————. Seventh Session, 1952.

————. ————. Eleventh Session, 1956.

————. ————. First Emergency Special Session, November, 1956.

————. ————. Second Emergency Special Session, November, 1956.

————. ————. Twelfth Session, 1957.

————. ————. Fifteenth Session, 1960.

————. Verbatim Record of 564th Mtg., November 4, 1956.

————. Verbatim Record of 577th Mtg., November 9, 1956.

————. Verbatim Record of 587th Mtg., November 21, 1956.

————. Verbatim Record of 608th Mtg., December 4, 1956.

————. Verbatim Record of 618th Mtg., December 12, 1956.

————. Verbatim Record of 636th Mtg., January 10, 1957.

UN Doc. A/1365, September 19, 1950.

————. A/C. 1/572, October 4, 1950.

————. A/C. 1/641, December 12, 1950.

————. Resolution 384(V), December 14, 1950.

————. Resolution 498(V), February 1, 1950.

————. Resolution 610(VII), December 3, 1952.

————. A/PV 571, November 9, 1956.

————. A/3368, November 19, 1956.

————. A/PV 576, November 21, 1956.

————. A/PV 608, December 4, 1956.

————. A/PV 618, December 12, 1956.

17

UN Doc. A/PV 636, January 10, 1957.

————. A/4510, September 20, 1960.

————. A/Res/1599, April, 1961.

————. A/Res/1619, April 21, 1961.

Security Council. *Official Records.* Third Year, 1948.

————. ————. Fifth Year, 1950.

————. ————. Eleventh Year, 1956.

————. ————. Twelfth Year, 1957.

————. ————. Sixteenth Year, 1961.

UN Doc. S/995, August 2, 1948.

————. S/1501, June 25, 1950.

————. S/1511, June 27, 1950.

————. S/3675, October 13, 1956.

————. S/3712, October 29, 1956.

————. S/3719, October 31, 1956.

————. S/PV 752, November 2, 1956.

————. S/PV 754, November 4, 1956.

————. S/3779, January 24, 1957.

————. S/3787, February 19, 1957.

————. S/3793, February 21, 1957.

————. S/3821, April 29, 1957.

————. S/3911, November 16, 1957.

————. S/4387, July 14, 1960.

————. S/4405, July 22, 1960.

————. S/4741, February 21, 1961.

————. S//5002, November 24, 1961.

BOOKS

Appadorai, A. *Indian Political Thinking : From Naoroji to Nehru.* Madras : Oxford University Press, 1971.

Arora, Satish K. and Lasswell, Harold. *Political Communication : The Public Language of Political Elites in India and the USA.* New York : Holt Rinehart, Winston, 1969.

Austin, Granville. *The Indian Constitution : The Cornerstone of a Nation.* Oxford : Clarendon Press, Oxford University Press, 1966.

Bains, J. S. *India's International Disputes.* Bombay : Asia Publishing House, 1962.

Bandyopadhyay, Jayantanuja. *The Making of India's Foreign Policy.* Bombay, Calcutta : Allied Publishers, 1970.

Baxter, Craig. *The Jana Sangh : The Biography of an Indian Political Party.* Philadelphia : University of Pennsylvania Press, 1969.

Berkes, Ross N., and Bedi, Mohinder Singh. *The Diplomacy of India : Indian Foreign Policy in the United Nations.* Stanford : Stanford University Press, 1958.

Bhutto, Zulfiqar Ali. *Foreign Policy of Pakistan,* Karachi. Pakistan Institute of International Affairs, 1964.

Brecher, Michael. *India and World Politics : Krishna Menon's World View.* New York : Praeger, 1968.

————. *Nehru : A Political Biography.* London : Oxford University Press, 1959.

————. *The New States of Asia : A Political Analysis.* London : Oxford University Press, 1966.

Burton, J. *International Relations : A General Theory.* Cambridge : Cambridge University Press, 1965.

————, ed. *Nonalignment.* London : Andre Deutsch, 1966.

Burton, J. "Nonalignment and Stability."
Sidhanta, Ramjana, "India's Nonalignment."

Calvocoressi, Peter. *Survey of International Affairs, 1949-50.* London : Royal Institute of International Affairs, 1951.

Cohn, George. *Neo-Neutrality.* New York : Columbia University Press, 1939.

Crabb, Cecil V. *The Elephants and the Grass.* New York : Praeger, 1965.

Crankshaw, Edward. *The New Cold War : Moscow vs. Peking.* Baltimore : Penguin Books, 1963.

Das, M. N. *The Political Philosophy of Nehru.* London : Allen and Unwin, 1961.

Dutt, V. P. *China and the World : An Analysis of Communist China's Foreign Policy.* New York : Praeger, 1964.

Eekelen, W. F. Van. *Indian Foreign Policy and the Border Dispute with China.* The Hague : Martinus Nijhoff, 1964.

Gupta, Karunakar. *India in World Politics : A Period of Transition.* Calcutta : Scientific Book Agency, 1969.

Gupta, Sisir. *Kashmir—A Study in India-Pakistan Relations.* Bombay : Asia Publishing House for Indian Council of World Affairs, 1966.

Halle, Louis J. *The Cold War as History.* New York : Harper and Row, 1967.

Halpern, A. M., ed. *Policies Toward China : Views from Six Continents.* New York : McGraw-Hill for Council on Foreign Relations, 1965.

Hammond, Paul Y. *The Cold Years : American Foreign Policy Since 1945.* New York : Harcourt, Brace, and World, Inc., 1965.

Hanson, Arthur H. *The Process of Planning : A Survey of India's Five Year Plans*. London : Oxford University for Royal Institute of International Affairs, 1966.

Hoskyns, Catherine. *The Congo Since Independence, January 1960—December 1961*. Oxford : Royal Institute of International Affairs, Oxford University Press, 1965.

Indian Council on Current Affairs. *Foreign Aid : A Symposium, A Survey, An Appraisal*. Calcutta : Oxford Book and Stationery, 1968.

Indian Council of World Affairs (Study Group). *Aspects of Indian Foreign Policy*. New Delhi : the author, 1958.

Verma, S. N. "Trends in India's Foreign Policy 1954-57" (Paper No. 1).

———. *Defence and Security in the Indian Ocean Area*. New Delhi : the author, 1958 (India Paper No. 4).

Jan, George P. *International Politics of Asia : Readings*. Belmont, California : Wadsworth Publishing Co., 1969.

Eldridge, P. J. "India's Nonalignment Policy Reviewed".

Jansen, G. H. *Nonalignment and the Afro-Asian States*. New York : Praeger, 1966.

Karunakaran, K. P. *India in World Affairs : February 1950 to December 1953*. London : Oxford University Press, 1958.

Kavic, Lorne J. *India's Quest for Security*. Berkeley : University of California, 1967.

Khrushchev, Nikita S. *Khrushchev Remembers*. Boston : Little Brown and Co., 1970.

Kidron, Michael. *Foreign Investments in India*. London : Oxford University Press, 1965.

Kundra, J. S. *Indian Foreign Policy, 1947-1954.* Groningen, Netherlands, J. B. Wolters, 1955.

Lamb, Alastair. *The Kashmir Problem.* New York : Praeger, 1966.

Lasswell, Harold ; Lerner, Daniel ; and Sola Pool, Ethiel de. *The Comparative Study of Symbols.* Stanford : Stanford University Press, 1952.

Lefever, Ernest E. *Crisis in the Congo : A United Nations Force in Action.* Washington, D. C. : Brookings Institution, 1965.

Lerche, Charles O. *The Cold War and After.* Englewood Cliffs, New Jersey : Prentice-Hall, Inc., 1965.

Lewis, John P. *Quiet Crisis in India : Economic Development and American Policy.* Garden City, New York : Anchor Books, Doubleday and Co., 1964.

London, Kurt. *The Making of Foreign Policy East and West.* Philadelphia and New York : J. B. Lippincott, 1965.

Lyon, Peter. *Neutralism.* Leicester : Leicester University Press, 1963.

Macridis, Roy C., ed. *Foreign Policy in World Politics.* Englewood Cliffs, New Jersey : Prentice-Hall Inc., 1967.

Aspaturian, Vernon C. "Soviet Foreign Policy".

Mallik, Dev Narayan. *The Development of Nonalignment in India's Foreign Policy. Allahabad :* Chaitanya Publishing House, 1967.

Martin, Laurence, ed. *Neutralism and Nonalignment.* New York : Praeger, 1962.

Good, Robert C. "Statebuilding as a Determinant of Foreign Policy".

Lefever, Ernest. "Nehru and Nkrumah on Neutralism."

Liska, George. "The Third Party : The Rationale of Nonalignment".

Wilcox, Francis. "The Nonaligned States and the United Nations".

Maxwell, Neville. *India's China War*. New York : Pantheon Book, 1970.

Mende, Tibor. *Nehru*. New York : Braziller, Inc., 1956.

Menon, K. P. S. *Many Worlds*. Bombay : Oxford University Press, 1965.

Moraes, Frank. *Jawaharlal Nehru*. New York : MacMillan Co., 1958.

Morris-Jones, W. H. *The Government and Politics of India*. London : Hutchinson University Library, 1971.

Mukerjee, Sadhan. *Who Really Aids India : The USA or the USSR ?* New Delhi : People's Publishing House, 1972.

Murti, B. S. N. *Nehru's Foreign Policy*. New Delhi : Beacon, 1953.

Murty, K. Satchidananda. *Indian Foreign Policy*. Calcutta : Scientific Book Agency, 1964.

————. *Readings in Indian History, Politics and Philosophy*. London : George Allen and Unwin, 1967.

Nehru, Jawaharlal. *A Bunch of Old Letters*. New York : Asia Publishing House, 1960.

————. *Discovery of India*. London : Meridian Books, 1951.

————. *Independence and After : A Collection of Speeches*, I. New York : The John Day Co., 1950.

————. *The Unity of India : Collected Writings, 1937-1940*, Third Impression. London : Lindsay Drummond, 1948.

Norman, Dorothy, ed. *Nehru : The First Sixty Years*, II. New York : The John Day Co., 1965.

Overstreet, Gene, and Windmiller, Marshall. *Communism in India*. Berkeley and Los Angeles : University of California Press, 1959.

Palmer, Norman D. *South Asia and the United States Policy*. Boston : Houghton Mifflin Co., 1966.

Panikkar, K. M. *The Problems of Indian Defence*. Bombay : Asia Publishing House, 1960.

————. *In Two Chinas : Memoirs of a Diplomat*. London : Allen and Unwin, 1955.

————. *India and the Indian Ocean*. London : George Allen and Unwin, 1951.

Poplai, S. L., ed. *Select Documents on Asian Affairs : India 1947-1950*, I. Bombay : Oxford University Press ?

Power, Paul F., ed. *India's Nonalignment Policy : Strengths and Weaknesses*. Boston : D. C. Heath Co., 1967.
Edwards, Michael. "Illusions of the Nehru Bequest."
Karunakaran, K. P. "Domestic and Afro-Asian Requirements."
Krishna, Raj. "A Need for Nuclear Arms."
Rajan, M. S. "Nonalignment Without Myth."

Rajkumar, N. V. *The Background of India's Foreign Policy*. New Delhi : All India Congress Committee, 1952.

Rahman, M. M. *The Politics of Non-Alignment*. New Delhi : Associated Publishing House, 1969.

Range, Willard. *Jawaharlal Nehru's World View*. Athens : University of Georgia Press, 1961.

Rosecrance, Richard. *International Relations : Peace or War ?* New York : McGraw-Hill Book Co., 1973.

Rosen, George. *Democracy and Economic Change in India*. Berkeley : University of California Press, 1967.

Rothermund, Indira. *The Philosophy of Restraint*. Bombay : Popular Prakashan, 1963.

Rowland, John. *A History of Sino-Indian Relations : A Hostile Coexistence*. Princeton, New Jersey : D. Van Nostrand, Inc., 1967.

Rubinstein, Alvin Z. *The Foreign Policy of the Soviet Union*. New York : Random House, 1960. Varga, E. "A Post-Stalinist View of India."

Sarbadhikari, Pradip R. *India and the Great Powers : A Study of the Politics of Nonalignment and of India's Relations with the USA and the USSR, 1947-1961*. London : By the Author. Printed in the Netherlands by J. C. Baan, The Hauge, 1962.

Sayeed, Khalid B. *The Political System of Pakistan*. Boston : Houghton Mifflin Co., 1967.

Schuman, Frederick L. *International Politics*, Seventh Edition. New York : McGraw-Hill, 1969.

Segal, Ronald. *The Anguish of India*. New York : Stein and Day, 1965.

Selltiz, Claire *et al*. *Research Method in Social Relations*. New York : Holt, Rinehart and Winston, 1967.

Sengupta, Bhabani. *Communism in Indian Politics*. New York : Columbia University Press, 1972.

————. *The Fulcrum of Asia*. New York : Pegasus, 1970.

Sheean, Vincent. *Nehru : The Years of Power*. New York : Random House, 1960.

Sherwani, Latif Ahmed. *India, China and Pakistan*. Karachi : Council for Pakistan Studies, 1967.

Siegel, Richard. *Evaluating the Results of Foreign Policy : Soviet and American Efforts in India*, Denver : University of Colorado, 1969.

Sinha, S. L. N. *Development with Stability : The Indian Experiment*. Bombay : Vora and Co., 1963.

Sitaramayya, B. Pattabhi. *History of the Indian National Congress*, I and II. Bombay : Padma Publications, 1946.

Soon Sung Cho. *Korea and World Politics*. Berkeley : University of California, 1967.

Stein, Arthur. *India and the Soviet Union : The Nehru Era*. Chicago : University of Chicago Press, 1969.

Stoessinger, John. *The Might of Nations*. Third Edition. New York : Random House, Inc., 1969.

————. *The United Nations and the Super Powers*. Second Edition. New York : Random House Inc., 1970.

Streeten, Paul, and Lipton, Michael. *The Crisis in Indian Planning*. London : Oxford University Press, 1968.

Tagore, Rabindranath. *Nationalism*. London : Macmillan, 1920.

Talbot, Phillips, and Poplai, S. L. *India and America : A Study of their Relations*. New York : Published for Council on Foreign Relations by Harper and Bros., 1958.

Tansky, Leo. *US and USSR Aid to Developing Countries : A Comparative Study of India, Turkey and the UAR*. New York : Praeger, 1967.

Tyson, Geoffrey. *Nehru : The Years of Power*. London : Pall Mall, 1966.

Verma, Shanti Prasad. *Struggle for the Himalayas*. Jullundur, Ambala : University Publishers, 1968.

Weekes, Richard. *Pakistan : Birth and Growth of a Muslim Nation*. New York : The Asia Library, 1964.

Whiting, Allen. *China Crosses the Yalu*. Stanford : Stanford University Press, 1960.

Wint, Guy. *The British in Asia*. London : Faber and Faber, 1947.

ARTICLES

Anabtawi, Samir. "Neutralists and Neutralism." *Journal of Politics,* XXVII (May, 1965), pp. 351-361.

Bailey, David H. "Public Protest and the Political Process in India." *Pacific Affairs,* XLII (Spring, 1969), pp. 5-16.

Bajpai, G. S. "India and the Balance of Power." *Indian Yearbook of International Affairs,* 1952, II. Madras : University of Madras, 1952, pp. 1-8.

Berkes, Ross N. "India and the Communist World." *Current History,* XXXVI (March, 1959), pp. 146-152.

Bell, Coral. "Nonalignment and the Balance of Power." *The Australian Outlook,* XVII (August, 1963), pp. 117-129.

Bowles, Chester. "America and Russia in India." *Foreign Affairs,* XLIX (July, 1971), pp. 636-651.

Bozeman, Adda. "India's Foreign Policy : Reflections Upon Its Source." *World Politics,* X (January, 1958), pp. 256-73.

Brecher, Michael. "Neutralism : An Analysis." *International Journal,* XVII (1961-62), pp. 224-36.

Brown, Judith. "Foreign Policy Decision-making and the Indian Parliament." *Journal of Constitutional and Parliamentary Studies,* III (April-June, 1969), pp. 15-52.

Burton, J. W. "Rights and Obligations of Nonalignment." *The Australian Outlook,* XVI (December, 1962), pp. 292-303.

C. K. "Review of Ross N. Berkes and Mohinder Singh Bedi, The Diplomacy of India." *India Quarterly,* XVI (April-June, 1960).

Choucri, Nazli. "The Nonalignment of Afro-Asian States : Policy, Perception, and Behavior." *Canadian Journal of Political Science,* II (March, 1969), pp. 1-17.

Deshpande, N. R. "National Interests and India's Policy of Nonalignment." *Indian Journal of Political Science,* XXV (January-March, 1964), pp. 68-75.

Devdutt. "Nonalignment and India." *Indian Journal of Political Science,* XXIII (1962), pp. 380-397.

———. "A Reappraisal of Nonalignment." *United Asia.* XV (November, 1963), pp. 765-778.

Ehrenfels, U. R. "The Culturological Approach to Nonalignment." *The Indian Yearbook of International Affairs, 1955,* IV. Madras : University of Madras Press, 1955, pp. 124-36.

Fick, Holla. "From Neutralism to Nonalignment." *The Spectator,* No. 6960, September 8, 1961.

Erdman, Howard L. "The Foreign Policy Views of the Indian Right." *Pacific Affairs,* XXXIX (Spring and Summer, 1966), pp. 5-18.

Fisher, Margaret W. "Goa in Wider Perspective." *Asian Survey,* II (April, 1962), pp. 3-10.

———. "India in 1963 : A Year of Travail." *Asian Survey,* IV (March, 1964).

Frankel, Francine R. "Ideology and Politics in Economic Planning : The Problem of Indian Agricultural Development Strategy." *World Politics,* XIX (July, 1967), pp. 621-645.

Frankenstein, Marc. "Les Initiatives de l'Inde pour le Réglement du Conflit Coréen." *Revue Politique et Parlementaire,* CCIIICCV (1951), pp. 53-62.

Gupta, Krishna Prakash. "Indian Approaches to Modern China—I." *China Report,* VIII (July-August, 1972), pp. 36-51.

————. "Indian Approaches to Modern China—II." *China Report*, VIII (September-October, 1972), pp. 38-57.

Hansen, Eric. "The Impact of the Border War on Indian Perceptions of China." *Pacific Affairs*, XL (Fall and Winter, 1967-1968), pp. 235-249.

Henderson, William. "The Roots of Neutralism in Southern Asia." *International Journal*, XIII (Winter, 1957-58), pp. 30-40.

Ilchman, Warren F. "Political Economy of Foreign Aid : The Case of India." *Asian Survey*, VII (October, 1967), pp. 667-688.

————. "Political Development and Foreign Policy : The Case of India." *Journal of Commonwealth Political Studies*, IV.

Jain, G. L. "Indian Nonalignment and the Balance of Power." *India Quarterly*, XLII (April-June, 1966), pp. 177-179.

Jangam, R. T. "The Problem of Neutrality in World Politics." *United Asia*, XIII (1961), pp. 145-150.

Kapur, Ashok. "Indo-Soviet Treaty and the Emerging Asian Balance." *Asian Survey*, XII (June, 1972), pp. 463-474.

————. "Peace and Power in India's Nuclear Policy." *Asian Survey*, X (September, 1970), pp. 779-788.

Karunakaran, K. P. "Nonalignment." *Seminar*, No. 19 (March, 1961).

Korbel, Josef. "Danger in Kashmir." *Foreign Affairs*, XXXII (April, 1954), pp. 482-490.

Lall, Arthur. "Reinvigorated Nonalignment." *Seminar*, No. 77 (January, 1966), pp. 15-18.

Levi, Werner. "Indian Neutralism Reconsidered." *Pacific Affairs*, XXXVII (Summer, 1964), pp. 137-147.

Lyon, Peter. "Neutralism and the Emergence of the Concept of Neutralism." *The Review of Politics*, XXII (April, 1960), pp. 255-268.

Mack, Doris, and Mack, Robert T. "Indian Foreign Policy Since Independence." *Australian Outlook*, XI (March, 1957), pp. 23-32.

Menon, K. P. S. "India's Relations with the Soviet Union." *International Studies*, V (July-October, 1963), pp. 151-155.

Mezerik, A. G. "Hungary and the United Nations." *International Review Service*, IV : No. 40, pp. 1-21.

————. "Suez Canal" (A Chronology). *International Review Service*, III : No. 30.

Misra, K. P. "India's Policy of Recognition of States and Governments." *American Journal of International Law*. LV (April, 1961), pp. 398-424.

Morgenthau, Hans J. "Critical Look at the Neutralism." *The New York Times Magazine* (August 27, 1961), pp. 25, 76-77.

Nayar, B. R. "Community Development Programme : Its Political Impact." *Economic Weekly*, XII (September 17, 1960), pp. 1401-12.

Nayar, N. Parameswaran. "Growth of Nonalignment in World Affairs." *India Quarterly*, XVIII (January-March, 1962), pp. 28-53.

————. "Nationalism as a Factor in India's Foreign Policy." *Indian Yearbook of International Affairs, 1962*, XI. Madras : University of Madras, 1962, pp. 433-458.

P. "Middle Ground Between Russia and America : An Indian View." *Foreign Affairs*, XXXII (January 1954), pp. 259-269.

Palmer, Norman D. "India's Foreign Policy." *The Political Quarterly*, XXXIII (October-December, 1962), pp. 391-403.

Pandit, Vijayalakshmi. "India's Foreign Policy." *Foreign Affairs*, XXXIV (April, 1956), pp. 432-440.

Panikkar, K. M. "The Himalayas and Indian Defense." *India Quarterly* III (July-September, 1947), pp. 233-238.

Rajan, M. S. "Indian Foreign Policy in Action, 1954-56." *India Quarterly*, XVI (July-September, 1960), pp. 203-236.

———. "India's Non-Alignment Policy." *International Studies*, V (July-October, 1963), pp. 115-132.

Rana, A. P. "The Intellectual Dimensions of India's Non-alignment." *Journal of Asian Studies*, XXVIII (February, 1969), pp. 299-312.

———. "The Nature of India's Foreign Policy." *India Quarterly*, XXII (April-June, 1966), pp. 101-139.

Rao, B. Shiva, and Kondapi, C. K. "India and the Korean Crisis." *India Quarterly*, VII (October-December, 1951), pp. 295-315.

Scalapino, Robert A. "Neutralism in Asia." *American Political Science Review*, XLVIII (March, 1954), pp. 49-62.

Schwarzenberger, Georg. "The Scope for Neutralism." *The Yearbook of World Affairs*, 1961, XV. New York : Praeger, 1961, pp. 233-244.

Shridharani, Krishnalal. "The Philosophic Bases of India's Foreign Policy." *India Quarterly*, XXIV (April-June, 1958), pp. 196-202.

Stein, Arthur. "India and the USSR : The Post-Nehru Period." *Asian Survey* VII (March, 1967), pp. 165-175.

Steinberg, Blema. "The Korean War : A Case Study in Indian Neutralism." *Orbis,* VIII (Winter, 1965), pp. 937-954.

Subrahmanyan, K. "1962 : The Causes and Lessons." *International Studies,* II (October, 1969), pp. 149-166.

————. "U.S. Policy Towards India." *China Report,* VIII (January-April, 1972), pp. 36-53.

Venkatasubbiah, H. "An Approach to Sino-Indian Relations." *Asian Affairs,* Vol. 60 (New Series Vol. IV), pp. 140-150.

Wells, Alan. "Mass Violence in India Since 1960." *The Indian Political Science Review,* VII (April-September, 1973), pp. 125-130.

Wilcox, Francis. "UN and the Nonaligned States." *Headline Series,* (September-October, 1962).

UNPUBLISHED MATERIALS

Amini, Bahman. "Indian Foreign Policy with Particular Reference to Asia and Africa." Unpublished Ph.D. dissertation, University of Maryland, 1959.

Ballard, James L., III. "The United Nations in the Congo Crisis." Unpublished Master's thesis, University of Texas at Austin, 1962.

Boland, Gertrude. "India and the United Nations : India's Role in the General Assembly." Unpublished Ph.D. dissertation, Claremont College, 1961.

Faust, John Rose. "Foreign Policy Positions of Selected States as Expressed in the General Assembly of the UN." Unpublished Ph.D. dissertation, North Carolina University, Chapel Hill, 1960.

Holly, David C. "The National Interests as Perceived by US Policymakers." Unpublished Ph.D. dissertation, The American University, 1964.

King, May Coates. "Nonalignment and the United Nations : The Congo Crisis." Unpublished Ph.D. dissertation, University of Idaho, 1968.

Parham, Paul B. "The Content Analysis." Unpublished Master's Thesis in Journalism, University of Missouri at Columbia, 1970.

Satyapalan, C. N. "India's China Policy : The First Decade." Unpublished Ph.D. dissertation, University of Pennsylvania, 1964.

NEWSPAPERS

Hindustan Times (New Delhi). December 31, 1949 (cited) January 28, 1962.

The New York Times. Magazine. August 27, 1961, pp. 25, 76-77.

The Spectator. No. 6960, September 8, 1961, p. 310.

The Statesman (Calcutta). October 26, 1962.

The Times of India. May 20, 1961 ; December 1, 1955 ; February 1, 1957 ; November 8, 1961.

MISCELLANEOUS

Asian Recorder. I (1956), and VI (1961).
Facts on File. XII (1952), and XXI (1961).

INDEX

ERRATA

Page	Line	For	Read
38	1 (fn 18)	African	Afrikaaner
40	4 (fn 27)	Noorji	Naoroji
48	30	maintance	maintenance
83	12	observe	observer
108	17	presisted	persisted
151	27	650,00	650,000
167	2	conicided	coincided
177	25	Columbia	Colombia
185	30	on this instance	in this instance